World Military Aircraft
Since 1945

Robert Jackson

Charles Scribner's Sons
NEW YORK

1 3 5 7 9 11 13 15 17 19 I/C 20 18 16 14 12 10 8 6 4 2

Printed in Great Britain

Library of Congress Catalog Card Number 79-53086
ISBN 0-684-16265-2

Contents

Photo Credits

Agababian 139(T)
Air Portraits 138(T), 146(B), 158(TR & BR)
J. P. Alexander 149(C)
APN 5,141(C)
Avions Marcel Dassault-Breguet Aviation, 15, 16, 25
   26, 27, 28, 29, 30, 31, 142(TC)

BAC 120, 134(T)
G. Bain 18
P. Beaver 143(TC)
Beech 153(TR)
Boeing 13, 14
N. F. Box 143(B)
Bristol Aeroplane Co 17
British Aerospace 10, 46, 47, 67, 69, 155(BR)
A. J. Brown 53

Camera Press 74
Canadair 153(BR)
A. B. Carlaw 126
Cessna 154(TL)
Convair 22
Crown Copyright 143(BC), 152(TC), 155(TR),
   156(C), 158(BR)

De Havilland 144(C), 144(B)

Fairchild 48, 111, 112, 113
S. A. Fenn 35
Flight 36, 66, 153(C)
Flightlines International 145(T), 152(T)
Fokker-VFW 147(T)
Fricker 96, 146(C)

Gloster Aircraft 62
D. Goodwin 24, 141
J. M. G. Gradidge 142(B)
Grumman 1, 55, 57, 58, 59, 60, 61,
   147(TC), 147(B)
J. Guthrie 145(C)

M. J. Hardy 139(BC), 140(T), 142(T), 149(T)
M. Hooks 75(B), 100(T), 110(T)
P. J. Howard 139(TC)
HS Aviation 11, 34, 37, 38, 68, 71, 140(C), 154(R)

A. F. Jarvis 54

N. Lewis 141(T)
R. Lindsay 155(BL)
Lockheed 77, 78, 79, 80, 81, 82, 83, 84, 85(T),
   150, 151(T), 156(R)

J. A. MacDonald 151(C)
P. R. March 148(BC)
F. Martin 139(B), 146(T), 147(BC)
J. McCarthy 154(CL)
McDonnell Douglas 43, 45(B), 88, 89(T), 90, 91, 92,
   145(B)
Messerschmitt-Bölkow-Blohm 110(B)
MOD 65, 99, 123(T), 130, 132, 155(TL)
J. Muriel 63

North American 100(B), 101, 102, 103, 104, 105,
   106, 107, 108, 157

Official US Navy 40

D. Robinson 148(T)

Saab 114, 115, 116, 117, 118, 119, 158(TL)
R. G. Sibson 93
Sissons 95
D. R. A. Spurzeon 144(T)

Tass 131, 149(B)
P. F. Thompson 42

USAF 12, 45(T)

Vickers 127
Vought 20, 21, 85(B)

Westland 49, 134(B)
R. Wiceen 97, 98, 138(B)
J. Wynne 89(B)

Introduction

In 1940, military aviation was dominated by two distinct and uncomplicated types of aircraft: the fighter and the bomber. Their roles were uncomplicated, too. The fighter's primary task was to destroy bombers, the majority of which were reserved for the tactical support of ground forces. Of all the belligerent nations, only Britain had formed the nucleus of a strategic bomber force.

The evolution of combat aircraft under the pressures of war during the next five years brought about profound changes. Existing fighter types were converted into fighter-bombers to provide battlefield support on a massive scale, while the strategic bomber had been forged into the mightiest and most devastating weapon in the history of warfare.

In the years immediately after World War II, the power and the menace of the strategic bomber led to the reawakening of old concepts. The jet age saw the rebirth of the pure interceptor, aircraft such as America's F-86 Sabre, Russia's MiG-15 and Britain's Hawker Hunter, high-speed gun platforms whose sole purpose, originally, was to climb fast enough and high enough to destroy the strategic bomber. But such a task had to be undertaken in all weathers, and this in turn led to the evolution of the 'weapon system', a fully integrated combination of airframe, engine, weapons, fire control systems and avionics. Early examples of the weapon system were the F-89 Scorpion, the F-94 Starfire and the Gloster Javelin.

In the mid-1950s yet another concept of air warfare came about, partly as a result of the lessons learned during the Korean War, and partly because of the wildly escalating cost of developing new combat types. This concept, the multi-role combat aircraft, was to dominate military design for the next 20 years, and reached fruition in such highly successful types as the F-4 Phantom and the Mirage family, whose basic airframe/engine combination was designed from the outset to support long-term development compatible with a wide variety of operational requirements. The high cost of developing new and complex airborne weapon systems also brought about international co-operation on an unprecedented scale, with a highly beneficial pooling of brains, expertise and financial resources which has so far resulted in the production of advanced and versatile military aircraft such as the Panavia Tornado, to name the most appropriate example.

The list of success stories in the field of military aircraft production since 1945 is a long one. In terms of longevity Britain's Canberra is unmatched, refurbished examples still being supplied to foreign customers some 30 years after the prototype first flew, while for sheer proliferation Russia's robust MiG-15 remains unsurpassed, having been produced in far greater quantities than any other combat type. Then there have been the postwar export successes of France's military aircraft industry, whose products have admirably upheld the French tradition for building machines which combine a high degree of potency with aesthetic appeal.

Against the successes, however, must be measured the many failures, some resulting from changing policies, others from prohibitive costs, and still others from political misconceptions — or a combination of all three. Some of the greatest political misconceptions of all time were contained in the British Defence White Paper of 1957, which announced the phasing out of manned aircraft in favour of missiles and sounded the death-knell of several promising projects which might have become Britain's military best-sellers in the 1960s. None of them, however, had such a profound and damaging effect on the British aerospace industry as the later demise of the superb TSR-2, leaving a gap which was still unfilled more than 10 years later. The Americans have had their troubles too, as have the Russians, but the budgets of both these powers have been far better placed to support the cancellation of advanced aircraft projects than those of economically weaker nations. Nevertheless, the abandonment of the very advanced Rockwell B-1 bomber in favour of cruise missiles will doubtless be keenly felt by the USAF in the future, when policy changes yet again — as it surely must. The Russians seem to have a keener appreciation of defence requirements in many respects, adhering to well-tried formulae. Their faith in the manned bomber is undiminished, as the variable-geometry Tupolev Tu-26 'Backfire' clearly shows.

The Tu-26 is designed to carry out a specialised role, and specialisation is slowly returning to the whole spectrum of military aviation. During World War II, the Germans designed the heavily-armoured Henschel Hs129 specifically to kill tanks; now the Americans are producing a modern counterpart, the Fairchild A-10 Thunderbolt II. In 1940, the Spitfire, Hurricane and Messerschmitt Bf109 were all what would now be clearly defined as air superiority fighters; now this category of combat aircraft is back again, after four decades, in the shape of such types as the F-15 Eagle. The wheel has turned full circle.

The story of military aviation since 1945 has been one of enormous technological progress — the V/STOL Harrier, to name but one example — but also one of compromise, with defence cuts dictating the need to adapt and uprate existing designs to fill the gap created by the cancellation of more advanced projects, usually for reasons of soaring cost. Compromise is very evident in the field of maritime aviation, where all the major powers with the exception of France use long-range maritime patrol aircraft developed from civil airliners, but this is nothing new; the Lockheed Hudson, Consolidated Catalina and Short Sunderland were all based on civil designs.

What is new, or relatively so, is the current tendency to develop low-cost strike aircraft from trainers (the BAC Strikemaster and the Cessna A-37, for example), providing limited offensive capability for small nations and opening up vital overseas markets. As the complexity of the weapon systems of the super-powers continues to grow, the potential of such aircraft — small, fairly cheap, manoeuvrable and with the ability to carry a high weapons load — is often ignored; yet over the next two decades, it is precisely this type of combat aircraft which will assure the internal security of the rapidly expanding Third World.

Part One

Avro Lincoln

UK

Role: Strategic Heavy Bomber
Specification: B14/43
Operational: 1945-55
Data: B2

Engines: Four Rolls-Royce Packard-Merlin 68As
Span: 120ft 0in
Length: 78ft 3½in
Weight: 44,188lb (empty)
82,000lb (loaded)
Crew: 7
Max speed: 290mph at 20,000ft
Service ceiling: 22,000ft
Range: 2,250 miles at 230mph with 14,000lb
bomb load
max 3,500 miles at 235mph and 20,000ft
Weapons: Max bomb load 22,000lb. Defensive
armament: Twin 0.5in Browning machine guns in
Boulton Paul Type F nose turret, remotely-controlled
from the bombardier's seat; twin 0.5in Brownings in
a Boulton Paul Type D tail turret; twin 20mm
Hispano Mk 4 or Mk 5 cannon in a Bristol B17 Mk 1
dorsal turret (Note: the dorsal turret was later
removed from most Lincolns in RAF service)

Developed to specification B14/43 to meet a
requirement for a Lancaster replacement, the
prototype Avro Lincoln flew for the first time on
9 June 1944. This aircraft, PW925, was followed by
two more prototypes, PW929 and PW932, which
differed from the first machine in that they were
fitted with Bristol dorsal gun turrets instead of the
Martin dorsal turret. The initial production model —
which was originally known as the Lancaster IV
before being given the name Lincoln B1 — was
powered by four 1,750hp Rolls-Royce Merlin 85
engines and first deliveries to the RAF took place in
the spring of 1945, when a Lincoln Flight was
formed within No 57 Squadron at RAF East Kirkby,
Lincolnshire. Other units to receive the Lincoln B1
during the immediate postwar years were Nos 7, 9,
12, 15, 35, 44, 49, 50, 61, 83, 90, 97, 100, 101,
116, 138, 148, 199, 207, 214, 527 and
617 Squadrons.

The Lincoln became operational too late to see
active service during World War II, although plans
had been made to send several squadrons to the Far
East as part of 'Tiger Force' for operations against
Japan. Lincolns, did, however, see action against
Communist terrorists during the Malayan
Emergency, and against the Mau-Mau in Kenya in
1954.

The Lincoln B2 (originally known as the
Lancaster V) differed from the B1 mainly in having
1,760hp Packard Merlin 68, 68A or 300 engines. It
was later re-engined with Merlin 85s and
redesignated Lincoln B4. The Lincoln B2 (IIIG) and
B2 (IVA) were fitted with H2S IIIG and H2S IVA,
Gee II and Rebecca II navigational aids, and the
Lincoln III was a projected maritime reconnaissance
aircraft which eventually became the
Shackleton MR1.

Plans were made to build the Lincoln in Canada
under the designation Lincoln B15, but only six
aircraft of this type were completed by Victory
Aircraft and all were subsequently converted as
freighters. The bomber was, however, produced by
the Beaufort Division of the Department of Aircraft
Production in Australia as the Lincoln B30; five
aircraft were assembled from British-built
components, the first flying on 17 March 1946, and
a further 68 machines were built entirely in Australia.
Production of the Lincoln B30, which was powered
by four Commonwealth-built Merlin 102 engines,
was terminated in 1953, but several aircraft were
converted to the long-range maritime
reconnaissance role by the addition of an extra nose
bay, lengthening the fuselage by 6ft and
accommodating two extra crew members and search
radar. Lincolns served with the RAAF in the maritime
role until the early 1960s when the last examples
were replaced by Lockheed Neptunes.

The Lincoln was retired from RAF Bomber
Command at the end of 1955, when the Command
became an all-jet force, although a small number
remained in service as bombing trainers for some
years after that. The last air arm to operate the
Lincoln as a bomber was the Argentine Air Force,
which received 12 B1s and used them until 1963.

Avro Shackleton

UK

Role: Long-Range Maritime Patrol
Specification: R5/46
Operational: 1951–
Data: MR3

Engines: Four Rolls-Royce Griffon 57As rated at 2,450hp each
Span: 119ft 10in
Length: 92ft 6in
Weight: 100,000lb (max loaded)
65,000lb (empty)
Crew: 10
Max speed: 300mph at 12,000ft
Service ceiling: 19,200ft
Range: 3,662 miles at 200mph and 1,500ft
Weapons: Two 20mm cannon in nose position; various internal loads of bombs, depth charges, sonobuoys and other anti-submarine or anti-surface vessel stores, plus airborne rescue equipment

Designed in 1946 to meet a requirement for a Liberator replacement in RAF Coastal Command, the Avro Type 696 Shackleton — originally designated Lincoln ASR3 — flew for the first time on 9 March 1949, powered by four Rolls-Royce Griffon 57 engines of 2,450hp each. It was the first British four-engined aircraft to fly with contra-rotating propellers. The prototype was armed with two 20mm cannon in nose barbettes, two cannon in a dorsal turret and two 0.5in machine guns in a tail turret, but the nose and tail armament was dropped on subsequent aircraft.

Seventy-seven production Shackleton MR1s were ordered, the first entering service with No 120 Squadron at RAF Kinloss, Scotland, in April 1951. A Shackleton Operational Conversion Unit, No 236, was also formed at Kinloss. The next Shackleton Squadrons to form were No 220, with MR1As, which were slightly modified to simplify engine changes, this unit moving from Kinloss to St Eval in Cornwall in November 1951, and No 224, which received its first aircraft in August of that year. By the end of 1952, Nos 240 and 269 Squadrons were operating Shackletons from Ballykelly in Northern Ireland, and Nos 42 and 206 had joined No 220 at St Eval, providing maritime coverage from Norway to mid-Atlantic, as far south as Gibraltar and westwards of Malta.

June 1952 saw the first flight of a new variant, the Shackleton MR2, which had a ventral ASV radar

'dustbin' in place of the MR1s chin radome, an elongated tail with an observation post and twin 20mm cannon in the nose. First units to re-equip with the MR2 were Nos 42 and 206 Squadrons, followed by Nos 220 and 204 Squadrons. Nos 37 and 38 Squadrons in Malta also received MR2s, extending coverage to the whole of the Mediterranean with the ability to deploy rapidly east of Suez. 69 MR2s were built, providing enough aircraft for the formation of another squadron, No 228.

The next Shackleton variant, the MR3, incorporated some radical design changes, with an altered wing shape and wingtip tanks that increased the total fuel capacity to 4,248gal. The mid-upper turret was deleted and the aircraft featured a tricycle undercarriage, improving its airfield performance.

By the end of 1957 Coastal Command's Shackletons were ranging world-wide, carrying out a variety of tasks — including oceanic survey and trooping — in addition to their usual maritime reconnaissance role. In 1958 15 squadrons were equipped with the type, as well as the Maritime Operational Training Unit at Kinloss, which operated a mixture of MR1As and T4s, the latter being modified MR1s with dual controls. Only 34 Shackleton MR3s were built for the RAF, but a further eight were delivered to No 35 Squadron South African Air Force. During the next four years the remaining Shackleton MR1s and 1As were progressively phased out and replaced by MR2Cs, which were standard MR2s brought up to MR3 equipment standard. Most of the MR1s and 1As were modified as T4s and served with MOTU until 1968, when they were replaced by surplus MR2s.

In the mid-1960s, following defence economy measures in the UK, it was decided that although the Shackleton MR2 would be replaced by the Hawker Siddeley Nimrod, the MR3s would continue in the maritime role for some time to come, and the aircraft were given an additional boost by the installation of Bristol-Siddeley Viper turbojets in the outboard engine nacelles. These Shackletons, designated MR3 Phase 3, continued in service until the early 1970s, when the RAF's long-range maritime role was taken over entirely by the Nimrod. The last RAF squadron to operate the Shackleton was No 8, which reformed at Kinloss in January 1972 in the airborne early warning role with Shackleton AEW Mk 2s (converted MR2s.)

5

Avro Vulcan

Role: Strategic Medium Bomber
Specification: B35/46
Operational: 1956-
Photo and Data: B Mk 2

Engines: Four Bristol Siddeley Olympus Mk 201 or 301 turbojets or 17,000lb or 20,000lb thrust
Span: 111ft
Length: 99ft 11in
Weight: 180,000-200,000lb (loaded)
Crew: 5
Max speed: 645mph at 40,000ft
Service ceiling: 55,000ft
Range: 4,750 miles max
Weapons: Hawker Siddeley Blue Steel Missile, free-falling nuclear weapons or 211,000lb high explosive bombs

The world's first jet bomber to employ the delta-wing planform, the Avro Type 698 Vulcan prototype (VX770) flew for the first time on 30 August 1952, following extensive testing of its then radical configuration in the Avro 707 series of research deltas. The first prototype was fitted with four Rolls-Royce Avon turbojets and later re-engined with Bristol Siddeley Sapphires and finally Rolls-Royce Conways, but the second prototype (VX777) employed Bristol Siddeley Olympus 100s. This aircraft, which flew on 3 September 1953, featured a slightly lengthened fuselage and was later fitted with wings having redesigned leading edges with compound sweepback, flying in this configuration on 5 October 1955. It was later used to test the larger wing destined for the Vulcan B Mk 2, until it was finally retired in 1960.

The first Vulcan B Mk 1 was delivered to the RAF's No 230 Operational Conversion Unit in July 1956, and No 83 Squadron became the first to equip with the type in July 1957. The second squadron to receive the aircraft, in October that year, was No 101, followed in May 1958 by No 617, the famous 'Dam Busters'. By this time production of the greatly improved Vulcan B Mk 2 was well under way, and production of the B Mk 1 was terminated with the 45th aircraft (XH532), the remaining aircraft on order being completed to B Mk 2 standard.

The first production Vulcan B Mk 2 flew on 30 August 1958, powered by 16,000lb thrust Olympus 200 engines. The second production aircraft featured a bulged tailcone housing electronic countermeasures equipment, and this became standard on subsequent aircraft. This Vulcan was also fitted with 17,000lb thrust Olympus 201 engines. Delivery of the Vulcan B2 began on 1 July 1960 to No 83 Squadron, and Nos 9, 12, 27, 35 and 617 Squadrons also received this variant. Vulcan B2s were adapted to carry the Blue Steel air-to-surface missile, which was flight tested during 1957 in the United Kingdom and at Woomera, Australia.

Meanwhile, the 34 Vulcan B1s remaining in service were progressively withdrawn for conversion to B1A standard. This involved the fitting of new avionics, including full ECM. Conversion work was completed early in 1963. Units operating the B1A were No 44 Squadron, which was formed at Waddington on 10 August 1960 by renumbering No 83, No 50, which re-formed the following year, and No 101, as well as No 230 OCU. All three B1/1A squadrons were based at Waddington and later converted to B2s.

The first Vulcan squadron to become fully operational with the Blue Steel was No 617, in February 1963, followed later that year by Nos 27 and 83. These units formed the Scampton Wing, and by early 1964 the Vulcans of Nos 9, 12 and 35 Squadrons — the Coningsby Wing — were also operational with the missile. By this time, plans to equip the Vulcan B2 force with the American Skybolt missile had been abandoned, although aerodynamic and dropping trials with dummy Skybolts had been carried out successfully. In 1968 the Blue Steel squadrons reverted to conventional free-fall bombs and were allocated to the tactical rather than the strategic role, the British nuclear deterrent now being in the hands of the Royal Navy's Polaris submarine force. In 1969 Nos 9 and 35 Squadrons went to Cyprus to form CENTO's spearhead force, and in November 1973 No 27 Squadron took over the strategic reconnaissance role from the Victors of 543 Squadron.

During their service career, RAF Vulcans carried out several notable long-distance flights. In June 1961, for example, a Vulcan of No 617 Squadron made the first non-stop flight from the United Kingdom to Australia, and in November 1962 three Vulcans of Nos 27, 83 and 617 Squadrons made a round-the-world flight in which they covered 30,000 miles in 50 hours' flying time.

Avro Canada CF-100 Canada

Role: Long-Range All-Weather Interceptor
Operational: 1953-
Data: CF-100 Mk 5

Engines: Two Orenda II single-shaft turbojets each rated at 7,275lb thrust
Span: 60ft 10in
Length: 54ft 2in
Weight: 23,100lb (empty)
33,600lb (normal loaded)
Crew: 2
Max speed: 650mph at 10,000ft
Service ceiling: 54,000ft
Range: 2,000miles
Weapons: Fifty-two 2.75in rockets in wingtip pods

One of the largest fighter aircraft ever built, the Avro Canada CF-100 was designed in response to an operational requirement for a long-range interceptor for the air defence of Canada's Arctic regions. The prototype CF-100 Mk 1 flew on 19 January 1950, powered by two Rolls-Royce Avon RA3 turbojets, and was followed by 10 pre-series CF-100 Mk 2s with Avro Orenda Mk 2 engines rated at 6,500lb thrust. The first of these aircraft, which carried no armament, flew on 20 June 1951. One of them was converted as a two-seat trainer with the designation CF-100 2T.

In September 1950 an order was placed with Avro Canada for 124 CF-100 Mk 3s for the RCAF. These were powered by two Orenda Mk 8s and armed with eight .5in Colt-Browning machine guns. In fact only 70 were built, the first entering service with No 445 Squadron RCAF. Some Mk 3s were converted as two-seat trainers under the designation Mk 3T; these carried the same armament as standard Mk 3s.

Thd next production version of the CF-100 was the Mk 4A, powered by two Orenda 9s and equipped with a Hughes AGP-40 fire control radar in the nose. This variant could be armed with 48 'Mighty Mouse'

HVAR rockets, eight .5in machine guns or four 30mm cannon in a ventral pack, plus 58 HVAR rockets in wingtip pods. The first production Mk 4A flew on 24 October 1953 and the aircraft entered service with No 445 Squadron the following year. In November 1956, this unit moved from Upland RCAF base to Marville, in France, as part of NATO's western European commitment. In all, 510 Mk 4As and 4Bs (the latter with Orenda 11 engines) were produced, and by the end of 1957 nine RCAF squadrons were operating the type, providing round-the-clock air defence coverage of Canada's far north. During that year, three CF-100 Mk 4B squadrons, Nos 400, 419 and 423, moved to Germany. Like the CF-100 Mk 4A, the 4B was armed with either eight .5in machine guns or a pack of four 30mm Aden cannon, as well as HVAR rockets, but six Hughes GAR-98 Falcon missiles could also be carried.

The last production version of the CF-100 was the Mk 5, which differed from the Mk 4 mainly in having increased flying surface areas and its gun pack deleted. 53 Mk 5s were supplied to the Belgian Air Force, deliveries beginning on 1957, and equipped the 11e, 349e and 350e Escadrilles. The Belgian CF-100s remained in service until mid-1963, when they were flown to the BAF's principal maintenance and storage unit at Coxyde and subsequently scrapped. Replacement of RCAF Mk 5s with the McDonnell F-101B Voodoo began in 1961. At one time it was proposed to manufacture a further version, the CF-100 Mk 6, with Orenda 11R turbojets and a primary armament of Sparrow II homing missiles, but this was abandoned after tests of the missiles had been carried out on two modified Mk 5s (Mk 5Ms).

Production of the CF-100 ended in December 1958, with the 692nd example. A few CF-100 Mk 5s (known to their crews as 'Clunks') still equip No 414 Electronic Warfare Squadron, Canadian Armed Forces, whose task is to simulate attacks on North American targets. These aircraft, in addition to other ECM equipment, carry underwing pods containing 'Chaff' — radar-jamming aluminium foil.

Beriev Be-6

USSR

Role: Maritime Patrol
Operational: 1949-64
NATO Code-Name: Madge

Engines: Two Shvetsov ASh-73TK radials
developing 2,300hp each
Span: 108ft 3¼in
Length: 73ft 10in
Weight: 41,419lb (empty)
61,846lb (max loaded)
Crew: 8
Max speed: 258mph at 7,875ft
Service ceiling: 20,100ft
Range: 3,045 miles max
Weapons: (late production model) Twin 23mm
cannon in remotely-controlled dorsal turret;
provision for various maritime stores on pylons
outboard of engine nacelles

At the end of World War II, among the new combat
aircraft designs that were beginning to take shape on
the drawing boards of the various Soviet design
bureaux, considerable priority was given to the
development of a new long-range maritime patrol
flying boat. Since all seaplane development was now
concentrated in the bureau of Georgii M. Beriev at
Taganrog, the task of producing such an aircraft fell
to his team. Beriev had been designing seaplanes
since 1932 and had considerable experience in the
field; in 1945 his factory was building the Be-4 or
KOR-2, a flying boat for the Soviet Navy, and this
was followed in 1946 by the Be-8, a light utility

amphibian. Beriev's new design, designated LL-143
(the LL standing for Letayushchaya Lodka, or flying
boat) was fairly advanced for its day, and in the same
class as America's Martin PBM-5 Mariner. A large,
gull-wing monoplane, the LL-143 was powered by
two 2,000hp Shvetsov ASh-72 radial engines and
carried an armament of two 23mm cannon in tail
and dorsal turrets and a single 23mm cannon in the
bow. Normal crew was eight, but a relief crew could
also be carried on very long range flights. The
aircraft's offensive load of mines, depth charges or
torpedoes was carried on pylons outboard of the
engine nacelles.

Flight testing of the LL-143 was completed in the
autumn of 1947, and the aircraft was ordered into
production for the Soviet Navy as the Be-6.
Production machines, the first of which flew early in
1949, were fitted with uprated engines and had the
forward armament deleted, the fuselage nose being
redesigned. A retractable radome was placed aft of
the hull step, and on later production aircraft the
remotely-controlled 23mm tail gun position was
replaced by a 'stinger' tail housing magnetic anomaly
detection (MAD) equipment. The Be-6 formed the
mainstay of the Morskaya Aviatsiya's maritime patrol
squadrons during the 1950s, being used as a
transport and a fishery protection aircraft in addition
to its primary role. Some Be-6s appeared on the
Soviet civil register, carrying out a variety of tasks
which included long-range flights in connection with
oceanic survey, mainly in the Arctic and Antarctic, on
behalf of the Soviet Academy of Sciences.

Beriev Be-10

USSR

Role: Long-Range Maritime Patrol
Operational: 1961-65(?)
NATO Code-Name: Mallow

Engines: Two Lyulka Type AL-7PB turbojets each
rated at 14,330lb
Span: 80ft
Length: 108ft
Weight: 53,000lb (empty)
90,000lb (loaded)
Crew: 3-5
Max speed: 470mph at 25,000ft (estimated)
Service ceiling: 45,000ft (estimated)
Range: 2,800 miles max
Weapons: Two 23mm cannon mounted in tail
position; variety of conventional and nuclear ASW
stores

Although the Beriev BE-10 served with the Soviet
Morskaya Aviatsiya only in very small numbers, and
for a limited time, it deserves its place among the
annals of the world's combat aircraft in that it was
the only pure-jet flying boat ever to see operational
service. Designed as a successor to the Be-6, the
twin-jet Be-10, which featured sharply swept flying

surfaces, was first seen publicly at the Tushino air
display of 1961, when four aircraft of this type flew
past. During its development phase, the Be-10 —
alternatively designated M-10 — established a
number of FAI-approved records for seaplanes,
including a 566.69mph speed record over a
15-25km course, a 544.2mph speed record with a
11,023lb payload round a 1,000km closed circuit
course, and altitude records of 49,088ft without
payload, 46,135ft with an 11,023lb payload,
41,775ft with a 22,046lb payload, and 39,360ft
with a 33,069lb payload. During all these record-
breaking flights, the aircraft was piloted either by
Nikolai Andreivsky or Georgii Buryanov, and carried a
crew of two apart from the pilot.

The Be-10 carried a built-in armament of two
fixed 23mm cannon in the nose to provide covering
fire while running-in to the target, and two more
23mm guns in a rear turret, over which was
positioned a gun-laying radar. Offensive stores —
mines and depth-charges, including low-yield
nuclear anti-submarine weapons — were carried
internally, and appear to have been ejected
rearwards through the base of the fuselage step.
There may have been provision for further stores in
the undersides of the engine nacelles.

Fewer than 30 Be-10s are thought to have served with the Soviet Navy, and the type appears to have been generally unsuccessful. It was certainly replaced on Beriev's production line by the turboprop-powered Be-12, which became the standard Soviet ASW aircraft of the 1960s.

Beriev Be-12 Tchaika

Role: Long-Range Maritime Patrol
Operational: 1965-
NATO Code-Name: Mail
Photo: Iraqi Be-12

Engines: Two 4,000shp Ivchenko AI-20D turboprops
Span: 97ft 6in
Length: 99ft
Weight: 65,000lb (estimated loaded)
Crew: 8-12
Max speed: 380mph at 5,000ft
Service ceiling: 37,000ft
Range: 2,500 miles max
Weapons: Various maritime stores in internal bomb bay aft of the fuselage step; provision for external stores on underwing pylons

First seen publicly at the Tushino Air Display in 1961, the turboprop-powered Beriev Be-12 amphibian was the type selected to replace the elderly Be-6 flying boat in service with the Soviet Naval Air Arm, presumably in preference to the turbojet-powered Be-10. The Be-12, the prototype of which flew early in 1960, was at first believed to be simply a new variant of the Be-6, but it was later realised that the type was virtually a new design, although bearing a close resemblance to the basic configuration of its predecessor. Service deployment of the Be-12 was rapid, and by 1965 it was identified in service with the Soviet Northern and Black Sea Fleets. Later, Be-12s were also reported to be operating out of bases in Egypt and Syria, bearing the national markings of those countries.

In 1964, the Be-12 established six FAI-recognised records for turboprop-powered amphibians, including an altitude of 39,977ft without payload, 37,290ft with payloads of 2,205 and 4,409lb, and 30,682ft with a payload of 22,046lb. The aircraft also lifted a maximum payload of 22,266lb to an altitude of 6,560ft. In 1968, the Be-12 set up a series of fresh records; 343.169mph over a 500km closed circuit, 338.456mph over a 1,000km closed circuit, and a closed circuit distance record of 643.2 miles in this class. The 500km closed circuit speed record was raised later that year to 351.290mph by the same aircraft, and the distance record (closed circuit) to 666.54 miles. Six further records were established by the Be-12 in 1970.

The Be-12 features a sharply-cranked, high-set wing similar to the Be-6's, a configuration dictated by the need to raise the engines well clear of the water. The single-step hull has a high length-to-beam ratio and is fitted with two long strakes to keep spray away from the engines on take-off. There is a glazed observation position in the nose, surmounted by a long thimble-type radome, and a 'stinger' tail houses MAD equipment. No defensive armament is carried.

Blackburn (HS) Buccaneer

UK

Role: Low-Level Strike
Specification: M148T
Operational: 1962-
Photo and Data: S Mk 2

Engines: Two 11,100lb thrust Rolls-Royce Spey Mk 101 turbofans
Span: 44ft
Length: 63ft 5in
Weight: 32,000lb (empty)
62,000lb (max loaded)
Crew: 2
Max speed: 645mph at sea level
Service ceiling: 50,000ft
Range: 2,300 miles (normal strike configuration)
Weapons: Four 1,000lb bombs or one nuclear weapon in internal bay; four 1,000lb bombs, four Martel ASMs, 2/3in Glow Worm rocket packs, 36-cell MATRA rocket dispensers or AGM-12B ASM on underwing pylons

Designed in 1954 to meet a Royal Navy requirement for a high-speed strike aircraft capable of operating from existing carriers and packing sufficient firepower to destroy major Soviet surface units, the Blackburn B103 Buccaneer flew for the first time on 30 April 1958, a development batch of 20 aircraft having been ordered in July 1955. After tropical trials from Malta, carrier trials were completed on 1960 on HMS *Victorious* and *Ark Royal*, and on 7 March 1961 the first Buccaneer S1s were assigned to Z Flight of No 700 Squadron at Lossiemouth for intensive trials. The first operational Buccaneer S1 squadron was No 801, which commissioned on 17 July 1962 (HMS *Ark Royal*), and was followed by No 809 (HQ Squadron, Lossiemouth) and No 800 (HMS *Eagle*). 40 production S Mk 1s were built, powered by two Bristol Siddeley Gyron Junior turbojets.

The S Mk 2 was a developed version with two Rolls-Royce RB168 Spey turbofan engines and a greatly improved performance. The prototype, converted from an S1, flew for the first time on 17 May 1963, and production aircraft were delivered to Nos 801 and 809 Squadrons in 1965. 84 S2s were built, and the South African Air force acquired 16 examples of a variant designated S Mk 50 in 1965, basically similar to the S2 but with a Rolls-Royce Bristol BS605 rocket motor in the rear fuselage to improve take-off from hot and high airfields. Most Royal Navy S2s were later transferred to the RAF with the running-down of the Fleet Air Arm's fixed-wing squadrons, the first aircraft being delivered to No 12 Squadron on 1 October 1969. Buccaneers in RAF service are designated S Mk 2A and S Mk 2B, the latter carrying Martel TV-guided ASMs. The naval equivalents are designated S Mk 2C and S Mk 2D.

Forty-three new S Mk 2Bs were ordered for the RAF, the first flying in January 1970, and these equipped Nos 15 and 16 Squadrons in Germany. Three more S Mk 2Bs were assigned to the Royal Aircraft Establishment for weapons trials, two to the Royal Radar Establishment for use as radar test beds, and two were converted as part of the Panavia Tornado development programme.

Blackburn Firebrand

UK

Role: Naval Strike Fighter
Specification: N11/40
Operational: 1945-53
Photo: Mk 1
Data: TF Mk 5

Engines: One 2,500hp Bristol Centaurus IX radial
Span: 51ft 3½ftin
Length: 39ft 1in
Weight: 11,835lb (empty)
16,700lb (normal loaded)
Crew: 1
Max speed: 350mph at 15,000ft (clean)
Service ceiling: 28,500ft
Range: 740 miles max
Weapons: Four 20mm Hispano cannon in the
wings; one torpedo, rocket projectiles or two 1,000lb
bombs

In the summer of 1940, the British Admiralty issued
a requirement for a short-range interceptor equipped
with a heavy armament and suitable for carrier-borne
operation, designed around the most powerful piston
engine then available: the 2,305hp Napier Sabre III.
To meet this requirement, crystallised in
Specification N11/40, Blackburn Aircraft Ltd
submitted their Type B37, three prototypes of which
were ordered in January 1941. The first of these,
DD804, flew on 27 February 1942. It was unarmed,
and had a top speed of 357mph at 18,000ft. The
second aircraft (DD810), which flew in July that
year, was fully navalised and carried an armament of
four 20mm cannon, as did the third prototype,
DD815. Nine pre-series aircraft, designated
Firebrand F Mk 1, were ordered by the Admiralty. In
October 1942 DD810 underwent carrier trials
aboard HMS *Illustrious* in conditions of great
secrecy, and during these it was flown in mock
combat against the Supermarine Seafire. Although
the new aircraft's performance was good it did not,
however, present a substantial advance on that of

naval fighters such as the Seafire, and the Admiralty
began to consider the development of the Firebrand
— which possessed considerable strength and an
ability to carry a heavy load — as a torpedo fighter.
Accordingly, DD810 — which was severely
damaged in an accident — was virtually rebuilt and
modified to carry a torpedo, flying in this form on 31
March 1943 with the new serial NV636 and
designation TF Mk II. The aircraft was ordered into
production, but this was held up by a critical
shortage of the Sabre engines, which were
earmarked for the RAF's Typhoon and Tempest. 12
Mk IIs were built with available Sabres and these
were assigned to No 708 Squadron in the autumn of
1944, but they saw no operational service.

The engine problem was solved by redesigning
the forward part of the Firebrand's airframe to
accommodate the Bristol Centaurus radial, and the
first Centaurus-powered aircraft — designated
TF Mk III — flew in December 1943, being followed
by a production batch of 27 machines, most of which
served on trials. One of them underwent a number of
modifications, including an increase in rudder area,
and became the TF Mk IV, the first of which flew in
May 1945. The aircraft was intended for use in the
Pacific, but by the time the first T Mk IV squadron —
No 813 — formed in September 1945, the war was
over.

Production of the T Mk IV reached a total of 102
aircraft. At the beginning of 1946 the Firebrand was
fitted with new aileron tabs, horn-balanced elevators
and other small innovations and became the
TF Mk 5. The last production version was the
TF Mk 5A, with powered ailerons, and 68 Mks 5/5A
were built. No 813 Squadron went aboard HMS
Implacable with the TF 5 in October 1946. A second
Firebrand squadron, No 827, was formed the
following year, being subsequently based in Malta
and on HMS *Eagle*. Firebrand production ceased in
February 1947, after 225 aircraft of all marks had
been built. In 1953, the type was replaced in service
by the Westland Wyvern.

Boeing B-29/B-50 Superfortress　　USA

Role: Long-Range Heavy Bomber
Operational: 1944-56 (B-29)
1947-65 (B-50)
Photo: B-29s
Data: B-50D

Engines: Four Pratt & Whitney R-4360-55 Wasp major engines rated at 2,650hp each (3,500hp with water injection)
Span: 141ft 3in
Length: 99ft
Weight: 140,000lb (normal loaded)
180,000lb (max loaded)
Crew: 10+
Max Speed: 400mph at 25,000ft
Service ceiling: 40,000ft
Range: 6,000 miles with 10,000lb bomb load
Weapons: .5in machine guns in remotely-controlled turrets; three .5in machine guns in tail turret; up to 28,000lb of bombs

Famous as the bomber that brought the strategic air war to the Japanese home islands during the last year of the Pacific conflict, the Boeing B-29 Superfortress continued to be the mainstay of the US Strategic Air Command for several years after 1945, and saw constant action during the three years of the Korean War. The first B-29 strike of that conflict was carried out by the Guam-based bombers of the Twentieth Air Force's 19th Bombardment Wing on 13 July 1950, and the offensive was maintained against North Korean troop concentrations, communications and industrial targets throughout August, September and October. During that period, the B-29 squadrons dropped more than 30,000 tons of bombs on North Korean targets, bettering the record of the Far East Air Force's B-29s operating out of the Marianas against Japanese targets in World War II. From 1 November 1950, however, the B-29s operating over North Korea — particularly lone RB-29 reconnaissance aircraft — suffered heavily at the

hands of MiG-15 jets, and it became clear that the day of the piston-engined heavy bomber was over.

Production of the B-29 ended in May 1946, after 3,970 aircraft had been built, but the basic design subsequently underwent several modifications. These included the SB-29 (search and rescue), TB-29 (trainer), WB-29 (weather reconnaissance) and KB-29 (tanker). The KB-29M had British 'probe-and-drogue' flight refuelling equipment, and the KB-29P used the Boeing 'flying boom' method, which was standardised in the USAF. 'One-off' modifications were the XB-29E, which was used to test fire control systems, the XB-29G, which was adapted as a jet engine test bed and loaned to the General Electric Company, and the XB-29H, which was assigned to special armament tests. Two production variants, the B-29C and B-29D, were cancelled at the end of the war, but the design of the B-29D underwent substantial changes and became the B-50, which began to re-equip Strategic Air Command squadrons in 1947. Although retaining the general appearance and characteristics of the B-29, the B-50 was in fact 75% a new aircraft, with a new aluminium wing structure some 16% stronger and 26% more efficient than that of the B-29 while weighing 650lb less. The vertical tail surfaces were 5ft higher than those of the B-29, and were hinged to fold horizontally over the starboard tailplane to enable the B-50 to be housed in existing hangars. Wings, tail unit, landing gear and other items of equipment of the B-50 were interchangeable with the C-97A transport.

On 26 February 1949, a B-50A left Fort Worth, Texas, on a non-stop flight around the world, being refuelled in flight over the Azores, the Arabian Gulf, the Philippines and Hawaii, returning to Fort Worth on 2 March after covering 23,108 miles in 94hr 1min. The aircraft carried a 6,000lb bomb load, which was dropped on a range in the Pacific.

Variants of the B-50 included the EB-50B, an experimental aircraft fitted with track-tread landing gear; the RB-50B, a photographic reconnaissance version carrying up to nine cameras and improved radar equipment for day and night reconnaissance;

the YB-50C, a proposed variant with turboprops which was to have been redesignated B-54A, but which was cancelled; and the WB-50 weather reconnaissance version. The B-50D was a progressive development of the B-50A and B-50B production models, with increased bomb load or fuel capacity — carrying either two 700 US gallon external tanks or two 4,000lb bombs on underwing pylons outboard of the outer engines — and improved radar and avionics.

The B-50 was progressively retired in the mid-1950s as SAC Wings re-equipped with the B-47 Stratojet, but 16 RB-50Fs were still serving early in 1965 with the 1370th Photo Mapping Wing at Turner AFB, Georgia, these being replaced by RC-135s. WB-50s were also used well into the 1960s by the 9th Weather Reconnaissance Group of the US Air Weather Service.

Neither the B-29 nor the B-50 was exported outside the USA, but 70 B-29s were supplied to the Royal Air Force in 1951 as part of a NATO expansion scheme. Known as the Washington in RAF service, the type equipped Nos 15, 35, 44, 57, 90, 115, 149 and 207 Squadrons of Bomber Command until 1953, when it was replaced by the Canberra. One ex-RAF Washington was delivered to the Royal Australian Air Force. During the immediate postwar years the Soviet Union produced large numbers of a B-29 copy, the Tupolev Tu-4 (qv).

Boeing B-47 Stratojet

USA

Role: Strategic Medium Bomber
Operational: 1951-1966
Photo and Data: B-47E

Engines: Six General Electric J47-GE-25A turbojets rated at 7,200lb (wet)
Span: 116ft
Length: 109ft
Weight: 175,000lb (normal loaded)
202,000lb (max loaded)
Crew: 3
Max speed: 630mph at 20,000ft
Service ceiling: 42,000ft
Range: 3,200miles max
Weapons: Up to 20,000lb of conventional or nuclear weapons carried internally; defensive armament of two 20mm radar-directed cannon in tail (Note: some B-47s were modified to carry the Bell GAM-63 Rascal ASM on a rack mounted on starboard fuselage side, these aircraft being redesignated DB-47)

In September 1945 the Boeing Aircraft Company commenced design of a strategic jet bomber project designated Model 450. The aircraft, which was a radical departure from conventional design, featured a thin, flexible wing — based on wartime German research data — with 35 degrees of sweep and carrying six turbojets in underwing pods, the main undercarriage being housed in the fuselage. Basic design studies were completed in June 1946, and the first of two XB-47 Stratojet prototypes flew on 17 December 1947, powered by six 3,750lb thrust Allison J35 turbojets. On 8 February 1949 one of the Allison-powered XB-47s made a coast-to-coast flight over the United States, covering 2,289miles in 3hr 46min at an average speed of 607.8mph. Later, the J35s were replaced by General Electric J47-GE-3 turbojets, the XB-47 flying with these in October 1949.

Meanwhile, Boeing had received a contract for 10 B-47A Stratojets in November 1948, and the first of this pre-production batch flew on 1 March 1950. The B-47A was built in small numbers, being used mainly for service trials and crew conversion; the first production aircraft flew on 25 June 1950. In addition to its main J47-GE-11 power plants, the B-47A was fitted with 18 JATO solid fuel rockets to give an emergency take-off thrust of up to 20,000lb. The first major production model, the B-47B, had a strengthened wing and other structural modifications

and was powered by J47-GE-23 engines rated at 5,800lb, thrust. The B-47B first flew on 26 April 1951 and was fitted with underwing fuel tanks. A reconnaissance version, the RB-47B, carried a camera pod in the bomb bay.

The most numerous version of the Stratojet was the B-47E, which first flew on 30 January 1953. Powered by six 6,000lb thrust J47-GE-25s, this variant carried twin remotely-controlled 20mm cannon in the tail, earlier aircraft having been armed with .5in machine guns. By the end of 1954, when the 1,000th Stratojet was delivered to the USAF, the bulk of SAC's strategic bomber wings were re-equipping with the B-47E, and other variants were making their appearance. These included the RB-47E reconnaissance version, with a longer nose and provision for seven cameras for day and night photography; the QB-47E radio-controlled drone; and the ETB-47 crew trainer. Further variants were the RB-47H and RB-47K, which were modified for electronic intelligence gathering and had a pressurised compartment containing three electronics specialists in the bomb bay. On 1 July 1960, a RB-

47H was shot down over the Barents Sea by a Soviet MiG-19 fighter while on a 'ferret' mission to probe Russia's northern radar defences.

The last of some 3,000 Stratojets was completed in February 1957, and most aircraft then in service were modified to B-47E standard with a strengthened wing for low-level operations. The B-47E was claimed to be the first aircraft of its size capable of 'toss-bombing', in which the bomber pulls up vertically, releases its nuclear weapon and then half-rolls out of a loop, the bomb describing a high arc to its target a great distance from the point of release.

The Stratojets continued to be the mainstay of Strategic Air Command until 1960, when its role was progressively taken over by the B-52 Stratofortress and, to a lesser extent, the B-58 Hustler. The last units to use the type were the 9th, 40th, 100th, 303rd, 307th, 310th, 376th, 380th and 509th Wings (B-47E) and the 55th Strategic Reconnaissance Wing (RB-47K).

Boeing B-52 Stratofortress

USA

Role: Strategic Heavy Bomber
Operational: 1955-
Data: B-52G

Engines: Eight Pratt & Whitney J57-P-43W turbojets each rated at 13,750lb thrust
Span: 185ft
Length: 157ft 7in
Weight: 190,000lb (empty)
480,000lb (max loaded)
Crew: 6
Max speed: 665mph at 20,000ft
Service ceiling: 55,000ft
Range: 9,000 miles (unrefuelled)
Weapons: Two North American Hound Dog missiles on underwing pylons; various loads of free-falling conventional or nuclear weapons internally.
Defensive armament: Two 20mm cannon in remotely-controlled tail position

For many years the backbone of America's nuclear deterrent, the mighty Boeing B-52 had its origin in a USAF requirement, issued early in 1946, for a new jet heavy bomber to equip Strategic Air Command. Two prototypes were ordered in September 1949, the YB-52 flying for the first time on 15 April 1952 powered by eight Pratt & Whitney J57-P-3 turbojets. On 2 October 1952 the XB-52 also made its first flight, both aircraft having the same power plants, carrying a crew of five and armed with four tail-mounted .5in machine guns.

The B-52 was ordered into production even before the first prototype had flown, the first production B-52A flying on 5 August 1954. Three B-52As were built and served as test aircraft; one of them (serial 52-003) served as 'mother ship' for the X-15 rocket research aircraft, first flying in this configuration on 8 June 1959 under the designation NB-52A. The first series production version was the B-52B, which flew in January 1955; 30 were built at Seattle. The B-52B had a crew of six and was armed

with four .5in machine guns in an automatic Bosch-Arma MD-9 tail turret. It was powered by eight Pratt & Whitney J57-P-19W or -29W or -29WA engines. The RB-52B, 27 of which were constructed, was a bomber-reconnaissance version, adapted to carry a pressurised two-man capsule containing cameras and ECM equipment in the bomb bay. One of these aircraft (52-008) was converted to carry the X-15 and designated NB-52B.

The focus of B-52 production shifted to Wichita in 1956 with the appearance of the B-52D, the first of which flew on 14 May 1956 and which was destined purely for the long-range bombing role. This variant entered service with SAC at Castle Air Force Base, California, in June 1956. 170 were built, following 35 B-52Cs constructed at Seattle. The B-52E was also purely a strategic bomber, 42 being built at Seattle and 58 at Wichita. First flight of the B-52E was on 3 October 1957, and one of the Seattle batch later served as a test bed for the General Electric GE TF-39 turbofan engine. The last B-52 variant to be built at Boeing's Seattle plant was the B-52F, which flew in May 1958. 89 were constructed, and these served with SAC's 2nd, 7th, 91st and 454th Bombardment Wings.

In August 1956 Boeing received an order to build what was to become the major production version of the Stratofortress: the B-52G, which carried two NA AGM-28 Hound Dog air-to-surface missiles on underwing pylons and a pair of McDonnell ADM-20

Quail decoy missiles. The first B-52G was delivered to SAC at Travis AFB, California, in February 1959, and 193 were built in all. B-52Gs served with the 5th, 17th, 39th, 42nd, 68th, 70th, 72nd, 97th, 320th, 397th, 416th 461st and 465th Bombardment Wings.

The last B-52G was completed late in 1960, its place on the Wichita production line being taken by the considerably modified B-52H with eight 17,000lb thrust Pratt & Whitney TF-33-P-3 turbofan engines. 102 B-52Hs were built, the first being delivered to SAC at Wurtsmith AFB, Michigan, in May 1961, and the last to Minot AFB in October 1962. The B-52H was originally intended to carry the Skybolt missile, but when this was abandoned the aircraft was equipped with four AGM-28s. Defensive armament consisted of a Gatling six-barrel 20mm cannon in the tail position. SAC units toreceive the B-52H included the 19th, 319th, 379th, 410th, 449th, and 450th Bombardment Wings.

B-52s operating out of Guam participated in the Vietnam War, carrying up to 35 1,000lb high explosive bombs. Because of the aircraft's low survivability factor in a hostile SAM environment, these operations — apart from a few early incursions into North Vietnamese airspace — were restricted to bombing tracts of jungle in support of land operations in the south. Total production of the B-52 (all variants) was 704 aircraft.

Breguet Alize

France

Role: Carrier-Borne Anti-Submarine Warfare
Operational: 1959-

Engines: One Rolls-Royce Dart RDa21 turboprop rated at 2,100eshp
Span: 51ft 2in
Length: 45ft 6in
Weight: 12,566lb (empty)
18,100lb (normal loaded)
Crew: 3
Max speed: 285mph at sea level
Service ceiling: 20,000ft
Range: 1,785miles (max)
Weapons: Three depth charges or two torpedoes

internally; two depth charges and six 5in rockets or two Nord AS 11/12 missiles underwing; two torpedoes on underwing stations

In 1948 Breguet Aviation received a contract from the French Navy for two prototypes of a carrier-based strike aircraft, the Br960 Vultur. The first of these flew on 3 August 1951, powered by a 980shp Armstrong Siddeley Mamba turboprop and a 4,850lb thrust Hispano-Suiza Nene 101 turbojet, and was followed on 15 September 1952 by the second aircraft with an uprated Mamba AS3 and a Nene 104. This second machine was modified to serve as an aerodynamic test bed for an improved ASW design, which emerged as the Br1050 Alize(Tradewind).

The prototype Alize flew on 6 October 1956 and was followed by two more prototypes and two pre-production aircraft, these being powered by the Rolls-Royce Dart RDa21 turboprop. 75 were ordered for the Aeronavale, the first flying on 26 March 1959, and subsequent orders brought the total for the French Navy up to 100 machines. Alizes served with the Aeronavale's Flottilles 4F and 9F (ASW) at Lann-Bihoue, 6F (ASW and operational training) at Nimes-Garons, and escadrilles 2S, 3S and 10S (target facilities and trials), the ASW Flottilles rotating on a regular basis between their shore bases and the aircraft carriers Clemenceau, Foch and Arromanches. 12 Alizes were also supplied to the Indian Navy to provide an ASW squadron aboard the carrier *Vikrant*, the first being delivered in 1960. The French Navy's most experienced Alize unit, from the operational viewpoint, was Flottille 9F, which in the 10 years between 1960 and 1970 flew the equivalent of 250 times around the world, totalling 36,100 hours' flying time and 8,100 deck landings.

Breguet Atlantic

France

Role: Long-Range Martime Patrol
Operational: 1965-

Engines: Two Hispano-Suiza-built Rolls-Royce Tyne RTY20 Mk21 turboprops rated at 6,105ehp each
Span: 119ft $1\frac{1}{4}$in
Length: 104ft $1\frac{1}{2}$in
Weight: 55,000lb (empty)
95,900lb (max loaded)
Crew: 12-24
Max speed: 363mph at 19,685ft
Service ceiling: 32,800ft
Range: 4,150 miles
Weapons: Mk 43 Brush or LK4 homing torpedoes, standard NATO bombs, HVAR rockets, underwing ASMs or 385lb depth charges

In the early part of 1958, 25 designs were submitted by European aircraft manufacturers in response to a NATO Armaments Committee requirement for a new maritime patrol aircraft to replace the P-2 Neptune in service with NATO's European air forces. The design selected, in October that year, was the turboprop-powered Breguet 1150, and two prototypes followed by two pre-production aircraft were ordered under the name 'Atlantic'. The first prototype flew on 21 October 1961 and the second on 23 February 1962, but the latter was destroyed in an accident less than two months later. The Atlantic was a truly international project, about a third of the development cost being borne by the United States and the work shared between France, West Germany, the Netherlands and Belgium, with Britain contributing the Rolls-Royce Tyne engines and de Havilland propellers (both built under licence by the European consortium). An initial series of 40 aircraft was ordered for the French Navy, the first being delivered on 10 December 1965. The type subsequently equipped Flottille 24F at Lann-Bihoue and Flottilles 21F and 22F at Nimes-Garons. 20 Atlantics were also ordered for the German Kriegsmarine, these serving with Marine-fliegergeschwader 3, and all 60 of the initial series were completed by the middle of 1968. These were followed, however, by further orders, totalling nine for the Royal Netherlands Navy and 18 for the Italian Navy.

The Atlantic carries a normal flight crew of 12, seven of whom are accommodated in the tactical operations compartment. For very long range patrol, missions, a further 12 may be carried as a relief crew. All crew compartments are located in the upper, pressurised section of the Atlantic's 'double-bubble' fuselage, the lower unpressurised section being devoted to a wide variety of maritime stores. These include all standard NATO bombs, 385lb US or French depth charges, homing torpedoes, MVAR rockets, and underwing air-to-surface missiles with either nuclear or conventional warheads.

Bristol Brigand

UK

Role: Light Bomber
Specification: H7/42
Operational: 1946-58
Photo and Data: B1

Engines: Two 2,470hp Bristol Centaurus 57 radials
Span: 72ft 4in
Length: 46ft 5in
Weight: 25,598lb (empty)
39,000lb (max loaded)
Crew: 3
Max speed: 358mph at 16,000ft
Service ceiling: 26,000ft
Range: 2,800miles (max)
Weapons: Four fixed 20mm Hispano cannon in the nose; provision for 2,500lb bombs + 360lb RPs or 2,000lb of RPs

Tracing its ancestry directly to the famous Bristol Beaufighter, the Bristol 167 Brigand was originally developed as a torpedo bomber, the first of four prototypes flying on 4 December 1944. Powered by twin Centauras 57 radials, the Brigand TF1 carried a powerful armament of four 20mm cannon in the nose and one .5in machine gun in the rear cockpit, together with an offensive load of one torpedo, one mine, 2,500lb of bombs or up to 16 rocket projectiles. The war's end, however, brought about a change in requirements, and in fact only 11 TF1s were built, these entering service with Nos 36 and

42 Squadrons of RAF Coastal Command in 1946. A year later they were converted as light bombers, in keeping with the Brigand variant then appearing on the production line: the B Mk 1.

The Brigand B1 entered service with No 84 Squadron at Habbaniyah, Iraq, early in 1949, and later that year replaced the Tempests of No 8 Squadron in Aden. In 1950 they replaced the last of the RAF's operational Beaufighters with No 45 Squadron in Malaya, and during the next four years operated intensively against the communist terrorists in Operation Firedog. Two Brigand B1s were supplied to the Pakistan Air Force for evaluation, but the type was not adopted. The next Brigand variant was the Met Mk 3, an unarmed weather reconnaissance aircraft. 16 were built and allocated to RAF meteorological flights in various parts of the world.

The last Brigand version to leave the assembly line, when production ceased in 1950, was the T Mk 4, an unarmed variant equipped with AI radar and designed for the initial training of night-fighter navigators. Only nine T4s were built, but a number of B1s were converted to T4 standard. The T4 replaced the Wellington T10s of No 228 Operational Conversion Unit at RAF Leeming in July 1951, moving to Colerne the following year to form No 238 OCU. The last radar training variant was the T5, which was either a B1 or T4 fitted with improved AI. In 1957 the Brigands moved to North Luffenham, where 238 OCU was disbanded in March 1958 and the aircraft finally retired from service.

Canadair Argus

Canada

Role: Long-Range Maritime Patrol
Designation: CL-28/CP-107
Operational: 1958-

Engines: Four Wright Cyclone R-3350-EAI turbo-compounds rated at 3,400hp
Span: 142ft 3½in
Length: 128ft 9½in
Weight: 81,000lb (empty)
157,000lb (max loaded)
Crew: 15
Max speed: 288mph at sea level
Service ceiling: 25,700ft
Range: 4,000 miles (normal)
Weapons: Up to 8,000lb of offensive maritime stores

In 1952 the Royal Canadian Air Force issued a requirement for a new and advanced long-range maritime patrol aircraft to replace the Avro Lancaster Mk 10s which were then the mainstay of Canada's Maritime Air Command. In April 1954 Canadair received a development contract for a design based on the Bristol Britannia, the new aircraft retaining the Britannia's wings, tail, landing gear and flying controls. The fuselage was completely redesigned, with provision for a weapons bay and new internal installations. The prototype CL-28 Argus, as the type was known, flew for the first time on 28 March 1957

and was followed by six more aircraft, these being used for service trials and evaluation. The first fully operational Argus Mk 1 was delivered to No 405 Squadron RCAF in May 1958, followed by No 404 Squadron — both based at Greenwood, Nova Scotia — in April 1959. Other units to equip with the Argus were Nos 407 and 415 Squadrons, No 449 Maritime Training Squadron, and the Maritime Proving and Evaluation Unit. In all but No 415 Squadron, the Argus replaced the Lockheed Neptune, which was purchased as an interim aircraft.

Argus production totalled 33 aircraft, the final delivery being made in July 1960. Of these, 13 were Mk1s and 20 Mk2s, the two differing visually in the size of the chin radome, which was much larger on the earlier mark. In 1961 the Argus fleet assumed the search and rescue role in addition to its normal patrol duties, and the aircraft subsequently took part in several notable air/sea rescue operations. The Argus also had a transport capability, being able to carry 40 passengers in the emergency airlift role.

During its operational career the Argus made several noteworthy flights. In July 1961, for example, a No 415 Squadron aircraft set a Canadian endurance record of 30hr 20min, covering a distance of 5,200 miles, and in September 1959 a 405 Squadron Argus Mk2 established a new Canadian non-stop record by flying from Hawaii to RCAF Station North Bay, Ontario, in 20hr 10min, covering a distance of 4,570 miles.

CASA C2111

Germany (Spanish Conversion)

Role: Bomber/Reconnaissance
Operational: 1945-64
Data: C2111-B

Engines: Two 1,500hp Rolls-Royce Merlin 500-20 in-lines
Span: 74ft 1½in
Length: 54ft 5½in
Weight: 14,400lb (empty)
26,445lb (normal loaded)
Crew: 5
Max speed: 260mph at 14,764ft
Service ceiling: 27,890ft
Range: 1,553 miles
Weapons: One 20mm cannon in nose; five 7.9mm machine guns; up to 6,000lb bombs

In 1941 the Construcciones Aeronauticas SA (CASA) began licence production of the Heinkel He111H-16 at Tablada, Seville. 200 production aircraft were ordered by the Spanish Air Force, but the first of these did not fly until 1945, and by that time the supply of German-built Jumo 211F-2 engines had dried up. The Hispano HS-12Z-17 engine was considered as an alternative power source, but production of this powerplant was nearing completion and, in 1953, it was decided to adopt the Rolls-Royce Merlin 500-20 instead. Several experimental conversions were carried out and proved successful, and in April 1956 the Spanish Government placed an order for 173 Merlins. Re-equipment proceeded rapidly, some Heinkels being re-engined and the remainder

receiving the Merlins on the production line. In Spanish Air Force service, the Merlin-engined Heinkel was designated B21, with the manufacturer's designation C2111-B. Other variants were the C2111-D and-D1 reconnaissance bombers, with 1,600hp Merlin 500-29 engines and cameras mounted in the starboard section of the bomb bay. 15 aircraft were also converted as transports, with the designation T8. Many CASA C2111s were still flying in the 1960s, and some of the surviving aircraft were used in the making of the film *The Battle of Britain*.

Chance Vought F4U/AV Corsair USA

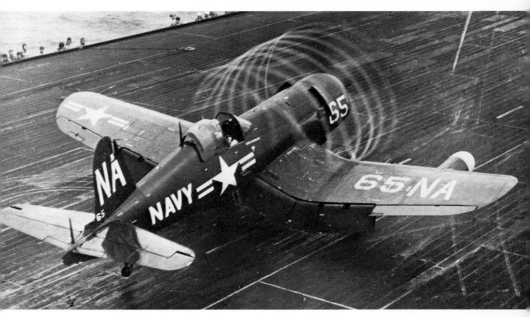

Role: Carrier-Borne Fighter-Bomber
Operational: 1943-64
Photo: F4U-5N
Data: F4U-7

Engines: One Pratt & Whitney R-2800-83WA radial rated at 2,100hp
Span: 40ft 11¾in
Length: 34ft 6½in
Weight: 9,230lb (empty)
12,399lb (loaded)
Crew: 1
Max speed: 450mph at 26,000ft
Service ceiling: 41,000ft
Range: 1,120miles
Weapons: Four 20mm cannon in wings; eight 5in rockets and two 1,000lb bombs, or two 1,600lb bombs under wings

Although the Chance Vought Corsair's place in aviation history properly belongs to the Pacific battlegrounds of 1943-45, where it achieved fame, it remained a significant combat aircraft for many years after World War II, by the end of which 12,681 aircraft had been built. Postwar developments included the F4U-5 fighter-bomber, F4U-5N all-

weather fighter, F4U-5P photo-reconnaissance aircraft, F4U-6 attack aircraft and F4U-7, the final variant. From 1946 to 1950 the Corsair formed the spearhead of the US Navy's carrier-borne fighter-bomber squadrons, having been replaced in the interceptor role by jet fighters, and was in the forefront of the fighting from the outbreak of hostilities in Korea. During the three years of the Korean War Corsairs accounted for nearly half the total sorties flown by the US Navy and Marine Corps, and one US Navy pilot, Lt Guy P. Bordelon, destroyed five enemy aircraft at night while flying an F4U-5NL Corsair (a winterised F4U-5N), becoming the Navy's only ace of the conflict. Noteworthy attack missions in which the Corsair took part included a strike on the Hwachon Dam in North Korea, which marked the first and only use of aerial torpedoes in the Korean War.

The Corsair was retired from the US Navy in December 1955, the last unit to use it being VC-4 with F4U-5Ns. A small number of F4U-6 Corsairs (later designated AU-1) were supplied to the French Navy, which used them operationally in Indo-China. 94 examples of the last production model, the F4U-7 — which was basically similar to the wartime F4U-4C but with a number of equipment changes — were also delivered to France under the Mutual

Defense Aid Programme of 1952-53, and the surviving aircraft equipped the Aeronavale's Flottilles 12F, 14F, 15F and 17F until the early 1960s, when they were replaced by the Dassault Etendard and, later, the Chance Vought Crusader. The last air arm to use the Corsair was El Salvador, which had a fighter-bomber flight of F4U-5s — the country's only combat type — in first-line service up to 1964.

Chance Vought F7U Cutlass

USA

Role: Naval Strike Fighter
Operational: 1954-58
Photo: F7U-1 prototype
Data: F7U-3M

Engines: Two Westinghouse J46-WE-8A turbojets rated at 4,600lb thrust each (6,100lb with reheat)
Span: 38ft 8in
Length: 43ft 1in
Weight: 18,210lb (empty)
27,340lb (normal loaded)
Crew: 1
Max speed: 705mph at sea level with reheat
Service ceiling: 40,000ft
Range: 660miles (clean)
Weapons: Four 20mm Mk 12 cannon installed above engines; four Sparrow I AAMs; pack containing 2.75in FFARs; up to 4,500lb of external stores

Although its service career was relatively short-lived, the radical Chance Vought F7U Cutlass had a claim to fame on several counts. It was the first production naval aircraft to achieve supersonic flight, the first to release bombs at supersonic speed and, in its day, the heaviest single-seat carrier fighter in service with any navy. It also set the pattern for future generations of multi-mission combat aircraft, being readily adaptable as an interceptor, an air superiority fighter, a low-level attack aircraft or for day and night reconnaissance.

The prototype XF7U-1 Cutlass flew on 29 September 1948 and was followed by a pre-production batch of 14 F7U-1s for service evaluation, the first of which flew on 1 March 1950. These aircraft were powered by a pair of Westinghouse J34-WE-32 turbojets developing a thrust of 3,000lb (4,200lb with reheat), and with these powerplants the F7U-1's performance fell considerably short of US Navy requirements. Chance Vought accordingly put forward proposals for a version with more powerful engines, the F7U-2, but this was doomed by the US defence cuts of 1949-50. Chance Vought nevertheless persevered with a much redesigned version, the F7U-3, and finally received a development contract in February 1950. Powered by two Allison J35-A-21A turbojets, the F7U-3 flew for the first time on 22 December 1951 and completed its carrier trials by July the following year. These demonstrated the Cutlass's extraordinary low-speed handling characteristics, vindicating Chance Vought's faith in their tailless configuration. The aircraft also proved to have good manoeuvrability and rate of climb.

First unit to equip with the Cutlass was Navy Fighter Squadron VF-81, in April 1954, and a dozen other carrier-based squadrons also received the type. Early production F7U-3s were still somewhat underpowered, and most operational Cutlasses were re-engined with the more powerful J46-WE-8A turbojets when these became available. On 12 July 1955, a new Cutlass variant made its appearance; this was the F7U-3M, with launching racks for four Sparrow I beam-riding AAMs and a central fuselage pack housing 2.75in Mighty Mouse FFARs. Another version, the F7U-3P, also flew in July 1955; this had a nose lengthened by just over 2ft and was equipped with up to five cameras for day and night reconnaissance.

In its attack configuration, the Cutlass could carry an underwing load of up to 5,400lb. By the end of 1958, the F7U had been largely phased out in favour of more advanced types such as the F8 Crusader, the last operational unit to use it being Attack Squadron VA-66. In March 1956, Attack Squadron VA-83, equipped with F7U-3Ms, became the first US Navy missile-armed squadron to deploy overseas, operating from the USS *Intrepid* as part of the Sixth Fleet in the Mediterranean.

Chance Vought F-8 Crusader

USA

Role: Naval Strike Fighter
Operational: 1957-
Photo: F8U-1
Data: F-8E

Engines: One Pratt & Whitney J57-P-20 turbojet rated at 18,000lb thrust with reheat
Span 35ft 8in
Length: 54ft 6in
Weight: 22,000lb (empty)
34,000lb (loaded)
Crew: 1
Max speed: 1,155mph at 36,000ft
Service ceiling: 55,000ft
Range: 1,000 miles
Weapons: Four 20mm cannon, various combinations of bombs or 24+rockets

The first carrier-borne aircraft capable of supersonic speed in level flight, the Chance Vought Crusader was the winner of a United States Navy competition for a new day fighter in May 1953. The first Crusader, designated XF8U-1, flew at Edwards AFB on 25 March 1955 and exceeded Mach 1 during its maiden flight, powered by a Pratt & Whitney J57-P-12 turbojet developing 13,000lb thrust. The first production F8U-1 flew on 30 September 1955 and by April the following year the aircraft had completed its carrier trials aboard the USS Forrestal. The type was formally accepted by the US Navy in December 1956, only 21 months after the first flight of the XF8U-1. The main reason for this rapid development was that virtually no changes were required in production aircraft, which had the same engine as the two prototypes. With this power plant, one of the early F8U-1s set up the first American national speed record above 1,000mph, reaching 1,015.428mph over China Lake, California, on 21 August 1956. F8U-1s (F8As) were later re-engined with the J57-P-4A. Armament was four 20mm cannon in the nose, with a belly pack containing 32 2.75in HVAR rockets. Two Sidewinder missiles were also carried on either side of the forward fuselage. Production of

the F8A ended in 1958, by which time 318 had been built.

The F8U1-E (F-8B) followed the F8A into production in September 1958. This version, of which 130 were built, had a larger nose radome and limited all-weather capability. Meanwhile, a reconnaissance version — the F8U-1P (RF-8A) — had flown in December 1956. This variant was capable of both day and night reconnaissance, and was used extensively for surveillance during the Cuban crisis of 1962 and its aftermath. 144 were built, of which 53 were later modernised in 1965-66 and redesignated RF-8G.

The F8U-2 (F-8C) was an improved version of the F-8A with a J57-P-16 turbojet, and flew in December 1957. Externally similar to the F-8A, it carried four Sidewinders as well as its cannon armament and had an improved fire control system. It entered service in April 1959 with Navy Squadron VF-84, and 187 were built. 87 F-8Cs were refurbished and designated F-8K; during the late 1960s, in fact, 375 Crusaders were modernised with structural alterations, improved avionics and fire control systems.

The F8U-2N (F-8D) Crusader, which first flew in February 1960, had a limited all-weather capability and was powered by a J57-P-20 turbojet with a thrust of 18,000lb with reheat, giving it a maximum speed approaching Mach 2. This variant had no belly rocket pack, but retained the 20mm cannon armament and four Sidewinders. Deliveries to the US Navy and Marine Corps were completed in January 1962 after 152 had been built. 89 were later completely refurbished, given an attack capability and designated F-8H.

The last Crusader variant to bear the old US Service nomenclature was the F8U-2NE (F-8E), which was basically similar to the F-8D but with more advanced APQ-94 search and fire control radar. The F-8E was the first Crusader to be developed for the strike role, being fitted with underwing pylons to carry a wide variety of loads including 12 250lb bombs, four 500lb bombs, two 1,000lb bombs, two 2,000lb bombs or 24 Zuni rockets, with provision for eight more Zunis instead of the fuselage-mounted Sidewinders. During trials,

an F-8E was launched from the carrier USS *Forrestal* at an all-up weight of 34,000lb, carrying full fuel, two 2,000lb bombs and eight Zunis. Over 250 F-8Es were built, and 136 were refurbished under the designation F-8J, the first of these flying on 17 July 1967.

The F-8E(FN) was a variant for the French Navy, 42 being ordered in August 1963 to equip two Aeronavale squadrons on the carriers *Clemenceau* and *Foch*. The last aircraft was delivered in January 1965, and this was the final new Crusader to be built. The F-8E (FN) had provision for two Matra R530 missiles in addition to Sidewinders.

Crusaders served extensively during the Vietnam War and, in company with A-4 Skyhawks (both operating from the USS *Hancock*) carried out the first air strike in the systematic US effort to destroy North Vietnam's fuel storage facilities on 16 June 1966. F-8s served with some 40 US Navy and Marine Corps squadrons, beginning with VF-32 towards the end of 1957.

Convair B-36 USA

Role: Strategic Heavy Bomber
Operational: 1947-57
Photo: RB-36E
Data: B-36H

Engines: Six 3,800hp Pratt & Whitney R-4360-53 radials and four 5,200lb thrust General Electric J47 turbojets
Span: 230ft
Length: 162ft
Weight:
358,000lb (max) loaded
Crew: 16
Max speed: 435mph over target
Service ceiling: 42,000ft
Range: 8,000miles
Weapons: Six retractable remotely-controlled turrets each housing twin 20mm cannon, plus two 20mm cannon in nose and two in tail; normal bomb load 10,000lb; maximum bomb load 84,000lb

The first bomber with truly global strategic capability to serve with any air force, the mighty Convair B-36 flew for the first time on 8 August 1946, powered by six Pratt & Whitney R-4360-25 engines developing 3,000hp each, The first XB-36 was followed by two more prototypes, the YB-36 and YB-36A, both of which flew in 1947. Unlike the two earlier aircraft, which had conventional undercarriages, the YB-36A had a bogie-type assembly and a modified cockpit, the canopy being raised above the line of the fuselage to improve visibility. An initial production batch of 22 B-36As was built, the first being delivered to Strategic Air Command in the summer of 1947. These aircraft were unarmed, and were used for crew training. The second production model, the B-36B, was powered by six 3,500hp Pratt & Whitney R-4360-41 engines with water injection, and was fully combat equipped with 12 20mm KM24A1 cannon in six turrets, together with nose and tail armament. 73 were built, the first flying on 8 July 1948. The B-36C was an abandoned project with six tractor engines in place of the normal B-36 'pusher' configuration.

The next variant, the B-36D, had four General Electric J47-GE-19 turbojets paired in pods under the outer wings to supplement the six piston engines and provide additional power for increased speed over the target area. The B-36D had snap-action bomb doors in place of the sliding type used in earlier models, and carried a 37mm cannon in the nose. First delivery to SAC took place at Eglin AFB on 19 August 1950. 22 aircraft were built, and 64 B-36Bs were modified to B-36D standard. The RB-36D was a long-range strategic reconnaissance version, equipped with 14 cameras and carrying a crew of 22 instead of the usual 16. 17 were built, and seven B-36Bs converted.

One of the more interesting B-36 variants was the GRB-36 Fighter Conveyor (FICON). 12 RB-36Ds were modified to carry an RF-84K Thunderflash on a special trapeze, the fighter being launched and retrieved in flight and recessed in the bomb bay. The GRB-36 served with the 91st Strategic Reconnaissance Squadron in 1955, but the idea was generally unsuccessful. Another strategic reconnaissance version, the RB-36E, was in fact the modified B-36A, all 22 of which were transformed together with the YB-36A production prototype. The RB-36E was re-engined and fitted with J47 turbojets, as in the B-36D.

The fourth production model, the B-36F, had six Pratt & Whitney R-4360-53 engines rated at 3,800hp, in addition to the J47s. 28 were built,

followed by 24 RB-36Fs. The YB-36G was a pure-jet project with a swept wing, and in fact became the YB-60, the unsuccessful competitor against Boeing's B-52.

Next on the production line was the B-36H, which was basically a B-36F with a modified flight deck layout and improved avionics. 81 were bulit, together with 73 examples of the reconnaissance version, the RB-36H. One B-36H (serial 51-5712) was modified to carry out tests of an airborne nuclear reactor and redesignated NB-36H. It carried a five-man crew. The final production version was the B-36J, of which 33 were built. The last example was delivered to SAC in August 1954, and the type continued in service until all SAC strategic heavy bomber wings had re-equipped with the B-52.

Convair B-58 Hustler

USA

Role: Strategic Medium Bomber
Operational: 1960-1970
Data: B-58A

Engines: Four General Electric J79-GE-5B turbojets rated at 10,000lb thrust (15,600lb with reheat)
Span: 56ft 10in
Length: 96ft 9in
Weight: 163,000lb (loaded)
Crew: 3
Max speed: 1,385mph at 40,000ft
Service ceiling: 60,000ft (zoom climb: 90,000ft)
Range: 2,400 miles
Weapons: One 20mm T-171E3 rotary cannon in extreme tail; conventional or nuclear weapons in detachable 'mission pod'

The first supersonic bomber to enter service with the USAF, the Convair B-58 originated in an Air Force design study competition of 1949, which was won by the Fort Worth division of General Dynamics. The design was given the designation B-58 in 1951, when Convair was awarded another contract to continue the study of the supersonic bombing

system concept, and in 1952 a third USAF contract gave the company the go-ahead to produce the B-58 as a viable weapon system. The aircraft was ordered into production in October 1954, and the prototype (55-0660) was flown on 11 November 1956. This was followed by a second prototype and a pre-production batch of 11 YB-58As for testing and service evaluation. The first operational Hustler entered service with Strategic Air Command's 43rd Bomb Wing in March 1960, followed by the 305th Bomb Wing in 1961. Originally, it was anticipated that the B-58 would replace SAC's B-47s, but in the event only enough aircraft were built to equip the two above-mentioned wings, a total of six squadrons. In addition to the prototypes and the pre-production aircraft, 103 B-58As came off the assembly line, eight of which converted as crew trainers with the designation TB-58A. Another conversion was the NB-58A, which was used as a test bed for the General Electric J93-GE-3 turbojet.

The B-58 was a bold departure from conventional design, having a delta wing with a conical-cambered leading edge, an area-ruled fuselage and four podded J79-GE-5B turbojets. The three-man crew were seated in tandem cockpits, and the B-58 was the

first aircraft in the world in which the crew had individual escape capsules for use at supersonic speed. The machine had no internal weapons bay, carrying a large under-fuselage pod housing weaponry, fuel, reconnaissance sensors and ECM equipment. Fuel was carried in the pod's lower component, which could be jettisoned under combat conditions when its contents were exhausted. The upper part of the pod was also jettisoned after weapon release, leaving the aircraft aerodynamically clean for the flight back to base.

During its relatively short career the Hustler established several international records. In 1961 it set up six records for speed with and without payload over 1,000km and 2,000km closed circuit courses, reaching a maximum speed of 1,430mph on one of the runs. In 1962 it attained an altitude of 85,360.84ft carrying an 11,023lb payload, and on 16 October that year it flew non-stop from Tokyo to London in 8hr 35min at an average speed of 938mph, being refuelled in flight five times.

Convair F-102 Delta Dagger/F-106 Delta Dart   USA

Role: All-Weather Interceptor
Operational: 1956-(F-102)
1959-(F-106)

	F-102A	F-106A
Engines:	One Pratt & Whitney J-57-P-23 turbojet rated at 11,700lb thrust and 17,200lb with reheat	One Pratt & Whitney J75-P-17 turbojet rated at 17,200lb thrust and 24,500lb with reheat
Span:	38ft 1½in	38ft 1½in
Length:	68ft 4in	70ft 8in
Weight (normal loaded)	28,600lb	35,000lb
Crew:	1	1
Max speed:	825mph at 36,000ft	1,525mph at 40,000ft
Service ceiling:	54,000ft	57,000ft
Range:	800 miles	2,700miles (max external fuel)
Weapons:	Three AIM 4A/E beam riding and three AIM-4C/F infra-red homing Falcon missiles	Two Douglas AIR-2A Genie or AIR-2B Super Genie nuclear AAMS or four Falcons

F-102 Delta Dagger

Designed in response to a 1950 USAF requirement for an all-weather interceptor incorporating the latest fire control system, the Convair F-102 was based on experience gained during the flight testing of the XF-92 delta-wing research aircraft. Two prototype YF-102s were built, the first flying on 24 October 1953. This aircraft was damaged beyond repair only a week later, but testing resumed with the second machine in January 1954. Eight more YF-102s were built for evaluation, and it soon became apparent that the aircraft's performance fell short of expectations. After substantial airframe redesign the machine re-emerged in December 1954 as the YF-102A, and the type was ordered into full production. The first F-102A was handed over to the USAF in June 1955, but it was another year before the type was issued to squadrons. Production of the Delta Dagger ended in April 1958 after 875 aircraft had been delivered, and several major modifications were subsequently carried out to update the machine's

combat capability. These included the installation of equipment providing full infra-red target acquisition capability.

During its lengthy operational career the F-102 equipped one Tactical Fighter Squadron (the 509th, based in the Philippines); nine all-weather interceptor squadrons within the North American Air Defense Command (the 57th at Keflavik, Iceland, the 59th, 64th, 82nd, 325th, 326th, the 332nd at Thule, Greenland, the 460th and 482nd. It also equipped one squadron (the 317th) of Alaskan Air Command; three Japan-based squadrons of Pacific Air Forces (the 4th, 16th and 40th); and six squadrons of USAFE, three in Germany (the 496th, 525th and 526th), one in Holland (the 32nd) and two in Spain (the 431st and 497th). Completing an impressive list, F-102s also served with 16 Air National Guard squadrons, and equipped two squadrons of the Turkish Air Force on NATO's southern flank. 63 examples of a subsonic two-seat trainer version, the

TF-102A, were produced as combat proficiency trainers. In Vietnam, F-102As were used for 'hot pad alert' defence of principal US air bases.

F-106 Delta Dart

The Convair F-106 Delta Dart was a straightforward development of the F-102 with redesigned fuselage and tail surfaces, the prototype flying on 26 December 1956. This was followed by 16 pre-production aircraft which were used for trials and service evaluation, and the first production aircraft entered service with the 539th Fighter Interceptor Squadron in June 1959. Production ended in 1962 after 257 aircraft had been built, and in the early 1960s the F-106A was the most important type on the inventory of Air Defense Command, with which it served exclusively. 13 Fighter Interceptor Squadrons

used the type: the 5th, 11th, 27th, 48th, 71st, 94th, 95th, 318th, 329th, 438th, 456th, 498th and 539th. On 15 December 1959 a Delta Dart established a new world air speed record of 1,525.95mph. Like the earlier F-102A, the F-106A had its systems progressively updated, and in 1967 the aircraft was equipped with external fuel tanks capable of being carried at supersonic speed. At the height of the aircraft's operational career its MA-1 fire control system, linked with the SAGE air defence network, made it one of the most sophisticated interceptors in the world. The F-106B was a two-seat training version which possessed full interception capability and carried advanced radar equipment in the rear cockpit. It first flew in April 1958, and production ended in 1960 with the 63rd machine.

Dassault Etendard   France

Role: Carrier-Borne Strike Fighter
Operational: 1962-

Engines: One 9,700lb thrust SNECMA Atar 8 turbojet
Span: 31ft 6in
Length: 47ft 3in
Weight: 13,000lb (empty)
22,650lb (max loaded)
Crew: 1
Max speed: 713mph at 36,000ft
Service ceiling: 49,200ft
Range: 1,860 miles (ferry)
Weapons: Two 30mm DEFA cannon; four underwing points for up to 3,000lb of rockets, bombs ASMs or Sidewinder AAMs

Originally designed to meet the requirements of a

mid-1950s NATO tactical strike fighter contest — which it lost to the Fiat G91 — the Dassault Etendard (Standard) nevertheless showed such outstanding qualities that a development contract was awarded on behalf of the French Navy, who at that time were looking for a strike aircraft capable also of undertaking high-altitude interception. Dassault had already produced three prototypes of the basic Etendard design, the last of which — designated Etendard IV — was developed as a private venture in the expectation of the NATO contracts, and it was this aircraft which was modified for naval use. Bearing the designation Etendard IVM-01 (the 'M' standing for Marine) — the first navalised prototype flew on 21 May 1958 and began service trials the following October. During this period it flew to the United Kingdom and underwent 'dry' deck landing trials at the Royal

Aircraft Establishment, Bedford. The prototype was followed by seven pre-production aircraft, one of them fitted with a Rolls-Royce Avon 51 engine and designated Etendard IVB and another serving as the prototype for the Etendard IVP reconnaissance variant.

The first of 69 production Etendard IVMs was delivered to the Aeronavale on 18 January 1962, the initial batch serving as OCU aircraft with Flottille 15F. Other units to equip with the Etendard IVM during the months that followed were Flottilles 11F, 14F, 17F and 59S, while Flottille 16F received the Etendard IVP photo-recce version. The latter was unarmed and served in the dual role of tanker, being equipped with the Douglas-designed hose-reel flight refuelling system. The Dassault Super Etendard, which first flew on 24 November 1977, is a transonic strike aircraft with an Atar 8K-50 engine, and is designed primarily for the low-level attack role.

Dassault Ouragan France

Role: Single-Seat Interceptor
Operational: 1952-68

Engines: One 5,070lb thrust Hispano-Suiza Nene 104B turbojet
Span: 40ft $3\frac{1}{2}$in
Length: 32ft $2\frac{1}{4}$in
Weight: 9,131lb (empty)
14,991lb (landed)
Crew: 1
Max speed: 584mph at sea level
Service ceiling: 49,000ft
Range: 600 miles
Weapons: Four 20mm Hispano Type 404 Mk 50 cannon; rockets and two 1,100lb bombs on underwing racks

The first jet fighter of French design to be ordered in quantity, the Dassault MD450 Ouragan began as a private venture in November 1947, and the first prototype flew on 28 February 1949 powered by a 5,000lb thrust Rolls-Royce Nene 102 turbojet, built under licence by Hispano-Suiza. A second prototype flew on 22 July 1949, followed by a third aircraft on 2 June 1950. The latter was fitted with an improved Nene 104B engine developing 5,070lb thrust. 12 pre-production and 350 production aircraft were ordered for the Armee de l'Air, equipping four fighter wings in 1952. Some of the pre-production aircraft were used for experimental purposes; the third was fitted with a 6,800lb thrust afterburning Nene 102B, the eleventh was fitted with lateral air intakes, and the eighth and twelfth machines were used to test early 30mm DEFA cannon.

The last Ouragan came off the assembly line in 1954. A year earlier, the Indian Air Force placed an order for 71 aircraft powered by the 5,180lb thrust Nene 105A, and in February 1957 13 more machines of this type were shipped to India aboard the French carrier Dixmude. Named Toofani (Whirlwind) in Indian service, the Ouragan began to be replaced by the Mystere IV in 1958, but remained in service as an operational trainer until well into the 1960s.

The second overseas customer was the Israeli Air Force, which received an initial batch of Ouragans in November 1955. During the next two years the number of Ouragans supplied to Israel rose to 75. The aircraft saw action during the Arab-Israeli war of 1956 and proved capable of absorbing considerable battle damage, although they were distinctly inferior to the MiG-15s used by the Egyptian Air Force. As in India, the Ouragan was used for some years in the operational training role after being phased out of first-line service. In 1975, Israel supplied 18 of her surviving Ouragans to El Salvador, and these were still operational in 1978.

Dassault Mirage III

France

Role: Multi-Role Combat
Operational: 1961-
Photo: IIIA
Data: IIIE

Engines: One SNECMA Atar 09C turbojet developing 13,670lb thrust with reheat, one optional and jettisonable SEPR 844 rocket motor of 3,300lb
Span: 27ft
Length: 49ft 3½in
Weight: 15,540lb (empty)
29,760lb (max loaded)
Crew: 1
Max speed: 1,460mph at 39,375ft, 851mph at sea level (clean)
Service ceiling: 55,775ft; 75,450ft with rocket motor
Range: 1,500miles
Weapons: Two 30mm DEFA cannon, two 1,000lb bombs, or one AS30 missile under fuselage and 1,000lb bombs under wings. Alternative underwing stores include JL-100 rocket pods, each with 18 rockets, and 250-litre fuel tanks. For interception, one MATRA R530 AAM can be carried under fuselage, plus two Sidewinder AAMs.

One of the biggest success stories in the field of post-1945 combat aircraft design, the Dassault Mirage III owes it origin to the Dassault MK550 Mirage I of 1954, which, together with the SE Durandal and SO Trident, was a contender in a French Air Force competition of a high-altitude interceptor. The Mirage I proved too small to carry an effective war load and its twin Viper turbojets failed to supply the necessary power, so the airframe was substantially redesigned and enlarged and fitted with a single 8,800lb thrust SNECMA Atar G1 engine. Designated Mirage III-001, the new aircraft made its first flight on 17 November 1956 and exceeded

Mach 1.5 in level flight on 30 January 1957. Later, equipped with a SEPR auxiliary rocket motor, it reached a speed of Mach 1.9.

Hopes that the Mirage III would be selected as an F-86 Sabre replacement in the Luftwaffe and other NATO air forces were shattered when the Lockheed F-104G Starfighter was chosen instead, and it became clear that the emphasis in the 1960s would be on versatility. Accordingly, the French Government instructed Dassault to proceed with the development of a multi-mission version of the Mirage, the IIIA, powered by a 9,370lb thrust Atar 09 engine. The prototype Mirage IIIA-01 flew on 12 May 1958, and a pre-series batch of 10 Mirage IIIAs was ordered, six of them equipped to production standard with Cyrano Ibis AI radar. On 18 June 1959 one of the Mirage IIIAs established a 100km closed circuit record speed of 1,109mph, and another zoom-climbed to 82,500ft with the aid of its SEPR 841 liquid rocket. The aircraft was capable of a speed of Mach 2.2 in level flight at 50,000ft.

The Mirage IIIC, which flew on 9 October 1960, was the first production version and was identical to the IIIA, with an Atar 09 B3 turbojet and a SEPR 841 or 844 rocket motor. 100 Mirage IIICs were ordered for the French Air Force, equipping the 2e and 13e Escadres de Chasse. 72 similar aircraft, without rocket motors or missiles, were also supplied to the Israeli Air Force, first deliveries being made to No 101 Squadron in 1963. These aircraft were designated Mirage IIICJ. 16 more aircraft in the IIIC series were supplied to South Africa as the Mirage IIICZ, equipping Nos 2 and 3 Squadrons. The SAAF also took delivery of three Mirage IIIBZ two-seaters, which carried the same armament as the IIIC. The first production IIIB flew on 19 July 1962; 73 were built, some being supplied to Brazil, Israel, the Lebanon and Switzerland, as well as South Africa.

The Mirage IIIE was a long-range tactical strike

variant capable of delivering a wide variety of conventional and nuclear weapons. The prototype Mirage IIIE-01 first flew on 5 April 1961 and 453 examples were subsequently produced for the French Air Force, where it equipped eight squadrons of FATAC (Force Aerienne Tactique), and the air forces of Brazil, the Lebanon, Argentina, South Africa, Pakistan, Libya and Spain. Among famous French units to use the IIIE were the 1/2 'Cigognes' and the 3/2 'Alsace' of the 2e Escadre de Chasse. A version of the IIIE, the Mirage IIIO, was manufactured under licence in Australia, the main differences being the fitting of a Sperry Twin Gyro Platform and a PHI 5CI navigation unit. The first two IIIOs were assembled in France and handed over to the RAAF in April 1963, and a further 98 were built in Australia. These machines equipped Nos 3, 75, 76 and 77 Squadrons RAAF, as well as No 2 OCU. The latter unit also received the Mirage IIID, the licence-built two-seat version of the IIIO for the RAAF; 10 were delivered in November 1966. Similar models were supplied to Argentina (III-DA), Pakistan (III-DP), Brazil (III-DBR), Spain (III-DE) and South Africa (III-DZ).

Dassault Mirage IV

Role: Medium-Range Tactical and Strategic Bomber
Operational: 1964-

Engines: Two SNECMA Atar 09K turbojets rated at 10,800lb thrust (15,435lb with reheat)
Span: 38ft 10in
Length: 76ft 11in
Weight: 32,000lb (empty)
66,140lb (normal loaded)
Crew: 2
Max speed: 1,520mph at 40,000ft
Service ceiling: 65,000ft
Range: 1,600 miles
Weapons: One 70-kiloton free-falling nuclear weapon recessed in underside of fuselage

In 1956, the French Air Force issued a draft specification for a new supersonic bomber capable of carrying France's first atomic bomb. There were two contenders: Sud Aviation, who offered a design based on their Vautour light bomber, and GAMD Marcel Dassault, who proposed a scaled-up development of the Mirage III. The Dassault proposal was selected, and a development contract signed in April 1957. The requirements surrounding the new design, known as the Mirage IV, called for an

The Mirage IIIR was the reconnaissance version of the IIIE, equipped with a battery of five OMERA Type 31 cameras in place of the nose radar. The two prototypes, the first of which flew in November 1961, were converted from IIIAs, and total production orders in 1978 stood at 153 aircraft, destined for the French, Pakistani, South African and Swiss Air Forces. An improved version, the Mirage IIIRD, had a Doppler navigation system, infra-red tracking equipment, gyro gunsight and automatic cameras. Twenty were built for the French Air Force.

Another variant developed from the IIIE was the Mirage IIIS, fitted with a Hughes TARAN electronic fire control system and carrying an armament of Falcon missiles. 36 were built for the Swiss Air Force, equipping Nos 16 and 17 Squadrons.

The Mirage IIICJs of the Israeli Air Force saw considerable action during the various Arab-Israeli conflicts since 1967. During the Indo-Pakistan war of 1969, the 17 Mirage IIIEPs of No 5 Squadron, Pakistan Air Force, destroyed nine Indian aircraft for no loss to themselves.

France

unrefuelled combat radius of about 1,000 miles and an over-target speed of at least Mach 1.7. The aircraft also had to be capable of operating from airfields used by existing jet fighter-bombers. Designated Mirage IVA in its definitive form, the design received final approval in the summer of 1959, a proposal for a still larger version with an increased combat radius — the Mirage IVB — having meanwhile been rejected.

The prototype Mirage IV-01, in fact, made its first flight in June 1959, while the merits of the two designs were still being considered, and in September an order was placed for three pre-production aircraft. The first of these flew in October 1961 and was later used for armament trials, dropping replicas of the operational version of the French A-bomb. The second pre-production machine was used mainly for flight refuelling trials, first with converted Vautours and later with Boeing KC-135s on loan from the USAF, and the last pre-production aircraft was a fully operational model.

The Mirage IVA entered service with the 91e Escadre de Bombardement in 1964 and ultimately equipped three Escadres, dispersed on airfields throughout metropolitan France and served by 12 KC-135F tankers. Each Escadre was composed of three Escadrons, each with four or five aircraft, and a centralised maintenance system ensured that at

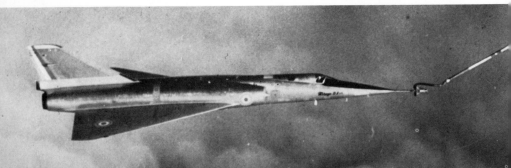

least 80% of the Mirage IV strike force was at operational readiness at all times. One Mirage in each Escadron was always kept in 15-minute readiness. Of the 60 Mirage IVs delivered to the Armee de l'Air, 45 were still serving in 1978, some of them in the strategic reconnaissance and electonic countermeasures role. From 1970, all Mirage IVs were withdrawn from their units on a rotation basis for structural tests and re-equipping compatible with low-level operations.

Dassault Mirage 5   France

Role: Multi-Role Combat
Operational: 1961–

Engine: One SNECMA Atar 9C turbojet rated at 9,436lb thrust (13,624lb with reheat)
Span: 26ft 11½in
Length: 52ft 0¼in
Weight: 14,550lb (empty)
29,760lb (max loaded)
Crew: 1
Max speed: 1,386mph at 40,000ft; 875mph at sea level
Service ceiling: 55,000ft
Range: 2,485 miles (max ferry)
Weapons: Two DEFA 30mm cannon plus up to 8,800lb of external stores

The Mirage 5 single-seat tactical fighter-bomber was derived from the Mirage IIIE, using the same airframe and engine, and intended primarily for export. Although having the same Mach 2+ capability of the Mirage III, it can also operate from rudimentary airstrips and its maintenance is simpler. The basic version can carry a wider variety of stores than the IIIE, has simplified avionics and increased fuel capacity. In its ground-attack configuration, the Mirage 5 can carry up to 8,200lb of external stores and can also be used as an interceptor, carrying two Sidewinder AAMs. Depending on customer requirements, the Mirage 5 can be equipped for full IFR operations, with a correspondingly reduced weapons load. The Mirage 5 was flown for the first time on 19 May 1967 and, up to 1978, was ordered for 11 air forces. In 1968 it successfully competed with the SAAB Draken and the McDonnell Douglas A-4 Skyhawk and was selected to re-equip the ground-attack squadrons of the Belgian Air Force, which had been operating F-84F Thunderstreaks. 106 Mirage 5s were ordered, in three versions: 63 ground-attack Mirage 5BAs, 27 fighter-reconnaissance 5BRs, and 16 two-seat 5BD trainers, the latter retaining the full combat capability of the 5BA. The Mirages equipped the BAF's Nos 1, 2 and 42 Squadrons, and No 8 (OCU) Squadron. The Mirage 5COA, 5COR and 5COD were variants for the Colombian Air Force, while 110 Mirage 5Ds, 5DDs, 5DEs and 5DRs were ordered by Libya, deliveries beginning in January 1971. The Israeli Air Force ordered 50 Mirage 5Js, but delivery was prevented by a French Government embargo. 12 Mirage 5Ps and two 5DP two-seat trainers were delivered to Peru, and a number of 5DM two-seaters were supplied to Zaire.

In 1975, an improved version of the Mirage 5 made its appearance, powered by a SNECMA Atar 9K-50 turbojet giving a 16% thrust increase over standard Mirage III/5s. Designated Mirage 50, the new aircraft is a multi-mission fighter which can be used in the air superiority role as well as for ground attack. The Sudan ordered 50 late in 1977. By the beginning of 1978, total orders for the Mirage III and 5 stood at 1,323 aircraft, the two types either in service with or on order for 20 different countries, including France.

29

Dassault Mirage F1

France

Role: Single-Seat Strike Fighter
Operational: 1973-
Data: F1C

Engines: One SNECMA Atar 9K-50 turbojet rated at
11,067lb thrust (15,785lb with reheat)
Span: 27ft 6¾in
Length: 49ft 2½in
Weight: 16,425lb (empty)
25,350lb (loaded)
Crew: 1
Max speed: 1,450mph at 40,000ft; 915mph at sea
level
Service ceiling: 65,700ft
Range: 2,050miles with max external fuel
Weapons: Two 30mm DEFA cannon, two Matra
R530/550 and two Sidewinder AAMs F1A:
14 250lb bombs, or various load combinations
including Martel and AS30 ASMs

In 1964 the French Government awarded Dassault a
contract to develop a replacement for the Mirage III,
and soon afterwards an order was placed for a
prototype aircraft designated Mirage F2, which had
originally been conceived as a test bed for the
SNECMA TF-306 turbofan engine and the armament
system of the Mirage III-V VTOL project. The
prototype F2 flew on 12 June 1966, and exceeded
Mach 2 on 29 December that year. A two-seat
attack fighter, the prototype F2 featured swept
wings in place of the Mirage III's delta, and had a
low-set all-moving tail. Only one prototype of the
Mirage F2 was built, its flight tests contributing
much to the development of the future members of
the Mirage family.

Concurrently with the F2, Dassault developed a
smaller single-seat strike fighter, the Mirage F1, as a
private venture. Powered by a SNECMA Atar 09K
turbojet, the prototype Mirage F1-01 flew for the
first time on 23 December 1966 and exceeded
Mach 2 on its fourth flight the following month.
Although the prototype crashed in May 1967, the
French Government ordered three pre-series F1s in
September 1967, and by the spring of 1971 these
had been extensively tested and evaluated by some
33 French and foreign pilots. The last pre-series
aircraft, the F1-04, served as the production
prototype, and an initial batch of 87 was ordered for
the French Air Force. The first unit to be equipped
with the type was the 30e Escadre, which became
operational at Reims early in 1974.

Roughly the same size as the earlier Mirage III, the
Mirage F1 has a swept wing which is a scaled-down
version of that used by the Mirage F2, and is fitted
with high lift devices permitting the aircraft to take
off over a distance of between 1,600 and 2,600ft at
normal combat weight. The type's primary role is all-
weather interception at any altitude, for which it is
produced in the F1C version, while the F1A is a
ground attack fighter with an extra fuel tank in place
of some of the interceptor's electronics. The F1B is a
two-seat trainer which made its first flight on
26 May 1976. By the beginning of 1978 total orders
for the Mirage F1 stood at 487 aircraft and 2,600ft air
forces, including France. In the latter country, Mirage
F1s have progressively replaced the Mirage III in the
air defence role, and are equipped with advanced
Matra Super-530 AAMs. Foreign customers for the
aircraft have included Spain, Iraq, Ecuador, Greece
and South Africa.

Dassault Mystere IIC

France

Role: Single-Seat Interceptor
Operational: 1954-58

Engines: One 6,600lb thrust SNECMA Atar 101D2 turbojet
Span: 38ft 1in
Length: 38ft 6in
Weight: 11,495lb (empty)
16,412lb (loaded)
Crew: 1
Max speed: 658mph at sea level
Service ceiling: 50,000ft
Range: 550 miles
Weapons: Two 30mm cannon in fuselage nose

The Dassault MD452 Mystere was a straightforward swept-wing version of the MD450 Ouragan, the first of three Mystere I prototypes flying for the first time on 23 February 1951, powered by a Hispano-Suiza-built Nene engine. The second and third aircraft employed the Rolls-Royce Tay turbojet, also built by Hispano-Zuiza under licence. A pre-production batch of 17 aircraft, designated Mystere IIs, was ordered in

April 1951. The first four were powered by Tay 250 engines, the first aircraft having an armament of four 20mm and the other three of two 30mm cannon, while the last 12 were equipped with the SNECMA Atar 101. The 11th and 12th machines were powered by an Atar 101F equipped with reheat, and designated IIC, the Tay-engined variants being designated Mystere IIA and IIB. The third pre-series aircraft, one of the Tay-powered machines, became the first French aircraft to exceed Mach 1, on 28 October 1952.

The production version of the Mystere IIC was powered by a SNECMA Atar 101 turbojet. Deliveries began to the Armee de l'Air during the second half of 1954, and 150 aircraft were built. The Mystere IIC's operational career with the French Air Force was relatively brief, the type being supplanted by the Mystere IV from early 1955, but it continued in service with various operational training establishments for some years after that. Israel had plans to acquire some Mystere IICs in 1954/55, but in view of the type's poor service record — several of the earlier French machines having been lost through structural failure — it was decided to buy the Mystere IV instead.

Dassault Mystere IV

France

Role: Fighter-Bomber
Operational: 1955-75
Photo and Data: IVA

Engines: One 7,000lb thrust Hispano-Suiza Verdon turbojet
Span: 36ft 5½in
Length: 42ft 1½in
Weight: 12,496lb (empty)
16,535lb (loaded)
Crew: 1
Max speed: 696mph at sea level
Service ceiling: 52,000ft
Range: 600 miles
Weapons: Two 30mm DEFA cannon; two underwing MATRA rocket pods (total of 38 RPs); two 1,000lb bombs or 12 T-10 AGMs

Although developed from the Mystere IIC, the Dassault Mystere IV was in fact a completely new design. The prototype Mystere IVA flew for the first time on 28 September 1952, and early tests proved so promising that the French Government placed an order for 325 production aircraft six months later in April 1953. Powered by a 7,000lb thrust Hispano-Suiza Verdon turbojet, the Mystere IVA was designed originally as an interceptor, being able to carry bombs, rockets or napalm on underwing points. The type entered service in 1955 with the 12e Escadre de Chasse, and equipped the Armee de l'Air's first-line interceptor units until supplanted by the Mirage III in the early 1960s. Several ground-attack units were also formed in France's Tactical Air Command (FATAC), and the 5e and 8e Escadres — part of the tactical strike force charged with providing support for the 1st Army, the spearhead of France's land forces — continued to use the Mystere IVA until 1975, when it was supplanted by the first Jaguars.

Late in 1955 Israel ordered an initial batch of 24 Mystere IVAs, quickly followed by a further 36. The first aircraft arrived in Israel in April 1956, where they began to replace the IDF/AF's Gloster Meteor Mk 8s, and during the Arab-Israeli war that October proved superior to the Egyptian MiG-15s on most counts. Two Mystere IVA squadrons also operated during the Six-Day War of June 1967 in the ground-attack role, but after that the type was progressively relegated to OTUs in Israeli service.

In 1957, the Indian Air Force received the first of 110 Mystere IVAs, which began to replace the Ouragan in first-line service. Many of the Mysteres were still first-line equipment in December 1971, when they were used in the ground-attack role during the Indo-Pakistan conflict. The last examples were replaced by the Sukhoi Su-7 in the mid-1970s.

Production of the Mystere IVA was completed in 1958, with the 421st aircraft. Variants of the basic type were the Mystere IVB, which had a redesigned front and rear fuselage and a Rolls-Royce Avon RA7R engine with reheat and which became the first French aircraft to exceed Mach 1 in level flight, the prototype flying on 16 December 1953 and subsequently serving as a test bed with a SEPR rocket motor mounted under the fuselage as part of the Mirage development programme; and the Mystere IVN, a two-seat version with a nose radome for night and all-weather interception.

Dassault Super Mystere B2

France

Role: Interceptor
Operational: 1957-

Engines: One 7,495lb thrust SNECMA Atar 101G-2 turbojet (9,700lb thrust with reheat); the last 54 production aircraft had a 9,370lb thrust Atar 9 (13,230lb with reheat)
Span: 34ft 5¾in
Length: 46ft 1in
Weight: 15,400lb (empty)
19,840lb (loaded)
Crew: 1
Max speed: 743mph at 36,000ft
Service ceiling: 55,750ft
Range: 1,100 miles
Weapons: Two 30mm DEFA cannon and 55 68mm SNEB FFAR in fuselage pack; up to 2,000lb of bombs under wings

The Dassault Super Mystere, a trans-sonic successor to the Mystere IVA with a thinner, more sharply swept wing, an improved air intake and modified cockpit, flew in prototype form as the Super Mystere B1 on 2 March 1955, powered by a Rolls-Royce

Avon RA7R turbojet. The next day, on its fourth flight, it exceeded Mach 1 on the level, becoming the first production aircraft of European design to do so. The production version, the Super Mystere B2, flew on 27 February 1957, powered by a 7,495lb thrust SNECMA Atar 101G turbojet, and the Atar became standard in subsequent machines. 180 Super Mysteres were produced before production ended in 1959 and the type equipped the Armee de l'Air's 10e and 12e Escadres de Chasse until the mid-1960s, when they were replaced by the Mirage III. 24 aircraft were also supplied to Israel in 1959-60 and these equipped two interceptor squadrons before being supplanted by the Mirage IIICJ, when they assumed a ground-attack role, carrying up to 55 68mm rockets. The Israeli Super Mysteres saw action during the Six-Day War of 1967 and during the skirmishes leading up to it, destroying several MiG-17s for the loss of six of their own number. Still with a reserve ground attack role, some Super Mysteres were serving as fighter trainers in Israel in 1978, and 12 refurbished aircraft — fitted with P&W J52s instead of Atar 101s — were supplied to Honduras in 1976.

De Havilland Hornet and Sea Hornet

UK

Role: Long-Range Fighter/Ground-Attack
Specification: F12/43
Operational: 1946-56
Photo: Sea Hornet NF Mk 21
Data: Hornet F Mk 3

Engines: One Rolls-Royce Merlin 130 in port nacelle (right hand rotation) and one Merlin 131 in starboard nacelle (left hand rotation); Maximum combat power output: 2,030hp at 3,000rpm
Span: 45ft
Length: 36ft 8in

Weight: 16,000lb (empty)
20,900lb (loaded)
Crew: 1 (Note: Sea Hornet NF21 carried 2 crew)
Max speed: 472mph
Service ceiling: 35,000ft
Max range: 3,000 miles
Weapons: Four 20mm Hispano cannon, eight 60lb rockets or two 1,000lb bombs

The de Havilland DH 103 Hornet, which was the fastest twin piston-engined aircraft to serve with any of the world's air arms, began life as a private venture in 1942 to meet the need for a long-range

escort fighter for service in the Pacific Theatre. Although it was basically a scaled-down single-seat version of the Mosquito and generally resembled the earlier aircraft, it was in fact an entirely new design. The prototype, RR915, flew on 28 July 1944, powered by two 2,070hp 'slim-line' Rolls-Royce Merlin engines driving de Havilland four-blade propellers. These gave the aircraft a climb rate of more than 4,500ft/min and a speed of 485mph in level flight. Armament of the production Hornet F Mk 1 was four 20mm cannon, with provision for two 1,000lb bombs on underwing pylons or two 200gall drop tanks, the latter extending the range to over 2,500miles. It was also intended to use the type for unarmed photographic reconnaissance under the designation PR Mk 2, with four cameras mounted under the fuselage. A production order for 500 mixed F1s and PR2s was placed, but this was cancelled with the end of the Pacific War after only five aircraft had been built.

The next Hornet variant to appear, in 1946, was the F Mk 3, which had a wider tailplane than the F1 and a dorsal fin, as well as increased internal tankage. One hundred and thirty-two F3s were built before production ceased in 1952.

The first batch of 60 Hornet F1s, meanwhile, had entered service with the RAF in 1946, a further 40 F1s having been cancelled. The first squadron to equip was No 64 at Horsham St Faith, followed by No 19 at Wittering and Nos 41 and 65 at Church Fenton. Hornet F1s also served with No 226 Operational Conversion Unit. In September 1949, one of 65 Squadron's Hornets flew from the United Kingdom to Gibraltar at an average speed of 357.565mph, establishing a British point to point record, and on the return trip a new record was set up with a speed of 435.823mph.

The Hornet was withdrawn from RAF Fighter Command in 1951 and many were sent to the Far East, where it equipped Nos 33, 45 and 80 Squadrons. The Singapore-based No 45 Squadron flew the type for five years, carrying out 4,500 air strikes against communist terrorists in the Malayan jungle. Hornets undertaking these missions were armed with eight rocket projectiles or a pair of 1,000lb bombs in addition to their cannon. No 45's Hornets were the last piston-engined fighters to see active service with the RAF, soldiering on until they were replaced by Vampires in 1956. The last 12 production Hornets were fitted with a vertically-mounted F52 camera and designated F Mk 4; these were divided between the three Far East Hornet squadrons.

The Hornet's potential as a carrier-based fighter had been recognised in the early stages of its development, and towards the end of 1944 two early production F1s were partly navalised with the installation of arrester hooks, catapult pick-up points and modified undercarriage legs. A third F1, PX219, was fully navalised with folding wings, and began trials on the carrier HMS *Ocean* in August 1945. A production order quickly followed for 79 Sea Hornet F Mk 20s, as the naval version was designated. It was the Royal Navy's first twin-engined, long-range escort strike fighter, and it carried an armament similar to that of its RAF counterpart — four Hispano 20mm cannon, two 1,000lb bombs or eight 60lb rockets.

The first Fleet Air Arm squadron to receive the Sea Hornet was No 801, in June 1947. It went to sea on board HMS *Implacable* in 1949, transferring to HMS *Indomitable* in 1951 before re-equipping with Sea Furies. Sea Hornet F Mk 20s also served briefly with No 806 Squadron on HMCS *Magnificent* in 1948, and with Nos 728 and 771 Fleet Requirements Units in Malta and the United Kingdom.

The Sea Hornet NF Mk 21 was developed in 1946 to meet an urgent need for a high-performance night fighter for the Royal Navy. After lengthy tests this variant entered service with No 809 Squadron at Culdrose in January 1949, the unit embarking on HMS *Vegeance* in May 1951. No 809 used the NF21 until 1954, when it re-equipped with Sea Venoms. After retirement from first-line service the Sea Hornet served in a training capacity with Nos 736, 738 and 759 Squadrons until 1956, when the majority were broken up.

The last mark of Hornet to be produced was the Sea Hornet PR Mk 22, which had its cannon armament removed in favour of two F52 cameras for day reconnaissance and one Fairchild K19B for night photography. 24 were built, bringing the total Sea Hornet production to 187 aircraft, including prototypes.

De Havilland Mosquito (postwar)   UK

Role: Fighter-Bomber/PR
Operational: 1941-63
Specification: B1/40
Photo: T3
Data: PR34

Engines: Two 1,700hp Rolls-Royce Merlin 76 in-lines
Span: 54ft 2in
Length: 40ft 6in
Weight: 16,631lb (empty)
25,500lb (loaded)
Crew: 2
Max speed: 425mph at 30,500ft
Service ceiling: 36,000ft
Range: 3,500 miles at 315mph
Weapons: None

One of the most versatile combat aircraft ever built, the famous de Havilland Mosquito continued in service with both the RAF and overseas air forces for many years after World War II. Of the total of 7,781 Mosquitos built, 1,071 were produced after the war, the last aircraft coming off the assembly line November 1950. In the immediate postwar years, the principal Mosquito variants equipping RAF squadrons were the PR34, a very long range development of the PR16 (a later version, the PR34A, having modified Gee and DR compass and Merlin 114A engines) and the B35, which was developed from the B16. The B35 operated at altitudes up to 34,000 feet, had a top speed of 422mph and a range of 2,050 miles with a 2,000lb bomb load. A further conversion was the PR35, which was used for night photo-reconnaissance, and

the TT35 was a target tug variant with belly winch. The NF36 was a night fighter, similar to the wartime NF30 but with higher-powered Merlin 113s, and the NF38 was the last Mosquito night fighter to serve with the RAF, with British AI Mk 9 radar in place of the American AI Mk 10. The 7,781st Mosquito was a Mk 38, built at Chester.

The Royal Navy became interested in the Mosquito following deck landing trials with a modified B Mk 6 in 1945, and in response to specification N15/44 de Havillands produced a fully navalised version, the TR33, with folding wings, nose thimble radome, and torpedo stations under the fuselage. The TR33 served with Fleet Air Arm shore establishments for a short period after the war. Another naval Mosquito was the TT39, a target-towing variant developed from the B16 to specification Q19/45. Modifications included a prominent 'glasshouse' nose, dorsal cupola and belly winch.

The last marks of Mosquito, 40-43 were built in Australia, the FB40 being an FB6 development with Merlin 31/33s, the PR40 an unarmed reconnaissance version, and the FB41 a re-engined FB40 with Packard-Merlin 69s. The T43 trainer was similar to the British T3, but with dual elevator trim.

Among the many foreign air forces to use the Mosquito during the postwar years were Yugoslavia and Israel, the Israeli Mosquitos — most of which were ex-French Air Force machines — seeing action as night bombers during the October 1956 conflict. The last Mosquitos in RAF service were seven TT35s of No 3 Civilian Anti-Aircraft Co-Operation Unit at Exeter, these being replaced by target-towing Meteors in 1963.

De Havilland Sea Vixen

UK

Role: Naval Strike Fighter
Specification: N40/46
N14/49
Operational: 1959-1973.
Photo: FAW Mk 1
Data: FAW Mk 2

Engines: Two 11,230lb thrust Rolls-Royce Avon
208 turbojets
Span: 51ft
Length: 55ft 7in
Weight: 26,000lb (empty)
37,000lb (loaded)
Crew: 2
Max speed: 640mph at sea level
Service ceiling: 48,000ft
Range: 1,200 miles
Weapons: Four Firestreak or Red Top AAMs and
various combinations of 500lb bombs, Bullpup
ASMs, 2in air-to-air rockets or 3in air-to-surface
rockets

In 1946, the Admiralty entered into discussions with
the de Havilland Aircraft Company to formulate the
design of a new twin-jet, two-seat, all-weather strike
fighter for the Royal Navy. The RAF had a similar
requirement for a night fighter, and de Havilland's
answer to both needs was the Type 110, an
advanced design using the basic twin-boom layout
of the DH Vampire but incorporating the latest ideas
in swept flying surfaces, recently tested on the
DH108. In April 1949 the Ministry of Supply ordered
seven night and two long-range fighter prototypes
for the RAF, and two night and two strike fighter
prototypes for the Navy. The naval order, however,
was cancelled in November 1949, the Sea Venom
being adopted instead, and the RAF order was cut
back to two prototypes.

The prototype DH110 (WG236) flew for the first
time on 26 September 1951, powered by two
7,500lb thrust Rolls-Royce Avon RA 7s, and
exceeded Mach 1 on 9 April 1952. The second
prototype (WG240) joined the test programme on
25 July 1952, but was grounded following the tragic

loss of the first aircraft at Farnborough on
6 September. In 1953 the RAF decided to adopt the
Gloster GA5 Javelin instead of the de Havilland
design, but the latter was rescued from oblivion
when Admiralty interest reawakened and
development continued under a new naval contract.
WG240 underwent structural modifications, the
result of the lessons learned from the Farnborough
crash, and resumed test flying in the spring of 1953.
In September, the aircraft underwent carrier trials on
HMS *Albion* and was later fitted with dummy missile
pylons. It was afterwards used as an instructional
airframe and ended its days in a scrap merchant's
yard in Wales in 1965.

More carrier trials were carried out in April 1956
aboard HMS *Ark Royal* with a semi-navalised
DH1110 pre-production aircraft, and the first fully
navalised machine — equipped with folding wings
and Rolls-Royce Avon 208 engines — flew on
20 March 1957. Known by the designation FAW20,
it was officially named Sea Vixen later that year and
then redesignated F(AW) Mk 1. This aircraft (XJ474)
was followed by nine production F(AW) Mk 1s,
(XJ475-583), all of which were allocated to trials
work of various kinds. The first operational Sea Vixen
F(AW)1 was delivered to RNAS Yeovilton on
3 November 1958, followed by seven more aircraft.
These formed No 700Y Trials Unit, which was
recommissioned in July 1959 as No 892 Squadron.

On 3 March 1960 the squadron embarked in HMS
Ark Royal for sea trials, transferring to HMS
Victorious later that year. No 892 also served aboard
the carriers *Hermes* and *Centaur*, and from the latter
base took part in the Indonesian confrontation and
carried out operations against rebel forces in the
Radfan.

By the beginning of 1960 all Sea Vixen
conversion training had been taken over by No 766
Squadron. In February that year a second operational
Sea Vixen squadron, No 890, was commissioned,
followed by No 899 in September. No 899 Squadron
was also formed in February 1961; this became the
Sea Vixen HQ Squadron, remaining at Yeovilton.

In 1961 two FAW1s were modified by the
installation of additional fuel tanks in forward

extensions of the tail booms, and these aircraft served as the prototypes for the FAW Mk 2 variant. Fleet Air Arm squadrons began to receive the FAW2 in 1965; the first was No 899, which went to sea aboard HMS *Eagle* in January that year. Nos 766, 890, 892 and 893 Squadrons also received Sea Vixen Mk 2s, No 890 — aboard HMS *Hermes* — covering the British withdrawal from Aden in 1967.

From 1968 the Sea Vixen was progressively phased out as the Phantom began to enter service as the Royal Navy's primary strike aircraft, and by 1970 only Nos 890 and 899 Squadrons still operated the type. Sea Vixens continued in operational service until 1973, when the carrier HMS *Eagle* was decommissioned. Total production of the Sea Vixen was 120 Mk 1s and 30 Mk 2s, and 67 Mk 1s were converted to Mk 2 standard.

De Havilland Vampire UK

Role: Fighter-Bomber
Operational: 1946-
Specification: E6/41
Photo: FB5
Data: Mk 1

Engines: One 3,100lb thrust DH Goblin DGn2 turbojet
Span: 40ft
Length: 30ft 9in
Weight: 6,372lb (empty)
8,578lb (loaded)
Crew: 1
Max speed: 531mph at 17,500ft
Service ceiling: 45,000ft
Range: 500 miles
Weapons: Four 20mm British Hispano cannon in nose

Design work on the DH100 Vampire, the second of Britain's jet fighters to enter service, began in May 1942, the prototype flying on 20 September 1943. In the Spring of 1944 it became the first aircraft produced in Britain or America capable of sustained speeds of over 500mph over a wide altitude range. The first production Vampire was flown in April 1945, the initial 40 Vampire F1s being powered by the 2,700lb thrust de Havilland Goblin DGn1 turbojet and subsequent F1s by the 3,100lb thrust Goblin DGn2. The Vampire F1 entered service with No 247 Squadron RAF Fighter Command in 1946, and this unit was joined by Nos 54 and 72 Squadrons to form the RAF's first Vampire Wing. After the first 50 aircraft the F1 was fitted with a pressurised cockpit

and a bubble canopy in place of the earlier three-piece hood. 70 aircraft were delivered to Sweden in 1946-47 and some of these were later purchased by the Republic of Dominica, serving with that country until the early 1960s. Four more were supplied to Switzerland. The Vampire Mk2 was a Mk 1 airframe fitted with a Rolls-Royce Nene turbojet and did not enter service, only three machines being converted. The Vampire F3 reverted to the Goblin 2 engine and was a long-range version, with extra internal fuel capacity and two drop tanks. The F3 flew for the first time on 4 November 1946 and entered production for the RAF. 85 were delivered to the Royal Canadian Air Force and four to Norway, and 12 served with the Mexican Air Force until 1976. The Nene-engined F Mk 4 was to have been the production version of the F2 and was developed into the F30, which was built under licence in Australia. The first F30 was delivered to the RAAF on 26 September 1949; 57 were built, followed by 23 FB31 fighter-bombers, and more than half the F30s were later modified to FB31 standard.

The first Vampire variant developed for ground attack was the FB5, which had squared wingtips, long-stroke naval pattern landing gear and strengthened wings to carry external stores. As the FB6, fitted with a Goblin 3 engine, it was exported to Switzerland and built under licence in that country, a total of 175 being delivered to the Swiss Air Force. Six were delivered to Finland as the FB52, being the Finnish Air Force's only postwar combat aircraft until the arrival of 12 Gnat Mk 1s in 1958; FB52s were supplied to the Royal Norwegian Air Force, serving with Nos 336 and 337 Squadrons from 1948; some were supplied to Sweden, replacing the elderly

Mk 1s; Mk 5s were supplied to the RNZAF, equipping No 75 Squadron, and to the Italian Air Force. The type also equipped a squadron of the Venezuelan Air Force.

In December 1949 the Egyptian Air Force received an initial batch of Vampire FB5s and deliveries went on spasmodically until March 1956, by which time 62 Vampires equipped four first-line squadrons. Egyptian Vampire FB52s — mainly drawn from No 2 Squadron at Fayid — took part in the early stages of the Sinai campaign of 1956, but they proved no match for Israel's Mysteres and suffered heavy losses. Others were destroyed on the ground by the Anglo-French air strikes. Vampire FB5s were also delivered to the South African Air Force from 1950, equipping Nos 1 and 2 Squadrons.

The Vampire FB9 was a tropicalised version of the Mk 5, fitted with refrigeration, de-icing and de-misting equipment. Produced in limited quantities, the FB9 was used by the RAF, the RNZAF, SAAF and the Royal Rhodesian Air Force as well as by the Indian Air Force. India, in fact, used Vampires on a large scale, the Mk 3 variant being licence-built.

The Vampire NF10 two-seat night-fighter version served with the RAF and the Italian Air Force, in whose service it was designated Mk 54. The Sea Vampire F20 and F21 were navalised versions of the Mk 1, the type completing its deck landing trials on HMS *Ocean* in December 1945. Only a small number were built for carrier trials and jet familiarisation. Vampire FB5s remained in RAF service until 1957, when the Royal Auxiliary Air Force was disbanded.

One of the biggest overseas users of the Vampire was France, which built the Nene-engined Mk 53 under licence. Known as the Mistral in Armee de l'Air service, the type was used operationally against rebel forces in Algeria during the 1950s in the ground-attack role. The two-seat Vampire T11 trainer is described separately.

De Havilland Venom

UK

Role: Fighter-Bomber
Specification: F15/49
Operational: 1952-
Photo: Sea Venom FAW Mk 22
Data: FB 1/4

Engines: One 4,850lb thrust DH Ghost 103 turbojet
Span: 41ft 9in
Length: 33ft
Weight: 15,610lb (loaded)
Crew: 1
Max speed: 597mph
Service ceiling: 48,000ft
Range: 1,075 miles (with tip tanks)
Weapons: Four 20mm Hispano Mk 5 cannon in fuselage nose; 2,000lb of bombs or eight RPs on underwing pylons

Designed as a successor to the famous Vampire, and originally known as the Vampire FB8, the de Havilland Venom was intended as an interim fighter/ground attack aircraft to fill the gap until the service debut of the new generation of swept wing RAF fighters, the Hunter and Swift. The prototype Venom (VV612) flew on 2 September 1949, joined by a second prototype (VV613) in July 1950, and the first six production aircraft underwent extensive service evaluation at Boscombe Down in 1951-52. The first squadron to equip with the Venom FB1 was No 11 at Wunstorf in Germany, which carried out operational service trials from August 1952, and by February 1954 No 226 (Rhodesia) and No 5 Squadrons had also re-equipped with the type. Two more 2nd TAF Venom Wings were formed in 1953-54: No 121 at Fassberg (Nos 14, 98 and 118 Squadrons) and No 139 at Celle (Nos 16, 94 and 145 Squadrons). In 1955 the original 2nd TAF Venom Wing, No 123, exchanged its FB1s for the improved FB4 with a redesigned fin and rudder, retaining these aircraft until 1957. In 1955 the squadrons of No 121 Wing began re-equipping with Hunters, and in 1957 No 139 Wing was disbanded.

In the Middle East, squadrons of MEAF began to receive Venom FB1s in 1954. These were Nos 6 and 73 at Habbaniyah, Iraq; No 249 at Amman, Jordan; No 32 at Shaibah; No 208 at Eastleigh; and No 8 at Khormaksar, Aden. In 1956 No 249 moved to Akrotiri, Cyprus, and No 32 went to Takali in Malta in 1955. In July 1955 No 6 squadron re-equipped with Venom FB4s, and on 1 November the following year this unit, now based in Cyprus, made the first RAF Venom strike against targets in Egypt during the Suez Crisis. In 1957, Venoms of Nos 8, 73 and 249 Squadrons carried out attacks on rebel tribesmen in the Trucial Oman and on the Aden-Yemen border. By August 1957 most MEAF Venom squadrons had re-equipped with Canberras; the exception was No 8, which used Venoms until it re-equipped with Hunter FGA9s in March 1960.

In the Far East, Venoms equipped No 28 Squadron at Kai Tak, Hong Kong, Nos 60 and 14 (New Zealand) Squadrons at Tengah, Singapore, and No 45 Squadron at Butterworth, Malaya. No 28 Squadron was the last RAF unit to operate Venoms, exchanging them for Hunters in June 1962. The other three carried out many strikes against the communist terrorists during the Malayan Emergency during 1955-57.

In 1950 de Havillands developed a night-fighter version of the the Venom as a private venture. The prototype (G-5-3) flew for the first time on 22 August 1950. Housing the pilot and radar observer side by side and with a lengthened nose accommodating AI radar, the aircraft was adopted by the RAF as the Venom NF2. 90 were built, and the type entered service with No 23 Squadron in December 1953. The NF3 was an improved version with a clear-view canopy and ejection seats; 129 were produced, and many NF2s were brought up to NF3 standard and redesignated NF2A. Other RAF squadrons using the Venom NF2/3 were Nos 33, 89, 141, 151, 219, and 253, the type being replaced by the Gloster Javelin in 1957. The last unit to use the Venom night fighter was No 151, which disbanded in September 1961.

The Venom was widely exported under the designations FB50 and NF51. Italy received two FB50s in January 1953, but plans to produce the type under licence were abandoned. FB50s also equipped two squadrons (Nos 5 and 6) of the Royal Iraqi Air Force and No 34 Squadron of the Venezuelan Air Force, where they served until the end of 1965. The largest overseas customer was Switzerland, who built 100 FB1s under licence and 150 FB4s, these aircraft equipping 14 ground-attack squadrons. Some were still serving in 1978, and were likely to continue for another two years. The other main export customer was Sweden, which acquired 62 NF51s (designated J33 in Flygvapnet service) between December 1952 and July 1957.

In 1950, the Royal Navy evaluated the Venom NF2 as a potential carrier-borne aircraft, and placed an order for three navalised prototypes. The first, designated Sea Venom NF20, flew for the first time on 19 April 1951, and deck trials were carried out aboard HMS *Illustrious*. 50 Mk 20 Sea Venoms were completed and the type became operational with the Fleet Air Arm's No 890 Squadron (HMS *Albion)* in July 1955. The next naval variant was the FAW21, fitted with more powerful DH Ghost 104 engines and American APS-57 AI radar. The FAW21 entered service in May 1955 with No 809 Squadron, followed by Nos 891, 892 and 893. All except No 891 took part in the Suez operation of 1956, carrying out strikes on targets in the Canal Zone. In January 1957 No 894 Squadron also formed with Sea Venom FAW22s, these aircraft having Ghost 105 turbojets. No 891 also re-equipped with FAW22s and saw action against the Yemeni rebels in Aden in 1960. Although No 891 was the last operational Sea Venom squadron, a few continued in service with second-line units well into the 1960s, and one was still flying at Yeovilton until October 1970.

In 1955 39 Sea Venoms, with the export designation FAW53, were supplied to the Royal Australian Navy, equipping Nos 724, 805, 808 and 816 Squadrons. Some were still in use as target tugs in the mid-1970s. The Sea Venom was also produced under licence in France by SNCASE for the Aeronavale, in whose service it was known as the Aquilon (North Wind). 25 production Aquilon Mk 20s were built, followed by a similar number of Mk 202s and 40 Mk 203s, the latter carrying Nord 5103 AAMs as their primary armament. The Aquilon entered service with Flottille 16F in January 1955, followed by 11F later that year. Both units saw extensive service in the ground-attack role in Algeria. The last Aquilons were withdrawn in 1965, following service with a fighter training unit, 59S.

Douglas AD/A-1 Skyraider

Role: Carrier-Borne Attack
Operational: 1946-
Photo: AD Skyraider
Data: A-1E

Engines: One 2,700hp Wright R-3350-26W radial
Span: 50ft
Length: 38ft 2in
Weight: 10,546lb (empty)
18,263lb (loaded)
Crew: 2
Max speed: 320mph
Service ceiling: 32,700ft
Range: 900 miles
Weapons: Four wing-mounted 20mm cannon and up to 8,000lb of bombs and rockets

Designed in 1944 and intended as a potent carrier-borne attack aircraft for use in the projected invasion of Japan, the prototype XBT2D-1 Skyraider flew for the first time on 18 March 1945 and an order was placed for 548 production aircraft, this being

USA

reduced to 277 after VJ-Day. After extensive service trials, which revealed a number of serious defects such as the failure of the main undercarriage legs, structural modifications were carried out and in December 1946 the first 20 AD-1 Skyraiders were allocated to Attack Squadron VA-19 for renewed tests. In the meantime, production AD-1s had begun to roll off the assembly line, the first examples being delivered to VA-3B and VA-4B. Carrier trials were undertaken aboard the USS *Sicily* in June 1947, and in October VA-1B became operational with the type aboard the USS *Midway*. The last 35 AD-1s were completed as AD-1Q radar countermeasures aircraft, with a search radar pod under the port wing and a 'window' dispenser under the starboard.

Following more structural modifications, a much improved Skyraider model, the AD-2, appeared in 1948, and an order was placed for 356 aircraft. In the event 156 AD-2s were delivered, together with 22 AD-2Q countermeasures aircraft, and some of the latter were converted for use as target tugs. The next variant was the AD-3, which featured a number of refinements including a redesigned cockpit canopy

and modified undercarriage. Total AD-3 production was 194 aircraft, including 125 basic AD-3s, 23 AD-3Qs, 15 AD-3Ns for night attack, and 31 AD-3W early warning aircraft. Some of the standard AD-3s were modified for anti-submarine warfare and redesignated AD-3s, while two were fitted with electronic intelligence equipment and designated AD-3E.

By mid-1949 the AD-3 had been replaced on the production line by the AD-4, which was equipped with APS19A radar and a P-1 autopilot. By the time AD-4 production ended in 1953, 1,032 aircraft had been delivered, including AD-4N night attack aircraft, AD-4Qs and AD-4Ws. Forty AD-4W early warning aircraft were supplied to the Royal Navy in 1953, equipping four flights of No 849 Squadron. The aircraft was known as the Skyraider AEW1 in Fleet Air Arm service. A further variant of the basic AD-4 was the AD-4B, which had four wing-mounted 20mm cannon and was capable of carrying nuclear weapons. The AD-4 saw considerable action during the Korean War, going into combat for the first time (Air Group 5, USS *Valley Forge*) on 3 July 1950. Quite apart from carrying a formidable weapons load, the Skyraider was quite capable of defending itself in combat; in one incident on 26 July 1954, two AD-4s from the USS *Philippine Sea* were attacked by Red Chinese La-9 fighters off Hainan Island, and shot down both communist aircraft.

Perhaps the most versatile Skyraider variant was the AD-5, which flew for the first time on 17 August 1951. By means of various equipment and weapons packages, the AD-5 could undertake several carrier-borne roles, including that of 12-seat transport, ambulance aircraft, and cargo aircraft with a 2,000lb payload. Production of the AD-5 ended with the 670th aircraft in 1956, but was followed by the AD-6, which was specially equipped for low-level attack bombing, and the AD-7, which had an improved engine and further structural strengthening to cope with heavier tactical loads. 713 AD-6s and 72 AD-7s were built, deliveries ending in February 1957.

Still in first-line service with the US Navy in the early 1960s, the Skyraider — redesignated A-1 in 1962 — received a new lease of life as the war in Vietnam intensified. In the late summer of 1962 two squadrons of A-1E (AD-5) Skyraiders were added to the inventory of the USAF's 1st Air Commando Group at Hurlburt AFB, Florida, and in 1964 an initial batch of 75 A-1Es was sent to Vietnam to replace the B-26s and T-28s of the 1st Air Commando Wing. The two-seat A-1E proved unsurpassed in the counter-insurgency role, and other aircraft were refurbished and sent to South-East Asia as they were withdrawn from US Navy attack squadrons.

Skyraiders were supplied to the air forces of France, South Vietnam, Cambodia and Sweden (where they are used as target tugs).

40

Douglas A30 Skywarrior/B-66 Destroyer USA

Role: Carrier-Borne Attack Bomber (A3D)
Bomber/Reconnaissance (B-66)
Operational: 1956- (A3D)
1956-65 (B-66)

	A3D	**B-66C**
Engines:	Two 10,500lb thrust Pratt & Whitney J57-P-10s	Two 10,200lb thrust Allison J79-A-11s
Span:	72ft 6in	72ft 6in
Length:	76ft 4in	75ft 1¼in
Weight (empty)	38,298lb	39,686lb
(Max loaded)	84,000lb	79,000lb
Crew:	3	3
Max speed:	610mph at 10,000ft	620mph at 10,000ft
Service ceiling:	41,000ft	45,000ft
Range:	2,100 miles on internal fuel	1,750 miles on internal fuel
Weapons:	Two 20mm cannon in tail barbette; up to 12,000lb of nuclear or conventional bombs	Two 20mm cannon in tail barbette

A3D Skywarrior

The Douglas A3D Skywarrior had its origin in a requirement for a long-range carrier-based attack bomber, issued by the US Navy Bureau of Aeronautics in 1947. The type's early evolution was closely connected with the development of the Westinghouse J40 turbojet and both XA3D-1 prototypes used this powerplant. By the time the first XA3D-1 flew on 28 October 1952, however, the numerous teething troubles attending the J40 had already led to a decision to replace it with the Pratt & Whitney J57, and the first pre-production aircraft flew with these engines on 16 September 1963. Deliveries of production A3D-1s began in the latter half of 1954 to the US Navy evaluation unit at Patuxent, and on 31 March 1956 five A3D-1s were flown from this location to Heavy Attack Squadron 1 at NAS Jacksonville, completing the first delivery of the type to a fleet unit. Initially deployed at sea aboard the USS *Forrestal*, with the Sixth Fleet in the Mediterranean, the Skywarrior — which, with a loaded weight of 31 tons, was the world's largest and heaviest shipboard aircraft — gave the United States Navy the capability to make nuclear attacks on cities as far away as Moscow, bringing a new strategic dimension to sea power. On 31 July 1956,

an A3D-1 Skywarrior demonstrated the type's potential by making a 3,200-mile flight from Honolulu to New Mexico in 5hr 40min, at an average speed of 570mph, without refuelling.

During 1956 the A3D-1 was replaced on the production line by the A3D-2, fitted with 10,500lb thrust J57-P-10 engines and incorporating some structural strengthening. This variant entered service with the US Pacific Fleet early in 1957. The A3D-2P was a photographic reconnaissance version, carrying a battery of 12 cameras, and the A3D-2Q was a radar countermeasures and electronic reconnaissance version, carrying a crew of seven and specialised equipment, some of it in an under-fuselage radome. The A3D-2T was a trainer for both bomber and reconnaissance crews, with accommodation for a pilot, instructor and six students. All A3D-2s had flight refuelling capability, and could be quickly converted into tankers by the installation of a refuelling pack in the bomb bay. Operating from carriers of the *Forrestal*, *Essex* and *Midway* classes, the Skywarrior — its variants redesignated A-3A, A-3B, RA-3B, EA-3B and TA-3B in 1962 — remained in first line service until the late 1960s.

B-66 Destroyer

In 1953, Douglas received an order from the USAF to modify the A3D as a land-based reconnaissance and bomber aircraft, and five RB-66As were produced for service evaluation during the first half of 1954. These were followed by the first production version, the B-66B, which flew for the first time on 4 January 1955 and began to enter USAF service in March the following year, preceded slightly by the first examples of the RB-66B reconnaissance version. This was followed by the RB-66C, which was equipped for all-weather reconnaissance and carried a crew of four, and the WB-66D, which was the first production aircraft ever designed specifically for weather reconnaissance. Carrying a crew of five and serving with the USAF from June 1957, the WB-66D

was instrumented to gather weather data over a wide area, either during combat operations or on normal weather surveillance, and was one of the first aircraft to carry an on-board computer. Fifty-five WB-66Ds were built out of a total of 209 B-66s, most of the remainder were reconnaissance aircraft. In the United States, RB-66Cs equipped the 363rd Tactical Reconnaissance Wing (9th and 16th TRS), and in Europe they served with the 10th TRW (1st, 19th, 30th and 42nd TRS) in the United Kingdom and France. They were replaced by the RF-4C Phantom in 1964-65. Both the Skywarrior and the B-66 were used in Vietnam in the ECM and reconnaissance roles, and as navigational 'lead ships' for the fighter-bomber formations.

Douglas A-4 Skyhawk

Role: Carrier-Borne Attack
Operational: 1956-
Data: A-4M

Engines: One 11,200lb thrust Pratt & Whitney J52-P-408A turbojet
Span: 27ft 6in
Length: 40ft 3$\frac{1}{4}$in
Weight: 10,465lb (empty)
24,500lb (loaded)
Crew: 1
Max speed: 645mph at sea level
Service ceiling: 49,700ft
Range: 2,055 miles with max fuel
Weapons: Several hundred variations of offensive load, including 3,500lb of bombs under fuselage, 4,500lb on inboard wing pylons and 2,000lb on outboard pylons. Nuclear or HE bombs, rockets, Sidewinder AAMs, Bullpup ASMs, gun pods, torpedoes and ECM packs may all be carried. Two 20mm Mk 12 cannon in wing roots (DEFA 30mm cannon optional on export versions)

In 1950, having abandoned the XA2D Skyshark as a potential turboprop-powered replacement for the

USA

legendary Skyraider, the Douglas Aircraft Company began design studies of a turbojet-powered shipboard attack aircraft capable of delivering nuclear weapons and performing the wide variety of conventional attack roles undertaken by the Skyraider in Korea. The result was the XA4D-1 Skyhawk, the prototype of which flew on 22 June 1954, only 18 months after the start of detailed engineering design. The prototype was, in fact, one of four pre-production aircraft ordered by the US Navy for evaluation, the normal practice of ordering two experimental aircraft and a static test machine being waived in this case. On 15 October 1955, one of these aircraft broke the Class C world air speed record, reaching an average speed of 695.127mph over a 500km closed circuit.

The first A4D-1 Skyhawks were delivered to the US Navy on 27 September 1956, equipping Attack Squadron VA-27 with the Atlantic Fleet. This initial variant was powered by a 7,800lb thrust Wright J65-W-4 engine, and 165 examples were produced. It was replaced on the production line by the A4D-2, which was powered by a J65-W-16A turbojet and featured a number of refinements, including a powered rudder and changes in cockpit layout. The

A4D-2 made its first flight on 26 March 1956, and production ran to 542 examples. Meanwhile, plans had been laid to re-engine the Skyhawk with a Pratt & Whitney J52-P-2 engine, and four aircraft were ordered for US Navy evaluation under the designation A4D-3. These, however, were cancelled, and the next Skyhawk variant to appear was the A4D-2N, which had a lengthened nose to accommodate terrain clearance radar and other all-weather electronics. The A4D-2N also had a rocket-boosted low-level ejection seat. Deliveries to the USN began in December 1959 and production ended in December 1962 after 638 aircraft had been built.

The 1,000th production Skyhawk was delivered in February 1961, and in July that year another variant, the A4D-5 (later redesignated A-4E) flew for the first time. Powered by a Pratt & Whitney J52-P-6 engine developing 8,500lb thrust, the A4E's offensive load was raised from 5,000lb to 7,000lb and the range increased by 27%. Cockpit refinements included a Douglas Escapac zero-height zero-speed rocket powered ejection seat. Deliveries began in November 1962, and 500 aircraft were built. The next model, the A-4F, was an attack bomber with a 9,300lb thrust J52-P-8A turbojet, and was furnished with extra flak- and bullet-resistant material around the cockpit. A 'hump' aft of the cockpit housed updated electronic equipment. The prototype flew on 31 August 1966 and production was completed in 1968 after 146 machines had been built. The TA-4F was a tandem two-seat dual control trainer, retaining the same weapons capability as the A-4F, and the A-4G and TA-4G were similar aircraft supplied to the Royal Australian Navy, 10 (including two TA-4Gs) being delivered in July 1967. The A-4H

was a variant supplied to Israel, 70 being delivered in 1967-68, together with two TA-4H trainers. The TA-4J was a simplified version of the TA-4F for the US Naval Air Advanced Training Command, with most of the weapons delivery systems deleted. Deliveries began to the USN in June 1969. Ten A-4Ks (basically A-4Fs) were supplied to the Royal New Zealand Air Force in 1970, and during that year the US Marine Corps received an initial batch of 50 A-4Ms, which were also similar to the A-4F but with an 11,200lb thrust J52-P-408A engine. The A-4L was a modified A-4C (A4D-2N) with uprated engine and avionics 'hump'.

During the 1960s the Skyhawk equipped some 40 USN and USMC squadrons, and saw extensive action during the war in Vietnam. It was also the mainstay of the Israeli Air Force's attack squadrons during the Yom Kippur War of October 1973, when about 40% of Israel's Skyhawks were lost in combat. Most of these losses were subsequently made good by the supply of A-4N Skyhawk IIs, a light attack variant, first flown in June 1972, which was ordered by the US Navy for export to Israel.

Other Skyhawk variants are the A-4P, a revised A-4B (A4D-2) for the Argentine Air Force, and the A-4Q, also a revised A-4B for the Argentine Navy. Fifty A-4Ps and 16 A-4Qs were ordered. 40 Skyhawks were also ordered for the Singapore Air Defence Command under the designation A-4S, these being converted from ex-USN A-4Bs by Lockheed, together with three TA-4S trainers. The last variant is the A-4Y, which is an updated A-4M for the US Marine Corps. The 2,900th Skyhawk was delivered in 1977, and the type is likely to remain in widespread service until well into the 1980s.

Douglas F4D-1 Skyray

USA

Role: Single-Seat Carrier-Borne Day Fighter/Attack Aircraft
Operational: 1956-64

Engines: One Pratt & Whitney J57-P-8 turbojet rated at 10,500lb thrust (14,500lb with reheat)
Span: 33ft 6in
Length: 45ft 8¼in

Weight: 20,000lb (normal loaded)
25,000lb (max loaded)
Crew: 1
Max speed: 720mph at sea level
Service ceiling: 55,000ft
Range: 950 miles with max external fuel
Weapons: Four 20mm MK-12 cannon and six underwing pods each containing seven 2.75in FFAR rockets, or four pods each containing 19 FFARs.

Provision for two Sidewinder missiles or two 2,000lb bombs

The Douglas F4D Skyray, which broke no fewer than seven world records during its operational career, owed much to the work of Dr Alexander Lippisch, whose wartime delta-wing designs made an impression on the US Navy's Bureau of Aeronautics. In 1947, the Douglas Aircraft Company was asked to investigate the possibilities of a delta wing in designing a short-range naval interceptor whose task would be to climb to 50,000ft in just over three minutes and destroy enemy bombers travelling at speeds in the order of 600mph before they could reach their targets. Design work began in 1948, the aircraft being originally designed around the Westinghouse J40 turbojet, but the development of this engine was subjected to serious delays and the prototype aircraft, designated XF4D-1, were powered by a 5,000lb thrust Allison J35-A-17. Two prototypes were ordered, the first flying on 23 January 1951, and flight tests revealed that they were underpowered. The test programme was therefore delayed until the aircraft · could be re-engined with the Westinghouse XJ40-WE-6 when it finally became available, and this in turn gave way to the 11,600lb thrust XJ40-WE-8 in the summer of 1953. Unexpected teething troubles, however, were encountered with the J40 (which was later cancelled) and it was decided to equip production F4Ds with the Pratt & Whitney J57-P-2.

On 3 October 1953, the second XF4D-1, flown by Lt-Cdr James Verdin of the US Navy and powered by an XJ40-WE-8 with reheat, gained the world air speed record with an average speed of 753.4mph in four timed runs over a salt lake in southern California, and on the 16th Douglas's test pilot Robert O. Rahn captured the 100km closed circuit record with a speed of 728.11mph. The second XF4D-1, meanwhile, had been completing the type's carrier trials, and when the first production F4D-1 exceeded Mach 1 in level flight on 5 June 1954, it seemed probable that the Skyray, as the aircraft was now officially named, would soon enter service. During further flight testing, however, serious problems arose, including a dangerous high-speed stall at altitudes over 40,000ft; these called for modifications, and it was not until 1956 that the F4D-1 entered service with the US Navy and Marine Corps, the first unit to receive it being VC-3. Deployment of the Skyray after that was rapid, the type being assigned to US heavy attack carriers in the Atlantic and Pacific Fleet Air Commands. Because of its excellent rate of climb and high altitude performance, the Skyray was also assigned to the North American Air Defense Command. The aircraft's astonishing climb characteristics, for its day, were publicly revealed when, on 22-23 May 1958, a production F4D-1 flown by Major Edward N. LeFaivre of the USMC and powered by an improved Pratt & Whitney J57-P-8 engine established five FAI climb records, reaching 9,842.5ft in 44.39sec, 19,685ft in 1min 6.13sec, 29,527.5ft in 1min 29.81sec, 39,370ft in 1min 51.23sec, and 49,212.5ft in 2min 36.05sec.

Production of the F4D-1 (F-6) Skyray terminated at the end of 1958 with the 419th aircraft, but the type remained in first-line service until well into the 1960s, the last combat squadron to use it being VMF-115.

Douglas B-26 Invader

USA

Role: Light Bomber
Operational: 1944-72
Data: B-26B

Engines: Two 2,000hp Pratt & Whitney R-2800-27/29 Double Wasp radials
Span: 70ft
Length: 50ft
Weight: 35,000lb (loaded)
Crew: 3
Max speed: 355mph
Service ceiling: 22,100ft
Range: 1,400 miles with max bomb load
Weapons: 10 .5in machine guns, six in nose and two each in dorsal and ventral turrets. Up to 4,000lb of bombs internally

First flown as the XA-26 in July 1942, the Douglas B-26 (formerly A-26) Invader light bomber saw extensive service in all theatres of war, replacing the earlier Martin Marauder in many USAF units. It was still first-line equipment in 1950, and saw further action during the Korean War with the 3rd Bombardment Wing (8th, 13th and 731st Squadrons), the 452nd Bombardment Wing (728th, 729th and 730th Squadrons), the 162nd Tactical Reconnaissance Squadron and the 6166th All-Weather Reconnaissance Squadron. It was the B-26s of the 8th Squadron which carried out the first UN air strikes against North Korean objectives on 27 June 1950, and an RB-26 of the 162nd Tactical Reconnaissance Squadron which flew the last UN sortie over North Korea shortly before midnight on 27 July 1953.

In November 1950 17 B-26Bs and eight B-26Cs were allocated on loan by the USAF to the French Air Force to help meet the emergency in Indo-China, Groupe de Bombardement 1/19 becoming operational with the type at Tan Son Nhut on 1 January. In August 1951 a second delivery, including four RB-26Cs, permitted the formation of a photographic reconnaissance flight. Designated ERB-26, it was attached to GB 1/19 in November. In February and March 1952 a second bomber group, GB 1/25 'Tunisie', also re-equipped with Invaders at Haiphong, having flown Halifax transports until then. The B-26s played a prominent part in all air operations over Indo-China.

Sixty more aircraft were acquired following the start of the Battle of Dien Bien Phu in November 1953 and these were hurriedly thrown into action against the enemy's lines of communication. On 1 June 1954 a third bomber group, GB 1/91 'Bourgogne', came into existence. After the ceasefire the bomber groups were disbanded and all airworthy B-26s returned to the USA. Of the 120 B-26s which served in the campaign, 10 were lost on operations and a similar number accidentally.

Hardly had the last shots died away in Indo-China when fighting broke out in Algeria, and the French Government once again requested American help. Forty B-26s were delivered before the end of 1956, followed by more in 1957 and 1959-60, until 110 aircraft were once more in French service. In Algeria, these equipped GB 1/91, GB 1/32 and GB 2/91. Other units partially equipped with the type were ECN 1/71 and ECTT 2/6 'Normandie-Niemen', which employed B-26Ns modified for night operations. On 1 January 1962 GB 1/32 'Armagnac' became ERP 1/32, equipped with 12 RB-26s and B-26P reconnaissance aircraft. The B-26N was equipped with nose radar and the B-26P with vertical and oblique cameras, both variants being modified from the B and C by the French. The B-26 combat units were disbanded in 1963, but ERP 1/32 remained operational until 1966. Surviving B-26s were assigned to various French Air Force test centres and some were used to train crews of the Mirage IV nuclear strike force. The final variant was the B-26Z target tug.

Several Latin American countries were still using the B-26 into the 1970s. The type equipped one light bomber group of the Brazilian Air Force, it was used by one flight of Dominica's sole bomber squadron, and equipped a squadron each of the Guatemalan, Colombian and Peruvian air forces. Cuba also had 18 B-26s prior to the Castro revolution, but these were soon replaced by modern Soviet equipment. Some B-26s were used by Katanga in the Congo conflict of the early 1960s.

In the United States, many Invaders were refurbished for the COIN role during the early 1960s, and served with the 1st Air Commando Wing in Vietnam before being replaced by A-1 Skyraiders in 1964. Others equipped Air National Guard units, the last aircraft of the type — a VB-26B-61-DL, serial 44-34610 — retiring in 1972 after service with the National Guard Bureau HQ at Andrews Air Force Base. A few were converted as target tugs for the US Navy, with the designation JD-1.

Douglas F3D Skynight   USA

Role: Naval All-Weather Fighter
Operational: 1950-57
Photo and Data: F3D-2

Engines: Two Westinghouse J46-WE-3 turbojets rated at 4,080lb thrust each
Span: 50ft
Length: 45ft 5in
Weight: 12,683lb (empty)
18,668 (normal loaded)
Crew: 2
Max speed: 543mph at 11,000ft
Service ceiling: 42,800ft
Range: 1,120 miles max
Weapons: Four 20mm cannon

The Douglas F3D Skynight was the first two-seat

carrier-borne jet fighter to be adopted by the United States Navy, serving with Marine Corps squadrons. Two XF3D-1 prototypes were ordered and the first of these flew on 23 March 1948, powered by two 3,000lb thrust Westinghouse J34-WE-22 turbojets mounted semi-externally on the lower fuselage beneath the wing. 28 F3D-1 Skynights were ordered in June 1948 and deliveries of production aircraft began in February 1950. 70 examples of an improved version, the F3D-2, were ordered in August 1949; this was to have been powered originally by a pair of Westinghouse J45-WE-3 turbojets of 4,800lb thrust each, but these engines required larger nacelles and installation difficulties led to the use of 3,400lb thrust J34-WE-36 engines instead. The first F3D-2 flew on 14 February 1951.

In November 1952 Marine Night Fighter Squadron VMF(N)513, which had been operating

F7F Tigercats over Korea, re-equipped with F3D-2s and were soon in action over North Korea, sweeping the night sky ahead of USAF B-29 bombers. On their second offensive patrol on 3 November 1952, one of the Skynights shot down a Yak-15, and five nights later another Skynight crew destroyed a MiG-15. Early in 1953 the Skynights revised their tactics, flying several thousand feet above the bomber stream on the lookout for enemy night fighters positioning themselves for an attack. Two enemy aircraft were destroyed in this way before the end of January 1953. During the weeks that followed, the Skynights worked in conjunction with F-94C Starfires, the latter having only just been cleared for

operations over the north because of the advanced radar they carried, and between them the Skynights and Starfires accounted for 15 communist night fighters during the first half of 1953.

Although Skynights were withdrawn from first-line service in 1955, a number continued to serve with reserve and trials units until the late 1950s. On 12 August 1957, an F3D-2 flown by Lt-Cdr Don Walker carried out the first shipboard test of the Automatic Carrier Landing System, designed to bring aircraft aboard in all weather conditions without help from the pilot, on the USS *Antietam* off Pensacola. More than 50 fully automatic landings were completed between 12-20 August.

English Electric Canberra

Role: Tactical Bomber/Reconnaissance
Specification: B3/45
Operational: 1951-
Photo: Argentine B62
Data: B(I)8

Engines: Two 7,500lb thrust Rolls-Royce Avon 109 turbojets
Span: 63ft 11½in
Length: 65ft 6in
Weight: 23,173lb (empty)
50,992lb (normal loaded)
Crew: 2
Max speed: 620mph at sea level
Service ceiling: 48,000ft
Range: 3,000 miles with wingtip tanks
Weapons: Gun pack comprising four 20mm Hispano cannon in rear weapons bay; six 1,000lb bombs internally and two 1,000lb bombs on underwing pylons

Originally designed for the radar bombing role, the English Electric (BAC) Canberra is one of the greatest success stories of Britain's postwar military aircraft industry. Four prototypes of the B1 model were produced and the first of these flew on 13 May 1949, powered by Rolls-Royce Avon turbojets. Problems with the radar bomb-aiming equipment, however, led to the redesign of the nose with a visual bomb-aiming position, and with this modification the fifth aircraft (VX165) became the Canberra B2, the type entering service with No 101 Squadron RAF Bomber Command in May 1951. By this time a photo-reconnaissance version, the Canberra PR3, had also flown; this was basically a B2 with seven cameras for the high-level photo-recce role, and

UK

entered service with No 540 Squadron in 1953.

In an attempt to speed up priority production of the B2, the type was built by A. V. Roe, Handley Page and Short Brothers & Harland, as well as English Electric. Avro and HP delivered 75 aircraft each, and Shorts 60. The Canberra's export potential now seemed promising; a sales tour of the USA resulted in plans being made to produce the bomber version under licence, and Venezuela ordered six at the end of 1952. The next variant was the T4 dual control trainer, which entered service with No 231 OCU in 1954; this was followed by the B5, a converted PR3 intended for target marking, but only a few examples were produced before it was superseded by the B6, a version with more powerful Avon 109 engines. This version entered RAF service in 1954, and six were ordered by Ecuador in May that year. Some B6s were also supplied to France for use at the Bretigny test centre. The B(I) Mk6 was an interim night interdictor version of the B6 with an underwing bomb armament and a 20mm cannon pack, while the PR7 was the photo-reconnaissance variant.

The Canberra B(I)8, which entered service with No 88 Squadron in May 1956, featured some radical modifications, the most notable being an entirely redesigned fuselage nose and offset fighter-type cockpit, the navigator being 'buried' in the starboard fuselage. In October 1955 Peru ordered eight B(I)8s and a similar number, together with two T4s, were ordered by Venezuela in January 1957. The Canberra PR9 high altitude photo-reconnaissance variant also had an offset cockpit and an increased wingspan, as well as RR Avon 206 engines. One PR9 was modified by Shorts as the SC9 for Red Top missile development.

In January 1957 the Indian Air Force became a major Canberra customer, ordering 54 B(I)58s and

eight PR57s. 12 more B(I)58s were ordered later in the year. Other overseas customers included the Royal Rhodesian Air Force, which acquired 15 B2s, and the RNZAF, which obtained 12 B(I)12s (basically B(I)8s). Also for the RNZAF, the T Mk 13 was a modified T4. A further trainer variant was the T11, which was converted from the B2 for the task of training pilots and navigators of all-weather fighters in AI interception techniques. Six were delivered to the RAF and two to the Swedish Air Force, designated Tp52.

The Canberra B Mk 15 was a modified B6 with underwing points for bombs or rocket packs. Designed for RAF service in the Near and Far East, it had updated navigational equipment and carried additional cameras. The B Mk 16, for RAF service in Germany, was similar, but retained many of the B6's radar aid . Other Canberra variants included the U Mk 10 unmanned target aircraft (modified B2), the T17 ECM trainer, the E15 electronic reconnaissance variant, the TT18 target tug, the T19 target facilities aircraft, and the T22 trainer for the Royal Navy. The Canberra was also built under licence in Australia as the Canberra B20 (48 produced) and the T21 (seven converted from B2/B20s).

During their lengthy career, Canberras have seen action in many parts of the world. RAF aircraft operated against Malayan terrorists during the Emergency and against Egyptian airfields during the Suez Crisis of 1956, Australian B20s saw combat during the war in Vietnam, and Indian Air Force machines fought in the Indo-Pakistan conflict of 1971. In the 1970s, Canberras were still being refurbished on a considerable scale for overseas air forces by the British Aircraft Corporation. In 1977, four Canberra B52s were used by Ethiopia in the war with Somalia.

English Electric (BAC) Lightning UK

Role: Interceptor
Specification: F23/49
Operational: 1960–
Photo and Data: F6

Engines: Two Rolls-Royce RB146 Avon 301 turbojets each rated at 12,690lb thrust (16,360lb with reheat)
Span: 34ft 10in
Length: 55ft 3in
Weight: 42,000lb (loaded)
Crew: 1
Max speed: 1,500mph at 40,000ft
Service ceiling: 70,000ft
Range: 800 miles with ventral tank only
Armament: Interchangeable packs for Firestreak or Red Top missiles, or two retractable boxes housing 22 Mk 1 2in rockets each

The English Electric (BAC) Lightning supersonic fighter had its origin in a Ministry of Supply specification (ER103) which was issued in 1947 and called for a manned supersonic research aircraft. English Electric's design, the P1, submitted in 1949, was quickly seen to have an operational application under the terms of Air Ministry specification F23/49 for a supersonic day fighter, and development of the aircraft for research and military purposes continued in parallel. Three research prototypes, designated P1A, were built, the first flying on 4 August 1954 powered by two Bristol Siddeley Sapphire ASSa5 turbojets. Also in 1954, work began on turning the Lightning into a complete weapons system; three operational prototypes were built, designated P1B, and the first of these (XA847) flew on 4 April 1957, powered by two Rolls-Royce Avons. The prototype P1B exceeded Mach 1 during its first flight, and on 25 November 1958 it became the first British aircraft to reach Mach 2.0, which it did in level flight. By this time the P1B had been given the name Lightning and ordered into production for RAF Fighter Command.

The first production Lightning F Mk 1 (XM134) flew on 29 October 1959, and fully combat-equipped Lightnings began entering service with No 74(F) Squadron at Coltishall on 30 July 1960. F Mk 1s were also supplied to Nos 56 and 111 Squadrons, and to No 226 OCU at Middleton St George. The F Mk 1 was powered by two Rolls-Royce Avon RA24R turbojets with reheat, and was equipped with Hawker Siddeley Firestreak air-to-air missiles. The final production aircraft in the F Mk 1 batch were fitted with flight refuelling equipment and improved avionics; these were designated F Mk 1A.

The Lightning F Mk 2 was an improved version of the Mk 1A, with a better range, speed and ceiling and more advanced avionics. The first F Mk 2 flew on 11 July 1961, and the variant entered service with Nos 19 and 92 Squadrons in Germany. Missile armament of the F2 was either the Firestreak or the Hawker Siddeley Red Top. A further development was the F Mk 3, which was powered by Rolls-Royce Avon 300-series turbojets and had a long range ferry

capability with two 1,182-litre overwing fuel tanks. The F3, which featured a larger tail fin with a square tip, first flew on 16 June 1962 and entered service with No 74 Squadron in 1964. Other units to re-equip with the F3 were Nos 23, 29, 56 and 111 Squadrons. The F Mk 3A, which became the Lightning F6, had a revised wing leading edge designed to reduce subsonic drag and improve range, and was fitted with a large ventral fuel pack with more than double the capacity of earlier packs. The first Lightning F6 flew on 17 April 1964 and the variant entered service with No 5 Squadron at Binbrook the following year.

In 1958 a two-seat operational trainer version of the Lightning was ordered into production for the RAF. This was generally similar to the fighter, except that the front fuselage was widened to take two side-by-side Martin-Baker ejection seats. The first trainer variant was the T Mk 4, which was complementary to the F1 and first flew on 6 May 1959. T4s were the first Lightnings to be exported,

being supplied to Saudi Arabia together with some F2s (seven aircraft in all). The T Mk 5 was complementary to the F3, and featured the same square-tipped fin. Deliveries to the RAF began in March 1955, and the export version was designated T Mk 55.

The Lightning F Mk 53 was a multi-mission export version of the F6 for Saudi Arabia and Kuwait, with two 30mm Aden cannon in a ventral pack, Firestreak or Red Top missiles, two 1,000lb bombs or two MATRA 155 launchers for 18 SNEB 68mm rockets. 44 2in rockets could also be carried, and later models had provision for twin MATRA launchers on each underwing pylon plus twin MATRA launchers on overwing pylons, giving a total of 144 68mm rockets.

Production of the Lightning F6 fighter for the RAF was completed in 1967, although some F3s were later brought up to F6 standard. Phantoms began to replace the Lightning in the air defence role in 1969.

Fairchild Republic A-10 USA

Role: Close Support
Operational: 1976-

Engines: Two 9,065lb thrust General Electric TF34-GE-100 turbofans mounted in pods on pylons on upper rear fuselage
Span: 57ft 6in
Length: 53ft 4in
Weight: 20,246lb (empty)
47,400lb (loaded)
Crew: 1
Max speed: 518mph at sea level (Vne)
Service ceiling: 25,000ft
Range: 2,647 miles (max ferry)
Weapons: One General Electric GAU-8/A Avenger 30mm seven-barrel cannon mounted in nose; external load up to 16,000lb, including 28 500lb Mk 82 retarded bombs, six 2,000lb Mk 84 GP bombs, four flare launchers, 20 Rockeye cluster bombs, 16 weapons dispensers, six Maverick missiles, Mk 82/84 laser guided bombs, two SUU-23 gun pods and ECM pods

In December 1970 Fairchild Republic and Northrop were each selected to build a prototype of a new close support aircraft for evaluation under the USAF's A-X programme, which had been initiated in 1967. Fairchild Republic's contender, designated YA-10A, flew for the first time on 10 May 1972, followed by a second aircraft in July that year. In

January 1973 it was announced that the A-10 had been chosen to meet the USAF requirement, and an order was placed for 10 pre-production aircraft for trials and evaluation, although this was later reduced to six. These, and subsequent production aircraft, were powered by two 9,050lb thrust General Electric TF34-GE-100 engines, and four of them were fitted with the General Electric GAU-8/A seven-barrel 30mm cannon, which was to be the type's standard fixed armament. 22 initial production A-10As were ordered in December 1974 and the first examples entered service with the 333rd Tactical Fighter Training Squadron at Davis AFB, Arizona, in the spring of 1976. By mid-1977 195 A-10As were on order, with plans to raise production to a total of 739 aircraft by April 1982.

The first fully operational unit to receive the A-10A was the 356th Tactical Fighter Squadron of the 354th Tactical Fighter Wing at Myrtle Beach, South Carolina, deliveries beginning in March 1977. This was followed by the 355th Wing at Davis AFB. Designed specifically for anti-tank operations, most of the A-10As are being assigned to USAF units in Europe, where the armoured threat is greatest. The first unit to be so equipped is the 81st Tactical Fighter Wing, based at Bentwaters and Woodbridge in the UK, which is exchanging its F-4D Phantoms for A-10As in 1978-79. The 81st will eventually have 108 A-10As, serving in six squadrons, and a second A-10A wing is scheduled to form in the UK in the

early 1980s. About 40% of the UK-based A-10A force will be deployed on the continent at any one time, the aircraft operating in 'cells' of four from forward airstrips.

The A-10A is stressed to absorb tremendous battle damage, and it is claimed that it can still fly even if it loses an engine and tail fin on the same side of the aircraft. It is also extremely manoeuvrable, with the ability to turn through 45 degrees in one second, and during trials it has shown itself easily capable of out-turning high-speed fighters such as the Phantom.

Fairey Firefly FR Mk 4 — U Mk 9   UK

Role: Carrier-Borne Fighter-Bomber
Specification: N5/40
Operational: 1943-57
Data: AS7

Engines: One 2,020hp Rolls-Royce Griffon 74 engine
Span: 44ft 6in
Length: 37ft 3in
Weight: 10,000lb (empty)
16,096lb (max loaded)
Crew: 3
Max speed: 386mph at 14,000ft
Service ceiling: 28,000ft
Range: 700 miles max with internal fuel
Weapons: None. Carried ASW detection equipment, sonobuoys etc

A wartime design which entered service with the Fleet Air Arm in 1943 and saw much operational service before the end of hostilities, including attacks on the German battleship *Tirpitz*, a strike on the Japanese-held oil refineries in Sumatra and missions over the Japanese home islands while operating with Task Force 57 in the Pacific, the Fairey Firefly equipped eight FAA squadrons on VJ-Day. Most of these were subsequently disbanded, but from October 1945 11 other FAA units re-equipped with the type: Nos 805, 812, 814, 824, 825, 826, 827, 837, 860, 861 and 1830. The first major postwar variant of the Firefly was the Mk 4, which entered service with No 825 Squadron in August 1947. 28 were later converted as target tugs, and by 1948 this variant had been replaced on the production line by

the Mk 5, No 814 Squadron being the first to re-equip. One squadron, No 827, was still using Firefly FR1s in 1949, and in December that year it began a series of strikes against terrorist hideouts in Malaya, flying from the light fleet carrier HMS *Triumph*. No 827 was also the first Firefly squadron to see action in Korea, on 30 June 1950. The Firefly continued to operate with considerable success throughout the Korean War, serving with No 810 Squadron (HMS *Theseus*), No 812 (HMS *Glory*), No 817 (HMAS *Sydney*), No 820 (HMS *Glory*) and No 825 (HMS *Ocean*).

The Firefly AS6 was a three-seat anti-submarine variant which entered service with No 814 Squadron in 1951 and subsequently equipped Nos 812, 817, 820, 825 and 826 Squadrons, as well as six squadrons of the RNVR. In 1954, the Fireflies of No 825 Squadron carried out a series of ground attack missions against terrorists in Malaya, the last occasion the type fired its guns in anger. In 1952 the Firefly AS7 made its appearance, being allocated initially to No 824 Squadron, but its operational career was relatively short and most of those built were converted as trainers with the designation T7. The last Firefly variant was the U Mk 8 target drone, but 54 Mk 5s were also converted to this role and redesignated U Mk 9.

Total production of the Firefly (all marks) was 1,702 aircraft, and the type was supplied to Australia, Canada, Denmark, Ethiopia, India, the Netherlands, Sweden and Thailand. The Danish, Indian and Swedish aircraft were target tugs, but the Dutch aircraft (FR1s) saw action with No 860 Squadron against rebel forces in the Dutch East Indies.

Fairey Gannet

UK

Role: Anti-Submarine Warfare
Specification: GR17/45
Operational: 1955-
Data: AS4

Engines: Armstrong Siddeley Double Mamba 102 developing 3,035ehp
Span: 54ft 4in
Length: 42ft 11in
Weight: 14,528lb (empty)
21,600lb (loaded)
Crew: 3
Max speed: 270mph at 5,000ft
Service ceiling: 25,000ft
Weapons: Two homing torpedoes or two 1,000lb parachute mines internally; 16 60lb rockets, six Mk 2 depth charges, 10 sonobuoys, two rotary dispensers, two 250lb No 2 Mk 3 bombs, two A Mk 9 mines or two homing torpedoes externally

The Fairey Gannet, its portly outline a familiar sight in many parts of the world during the late 1950s, originated in an Admiralty requirement, issued towards the end of 1945, for a new anti-submarine aircraft. Searching for a suitable powerplant, Fairey Aviation selected the Armstrong Siddeley Mamba turboprop and suggested the possibility of coupling two of these engine together, driving a co-axial propeller. Armstrong Siddeley agreed and the result was the Double Mamba. Each half of the powerplant could be separately controlled, giving the pilot the option of shutting down one half and feathering the propeller to extend cruise range and lengthen search time. Another advantage of the coupled engine arrangement was that in the event of one engine failing, a safe deck landing could be accomplished on the other with no assymetric problems.

Three designs were submitted by Fairey, one based on a Rolls-Royce Tweed single turboprop and the other two on the Double Mamba. One of the latter was selected, and the Admiralty placed a contract for two prototypes on 12 August 1946. The first aircraft (VR546) flew on 19 September 1949, and the second (VR577) on 6 July 1950. These two machines were both two-seaters, but a third prototype (WE488), which flew on 10 May 1951, had provision for three seats. Known officially now as the Gannet (previously the Type Q), the aircraft underwent competitive trials with the Blackburn

YB1, and emerged successful, being ordered into production as the Gannet AS1.

The first carrier landing had already been carried out by the prototype Gannet on HMS *Illustrious* on 9 June 1953, and carrier trials, including day and night deck landings and catapult launches, were completed by the first production Gannet (WN339) in October 1953 from HMS *Illustrious* and HMS *Eagle*. Four Gannet AS1s were allocated to No 703 (Service Trials) Squadron in April 1954, and the first operational Gannet squadron, No 826, formed at Lee-on-Solent in January 1955. On 16 August 1954 the Gannet T2, a dual control training version, made its first flight, the radar and radome being deleted, and this variant was produced in parallel with the AS1. In 1956, the 170th production AS1 received a more powerful 3,035ehp Double Mamba 101 engine and became the Gannet AS4, the parallel trainer version being designated T5. The AS4 entered service in 1957 and equipped the Royal Navy's first-line ASW squadrons until 1960. Two modified versions of the AS4 were the AS6 and AS7 with more advanced electronics, and one flight of AS6s continued to operate from RNAS Culdrose until 1962, being eventually replaced by ASW helicopters. Fifteen Gannet AS4s and one T5 were delivered to the Federal German Naval Air Arm, and continued in service until replaced by the Breguet Atlantic. Seventeen AS4s were also supplied to Indonesia in 1960.

The last operational version of the Gannet was the AEW3, which flew for the first time on 20 August 1958. Designed to succeed the Douglas Skyraider in the early warning role, the AEW3 was almost completely redesigned, retaining little more than the wing and tailplane of earlier marks, and was powered by the 3,875ehp Double Mamba 102. Carrier trials took place in November 1958 on HMS *Centaur* and production was completed in 1961 after 30 aircraft had been built. The aircraft carried the AEW radar in a large ventral radome and normal operating height was 25,000ft, giving all-round radar coverage of some 200 miles. The Gannet AEW3 equipped four flights of No 849 Squadron, the Royal Navy's largest flying unit during the 1960s, but by 1972 this had been reduced to one flight based on shore and another aboard the last remaining British carrier, HMS *Ark Royal*, and in April 1978 the squadron's last nine Gannets embarked on the carrier for their final tour.

FFVS J22

Role: Fighter
Operational: 1944-1952

Engines: One SFA-built STWC3-G (Pratt & Whitney Twin Wasp) rated at 1,065hp
Span: 32ft 9½in
Length: 25ft 7in
Weight: 4,400lb (empty)
6,300lb (loaded)
Crew: 1
Max speed: 358mph at 11,500ft
Service ceiling: 30,000ft
Range: 780 miles max
Weapons: Four 13.2mm M39A machine guns

Designed in 1941 by the Swedish Flygförvaltningens Verkstad (Air Board Workshop) to meet an urgent need for a modern fighter type to equip the squadrons of the Flygvapnet, the FFVS J22 was a small, orthodox machine developed around the most powerful engine then available in Sweden, a copy of the American Pratt & Whitney SC3-G Twin Wasp radial. Such was the urgency — the US Government having placed a sudden embargo on the supply of

Sweden

Republic EP-1 fighters to Sweden — that an initial batch of 60 J22s was ordered straight off the drawing board in March 1942, more than five months before the prototype flew on 1 September. The prototype proved to be highly manoeuvrable and met all its performance requirements, and after further extensive testing a small pre-production batch was delivered to the Flygvapnet for service evaluation in November 1943. The year's delay was caused, in part, by disputes among the various companies involved in the production of the J22's components, which — because of strict quality controls imposed by the FFVS — necessitated the development of new production techniques.

Early in 1944, production J22s were delivered to F9, replacing the unit's elderly Fiat CR42bis biplanes, and F13 and F16 followed suit soon afterwards. By the end of 1944 75 J22s were in service. By the time production ended in April 1946, 198 J22s had been built. Other Flygvapnet units to use the type were F3, F8, F10 and F18. The J22 remained in service until 1952, when it was finally replaced by the Vampire FB50 in F3.

Fiat G91

Italy

Role: Ground-Attack/Reconnaissance Fighter
Operational: 1959-
Photo: G91Y
Data: G91R

Engines: One 5,000lb thrust Fiat-built Bristol Siddeley Orpheus 803 turbojet
Span: 28ft 1in
Length: 33ft 9½in
Weight: 8,130lb (empty)
12,125 (max loaded)

Crew: 1
Max speed: 650mph at 5,000ft
Service ceiling: 40,000ft
Range: 400 miles
Weapons: Four .5in Colt-Browning machine guns or two 30mm guns; 500lb bombs, nuclear weapons, Nord 5103 AAMs, clusters of six 3in RPs, packs of 31 FFARs, or gun pods in various combinations on underwing pylons

The Fiat G91 lightweight ground-attack fighter was designed in response to a NATO requirement issued early in 1954, and the company was awarded a

51

contract for three prototypes and 27 pre-production aircraft while the project was still on the drawing board. Powered by a Bristol Siddeley Orpheus turbojet, the aircraft took part in the NATO evaluation trials at Bretigny, France, in the Autumn of 1957, the prototype having flown on 9 August the previous year. The G91 proved easily capable of meeting all the demands of the NATO specification, and as a result it was ordered into production as the standard NATO light tactical fighter. The basic G91 was evaluated by the Italian Air Force's 103rd Squadron from February 1959, and by the end of the year the unit was fully operational wih the type as part of the 5th Aerobrigata.

The G91 ground-attack version (comprising the prototypes and the 27 pre-production machines) was followed on the assembly line by a series of fighter-reconnaissance variants, the first of which was the G91R/1 with three Vinten cameras for low-level, high speed photography. The G91R/1A, R/1B and R/3 were basically similar to the R/1, with various equipment changes; 98 FR aircraft were delivered to the Italian Air Force and a further 50 R/3s to the Luftwaffe, the first unit to receive them

being Aufklärungsgeschwader 53 in May 1962. Fifty examples of a further reconnaissance variant, the G91R/4 — originally intended for the US Air Force — were also diverted to the Luftwaffe. The Federal German aircraft industry also built 294 G91R/3s under licence, and the last of these were delivered to the Luftwaffe in May 1966.

The G91T was a tandem two-seat advanced trainer, retaining a tactical fighter capability, and flew for the first time on 31 May 1960 with an Orpheus 803 turbojet. 76 G91T/1s were built for the Italian Air Force, and 44 G91T/3s for the Luftwaffe. The G91PAN, which was delivered in 1964, was a special aerobatic version for the Frecce Tricolori, the Italian AF Aerobatic Team.

The Fiat G91Y was a twin-engined development of the G91T, powered by two General Electric J85-GE-13A turbojets producing a 60% greater take-off thrust and permitting a greater tactical load. The first of two G91Y prototypes flew on 27 December 1966, followed by 20 pre-series and 45 production aircraft. In 1978, the G91Y equipped the Italian Air Force's 1st Group, 8th Wing, and 13th Group, 32nd Wing.

Folland Gnat Mk 1

UK

Role: Fighter/Ground-Attack
Specification: —
Operational: 1960-

Engines: One 4,520lb thrust Bristol Orpheus BOr2 (701) turbojet
Span: 22ft 2in
Length: 29ft 9in
Weight: 4,850lb (empty)
8,600lb (max loaded)
Crew: 1
Max speed: 695mph at 20,000ft
Service ceiling: 50,000ft
Range: 920 miles with external fuel
Weapons: Two 30mm Aden cannon in air intake fairings; two 500lb bombs or 12 3in RPs underwing

The Folland Fo141 Gnat began its career as a private venture and was conceived by Folland's Managing Director, W. E. W. Petter, who was also responsible for the design of the Canberra jet bomber. Work began in 1951 with the initial encouragement of the

Air Ministry, but this later waned when the Saturn turbojet around which the type was designed was abandoned. Undeterred, Follands modified the design to take the lower-powered Armstrong Siddeley Viper engine, and with this powerplant a prototype aircraft — named Midge — flew on 11 August 1954. The Midge subsequently underwent a rigorous flight test programme, and despite the low power of its engine — only 1,640lb thrust — it was dived at supersonic speed. Work on the Gnat resumed when, in November 1953, the Bristol Aeroplane Company announced its intention to build the Orpheus engine, and the prototype flew on 18 July 1955. This was followed by a batch of six aircraft for the Ministry of Supply, the first of these flying on 26 May 1956.

Production Gnat Mk 1s were powered by the Bristol Orpheus 701 turbojet of 4,520lb thrust and carried an armament of two 30mm Aden cannon plus up to 2,000lb of underwing stores, but despite the promise shown by the diminutive aircraft — which cost far less to manufacture than other combat aircraft of comparable performance — it was not adopted by the RAF. 25, however, were supplied

to India, together with 15 sets of components; 12 to Finland and two to Yugoslavia. In India, the Gnat Mk 1 was manufactured under licence by the Bangalore Division of Hindustan Aeronautics Ltd, the licence being acquired in September 1956 and a quantity production order placed in July 1958. One hundred Gnats were subsequently produced by HAL and the type saw considerable action during the 1971 war between India and Pakistan, where it proved quite deadly in high-speed, low-level combat. Gnat Mk 1 production ended in 1974, but the last

two aircraft were completed as the prototypes of a HAL-produced Mk II version known as the Ajeet (Unconquered), and the first of these flew on 30 September 1976. The Ajeet, which has an improved performance and more reliable control system, is in production for the Indian Air Force (1978).

Projected British versions of the basic Gnat design were the Mk 2 with an afterburning Orpheus BOr2, the Mk 3 carrier-borne variant, and the Mk 4 with an afterburning BOr12 and AI radar. The Gnat T Mk 1 trainer is described separately.

General Dynamics F-16 USA

Role: Air Superiority Fighter
Operational: 1980 (planned)
Photo: YF-16
Data: F-16A

Engines: One Pratt & Whitney F100-PW-100 turbofan rated at 25,000lb thrust with reheat
Span: 30ft
Length: 47ft $7\frac{1}{2}$in
Weight: 14,567lb (empty)
22,500lb (normal loaded)
Crew: 1
Max speed: Mach 2+
Service ceiling: 50,000ft+
Range: 2,303 miles (ferry)
Weapons: One 20mm M61A-1 cannon; one infra-red AAM on each wingtip; up to 15,200lb of external stores on underwing and under-fuselage stations.

The winner of a USAF contest for a lightweight air superiority fighter, the General Dynamics F-16 is

scheduled to replace the F-104 Starfighter in service with several air forces and is likely to be one of the most important combat types of the 1980s. The first of two YF-16 prototypes flew officially for the first time on 2 February 1974 (an unofficial first flight having been made on 20 January, when test pilot Philip Oestricher decided to take off after the aircraft's tailplane was damaged during taxi trials) and the type exceeded Mach 2 in level flight on 11 March 1974. During an 11-month evaluation programme, flying in competition with the Northrop YF-17, the YF-16 readily attained all its design objectives, and in July 1975 construction began of a batch of eight pre-production aircraft, comprising six F-16A single-seaters and two F-16B two-seaters. All pre-production aircraft were flying by mid-1978, and the USAF plans to procure an eventual total of 1,388 operational aircraft. Other nations planning to purchase the F-16A/B are Israel (75), Belgium (102), Denmark (48), the Netherlands (84), Norway (72) and Iran (160), with options for 42 more.

General Dynamics F-111 USA

Role: Tactical Strike
Operational: 1967-
Data: F-111F

Engines: Two 25,100lb thrust Pratt & Whitney TF30-P-100 turbofans
Span: 63ft (spread)
31ft $11\frac{1}{2}$in (fully swept)

Length: 73ft 6in
Weight: 47,481lb (empty)
100,000lb (max loaded)
Crew: 2
Max speed: 1,650mph at 40,000ft; 865mph at sea level
Service ceiling: 59,000ft+
Range: 2,925 miles with max internal fuel

Weapons: One M61 multi-barrel 20mm gun and two B43 bombs in internal weapons bay; three points for variety of external stores under each wing

In 1962 the General Dynamics Corporation, in association with Grumman Aircraft, was selected to develop a variable-geometry tactical fighter to meet the requirements of the USAF's TFX programme. An initial contract was placed for 23 development aircraft, including 18 F-111As for the USAF and five F-111Bs for the US Navy. Powered by two Pratt & Whitney TF30-P-1 turbofan engines, the prototype F-111A flew for the first time on 21 December 1964, and during the second flight on 6 January 1965 the aircraft's wings were swept through the full range from 16 degrees to 72.5 degrees. 160 production F-111As were built, the first examples entering service with the 4480th Tactical Fighter Wing at Nellis AFB, Nevada, in October 1967. On 17 March the following year five aircraft from this unit flew to Takhli base in Thailand for operations evaluation in Vietnam, making their first sorties on 25 March. Two were lost during the next five days, the cause being attributed to fatigue in the wing pivot fitting, and modifications were carried out to subsequent aircraft. Fifty F-111As were ordered by the British Government to replace the abandoned TSR-2 under the designation F-111K, but this order was subsequently cancelled. Two YF-111As served as prototypes for the British strike/reconnaissance version, and were subsequently used by the USAF for research and development.

The F-111B version for the US Navy, which was assembled by Grumman, flew for the first time on 18 May 1965, but was discontinued after seven aircraft had been built. Intended for fleet defence, with an armament of six Hughes Falcon missiles, original orders called for 24 production aircraft. The FB-111A was a strategic bomber version for the US Strategic Air Command, two prototypes being converted from F-111As. Designed to replace early models of the B-52 and the Convair B-58 Hustler, the first FB-111As were assigned to the 340th Bomb Group at Carswell AFB, Texas, on 8 October 1969. The FB-111A had an offensive armament of 50 750lb bombs or six SRAM missiles; 76 aircraft were built, equipping two SAC Wings. The F-111C, outwardly similar to the FB-111A, was a strike variant for the Royal Australian Air Force, 24 being delivered, while the F-111D was similar to the F-111A but with more advanced electronics. 96 F-111Ds were built, and the variant equipped the 27th Tactical Fighter Wing. The F-111E superseded the F-111A in service, having modified air intakes to improve performance above Mach 2.2; 94 were built, equipping the 20th TFW at Upper Heyford, UK, and the 474th TFW at Nellis AFB, Nevada. The F-111F was a fighter-bomber variant, combining the best features of the F-111E and FB-111A, and was fitted with more powerful TF-30-P-100 engines. 106 aircraft were built, serving with Tactical Air Command. Other variants of the F-111 are the RF-111A, a two-seat reconnaissance version of the F-111A equipped with cameras, radar and infra-red sensors, and the EF-111A electronic countermeasures aircraft. Total production of the F-111 (all variants) was 562 aircraft, including 23 development machines, and the last (an F-111F) was delivered to the USAF in November 1976.

Grumman AF-2 Guardian

USA

Role: Anti-Submarine Warfare
Operational: 1950-55
Photo: AF-2S

Engines: One Pratt & Whitney R-2800-48W radial rated at 2,400hp
Span: 60ft 8in
Length: 43ft 4in
Weight: 14,580lb (empty)
22,500lb (max loaded)
Crew: 3/4
Max speed: 315mph at 16,000ft
Service ceiling: 32,000ft
Range: 1,500 miles (normal)
Weapons: (AF-2S) Two 2,000lb torpedoes, or two

1,600lb depth charges, or two 2,000lb bombs plus two 20mm cannon

Originally designed as a torpedo-bomber, the prototype Grumman XTB3F-1 Guardian flew for the first time on 1 December 1945 with a composite powerplant consisting of one Pratt & Whitney R-2800-34W radial engine and one Westinghouse 19XB-2B turbojet in the rear fuselage, exhausting under the tail. The crew of two were seated side by side in a roomy cockpit forward of the wings and an internal weapons bay housed two torpedoes or a combination of bombs and depth charges. The turbojet was subsequently removed and the torpedo-bomber classification abandoned, the design being modified for anti-submarine warfare operations.

After considerable redesign, which resulted from extensive evaluation in 1948-49, two new prototypes made their appearance, bearing the designations XTB3F-1S and XTB3F-2S, the former being equipped as a submarine hunter and the latter as a 'killer'. Both types were ordered into production for the United States Navy under the service designations AF-1S and AF-2S, but the AF-1S was soon changed to AF-2W and the type officially named 'Guardian'. The AF-2W and -2S were intended to work in conjunction with one another, the -2W carrying out the actual search and directing the -2S on to the target, which was then attacked with torpedoes, depth charges or bombs, and cannon fire.

The first Guardians were delivered to Navy Squadron VS-25 on 18 October 1950 and the type remained in service until August 1955, the last unit to use it in first-line service being VS-37. Total production was 389 aircraft, including prototypes.

Grumman F7F Tigercat

USA

Role: Long-Range Carrier-Borne Fighter
Operational: 1944-54
Photo: F7F-1
Data: F7F-2N

Engines: Two 2,100hp Pratt & Whitney R-2800-22W radials
Span: 51ft 6in
Length: 45ft 5in
Weight: 16,190lb (empty)
23,881lb (max loaded)
Crew: 2
Max speed: 424mph at 19,200ft
Service ceiling: 36,000ft
Range: 1,630 miles with long-range tanks
Weapons: Four 20mm cannon and four .5in machine guns; up to 3,000lb of bombs, eight 60lb rockets, or one 18in torpedo (attack variants)

Although it appeared too late to see operational service during World War II, the Grumman F7F Tigercat was significant in that it was the first twin-engined carrier-borne aircraft with a tricycle undercarriage to enter series production. It began life as the Model G51 under a US Navy design contract placed in 1941 and two XF7F-1 prototypes were ordered in June that year, the first flying on 3 November 1943. Series production of the F7F-1 began in April 1944, an initial batch of 34 aircraft being produced under the designation F7F-1D. These were designed to carry out the role of long range fighter and tactical support, operating from 45,000 ton carriers of the Midway class in the Pacific with the US Marine Corps, and first deliveries were made to VMF-911 and VMF(N)-531 early in 1944. During the winter of 1944/45 VMF(N)-531 re-equipped with the F7F-2N night fighter version, which had some internal fuel tanks deleted to make room for a radar observer. 64 were built before the end of March 1945, and two of these were evaluated by the British Fleet Air Arm (serials TT346 and TT349).

The next variant, the single-seat F7F-3, had more powerful Pratt & Whitney R-2800-34W engines and was the major production version, 189 being built. The night fighter variant, the F7F-3N, had a longer nose to accommodate additional radar equipment; 60 were built, the first flying in February 1946. The F7F-3E carried special equipment for electronic

reconnaissance and countermeasures; the F7F-3P was a photographic reconnaissance version; and the F7F-4N, of which 13 were built, was the last night fighter variant, appearing in June 1946. Production of the F7F ended with the 364th aircraft.

During the Korean War, the Tigercats of VMF(N)-513 operated as night intruders, attempting to seek out enemy night fighters, but met with only limited success. They were eventually replaced in this role by the Douglas Skynight in November 1952. The last unit to use the Tigercat was VJ-64, which relinquished its F7F-3Ns and -4Ns in March 1954.

Grumman F8F Bearcat

USA

Role: Carrier-Borne Fighter-Bomber
Operational: 1945-1966
Data: F8F-1

Engines: One 2,100hp Pratt & Whitney R-2800-22W radial
Span: 35ft 10in
Length: 28ft 3in
Weight: 7,070lb (empty)
9,386lb (loaded)
Crew: 1
Max speed: 421mph at 19,700ft
Service ceiling: 38,700ft
Range: 1,105 miles
Weapons: Four wing-mounted .5in Colt-Browning machine guns; provision for two 1,000lb bombs under wings

Developed from the F6F Hellcat, which achieved fame in the Pacific during World War II, the Grumman F8F Bearcat flew for the first time on 6 October 1944 and entered service with the US Navy Squadron VF-19 in May 1945. It was destined never to see combat in World War II, but became one of the principal US Navy types in the immediate postwar years, equipping 24 squadrons by June 1949. The last aircraft was delivered to the US Navy in May that year, bringing total production to 1,268, including prototypes. This total comprised 765 F8F-1s, 100 F8F-1Bs — which carried an armament of four 20mm cannon in place of the earlier model's .5in machine guns — 36 F8F-1N night fighters, 293

F8F-2s, 12 F8F-2Ns and 60 F8F-2Ps, the latter being a photo-reconnaissance version with only two cannon. Both the F8F-1 and F8F-2 were phased out of service with the fleet by the end of 1950, being progressively assigned to reserve squadrons, but the F8F-2Ps remained in first-line service until the end of 1952. The last units to use the type in US service were Reserve Squadrons VF-921 and VF-859, which relinquished it in January 1953.

In 1951 the first of 100 Bearcats, all ex-US Navy F8F-1s and -1Bs, were delivered to the Armee de l'Air for use in the Indo-China conflict, equipping GC I/6 'Corse' and GC III/6 'Roussillon' at Saigon. In September 1951 GC I/6 left Indo-China and its aircraft were allocated to GC I/8 'Saintonge'. In February 1952, GC II/8 'Languedoc' also converted to Bearcats, followed by GC I/9 'Limousin', GC II/9 'Auvergne' and GC I/21 'Artois', while the Escadron de Reconnaissance d'Outre-Mer used the type with cameras installed in a belly tank. When the French withdrew from Indo-China following the ceasefire of July 1954, the surviving Bearcats were turned over to the embryo Vietnam Air Force.

Following the visit to Thailand of a US Military Air Advisory Group, it was decided to use the Bearcat in re-equipping the Royal Thai Air Force, and an initial batch of ex-USN F8F-1s was delivered aboard the carrier USS Cape Esperance. Later, 79 more aircraft were supplied to equip a number of tactical fighter-bomber squadrons, this total including 29 F8F-1Bs. The Bearcat continued to serve in Thailand until 1966, equipping four close-support squadrons.

Grumman F9F Panther/Cougar

USA

Role: Carrier-Borne Fighter-Bomber
Operational: 1949-58 (Panther)
1952-60 (Cougar)

	F9F-5	F9F-8
Engines:	One 6,250lb thrust Pratt & Whitney J48-P-4 turbojet	One 7,200lb thrust Pratt & Whitney J48-P-8A turbojet
Span:	38ft	34ft 6in
Length:	42ft	41ft 7in
Weight: (empty)	9,000lb	9,200lb
(Loaded)	15,750lb	17,500lb
Crew:	1	1
Max speed:	625mph at sea level	705mph at sea level
Service ceiling:	50,000ft	42,000ft
Range:	1,200 miles	1,000 miles
Weapons:	Four 20mm cannon. Underwing rockets and bombs	Four 20mm cannon. Up to 4,000lb of underwing ordnance

F9F Panther

In April 1946 the United States Navy signed a contract with the Grumman Aircraft Corporation for the construction of a prototype night fighter, designated the XF9F-1 and powered by four Westinghouse J30-WE-20 engines. The following

October, however, the Bureau of Aeronautics decided to abandon development of the XF9F-1 in favour of a single-engined naval day fighter which was to be designated XF9F-2 and powered by a Rolls-Royce Nene turbojet. Two XF9F-2 prototypes

were ordered, the first of which (Nene-engined) flew on 24 November 1947. The second prototype, designated XF9F-3, flew in August 1948 and was equipped with an Allison J33-A-8 engine.

The first production batch of F9F-2 Panthers (47 aircraft) featured the Pratt & Whitney J42-P-6 turbojet, the licence-built Nene. The F9F-2 carried an armament of four 20mm cannon in the nose, and carried underwing points for rockets and bombs. It entered service with Navy Squadron VF-51 in May 1949. The F9F-2 was replaced on the production line by the F9F-3, powered by the Allison J33-A-8, but this variant was converted retrospectively to F-9F-2 standard by the installation of the Pratt & Whitney engine. Total production of the F9F-2 and -3 was 437 aircraft.

The next variant was the F9F-4, powered by an Allison J33-A-C6 engine; 73 examples were built, followed by 655 F9F-5s. The latter version was fitted with a Pratt & Whitney J48-P-2/4 turbojet based on the Rolls-Royce Tay. Twenty-six examples of a photo-reconnaissance variant, the F9F-5P, were also produced.

The F9F-2 Panther became one of the workhorses of the US Navy during the Korean War, going into action for the first time on 3 July 1950 when aircraft of VF-51 (Air Group 5, USS *Valley Forge*) flew top cover for strikes on enemy airfields and supply lines near Pyongyang. During this mission, two VF-51 pilots shot down two Yak-9s, scoring the Navy's first kills in Korea. On 9 November that year, the CO of another Panther squadron, VF-111 (Lt-Cdr Amen)

became the first naval pilot in history to destroy a jet aircraft (a MiG-15). In April 1951, two F9F-2B Panthers of VF-191, each carrying four 250lb and two 100lb GP bombs, were launched from the USS *Princeton* for an attack on a railway bridge near Songjin; this was the US Navy's first use of a jet fighter as a bomber.

In the mid-1950s the Panther was progressively allocated to reserve squadrons, the last unit — VAH-7 — finally relinquishing its F9F-5s in October 1958.

F9F-8 Cougar

The Grumman F9F-6 Cougar was a logical development of the Panther, the prototype XF9F-6 being an F9F-5 airframe with swept flying surfaces. Both the prototype, which first flew on 20 September 1951, and the initial production Cougars used the 6,250lb thrust Pratt & Whitney J48-P-6A turbojet, but this was later replaced by the 7,250lb thrust J48-P-8. A small number of aircraft were also produced with the Allison J33-A-16A, under the designation F9F-7, but it was the J48-engined F9F-8 which became the standard variant in US Navy service. The Cougar first entered service with VF-32 in November 1952, and by the beginning of 1954 many US Navy and Marine Corps units were using the type. On 1 April that year, three Cougars of VF-21 made the first transcontinental crossing of the United States in less than four hours, refuelling once in flight, the best time being 3hr 45min 30sec. 400 F9F-8 Cougars were built, the last being delivered in

February 1960. The last variants in squadron service were the F9F-8P photo-reconnaissance aircraft and the F9F-8T trainer, which had tandem seats and was 3ft longer than the single-seat aircraft. The F9F-8T also carried a full armament and about half the

production batch were issued to fleet units as fighter-bombers, the last first-line unit to use it in this role being VMCJ-3. In its reconnaissance role, the F9F-8P Cougar served with recce squadron VFP-62 until February 1960.

Grumman F11F Tiger

USA

Role: Naval Air Superiority Fighter
Operational: 1957-61
Data: F11F-1

Engines: One Wright J65-W-6 or W-18 turbojet developing 7,800lb thrust (10,500lb with reheat)
Span: 31ft 7½in
Length: 44ft 6in
Weight: 13,428lb (empty)
21,174lb (normal loaded)
Crew: 1
Max speed: 890mph at 36,000ft
Service ceiling: 55,000lb
Range: 750 miles (normal)
Weapons: Four 20mm cannon and two AAM-N-7 Sidewinder missiles

Conceived by the Grumman Design Team in January 1953 as a supersonic successor to the Panther/Cougar series, the Grumman Tiger was originally designated F9F. The first of six pre-production F11F-1 Tigers flew for the first time on 30 July 1954, powered by a 7,500lb thrust Wright J65-W-7 turbojet, and 39 production aircraft were ordered in October that year. The aircraft displayed a number of serious

teething troubles which delayed its service debut, and it was not until 8 March 1957 that the first US Navy unit, VA-156, equipped with the type. Operational Tigers differed extensively from the pre-production aircraft, having a longer nose and extended inboard wing leading edges. A further variant was the F11F-1F, which was developed as a private venture and was powered by a General Electric J79-GE-7 turbojet developing a thrust of 15,560lb with reheat and boosting the fighter's performance to the region of Mach 2 at 40,000ft. The F11F-1F replaced the earlier model on the production line and remained in service until April 1961, the last units to use it being VF-33 and VF-111.

On 21 September 1956 an F11F-1 Tiger, piloted by Grumman test pilot Tom Attridge was involved in an extraordinary incident when it shot itself down during test firings off Long Island, running into 20mm cannon shells it had fired only seconds earlier. On 18 April 1958, the more powerful F11F-1F demonstrated its climbing ability when it broke the world altitude record twice in three days with a height of 76,939ft. Only 201 F11F-1s and -1Fs were built, the last delivery being made in December 1958.

Grumman F-14 Tomcat

USA

Role: Naval Air Superiority Fighter
Operational: 1974-
Photo: F-14A

Engines: Two Pratt & Whitney TF30-P-412A turbofans with a maximum rating of 20,900lb thrust
Span: 64ft 1½in (spread)
38ft 2½in (swept)
Length: 61ft 11in
Weight: 38,930lb (empty)
58,539lb (normal loaded)
Crew: 1
Max speed: Mach 2.4
Service ceiling: 50,000ft +

Range: Not available
Weapons: One General Electric M61A-1 Vulcan cannon on port side of forward fuselage; four Sparrow AAMs partly recessed under fuselage; four Sidewinder, or two Sidewinder plus two Sparrow or Phoenix AAMs on wing pylons; tactical weapons load of up to 14,500lb

Selected in January 1969 as the winner of a US Navy contest for a new carrier-borne fighter (VFX), the Grumman F-14 Tomcat is designed primarily to establish complete air superiority in the vicinity of a carrier task force and also to attack tactical objectives as a secondary role. Powered by two Pratt & Whitney TF30-P-412A turbofans, the prototype

F-14A flew for the first time on 21 December 1970, followed by 11 research and development aircraft. The variable-geometry fighter completed carrier trials in the summer of 1972 and first deliveries to the fleet began the following October, when F-14As were assigned to Replacement Training Squadron VF-124 at San Diego, California. The first two operational squadrons, VF-1 and VF-2, were commissioned in 1974 and sailed for the Western Pacific aboard the USS *Enterprise*, while squadrons VF-14 and VF-32 became operational on the USS *John F. Kennedy* in July 1975. By the end of 1977 270 F-14As had been delivered, equipping squadrons VF-24, VF-101, VF-142, VF-143 and VF-211 in addition to those listed above. Carriers on

which these units are operational in 1978 (except for VF-101, which is a training squadron) are the USS *America* and USS *Constellation*. The first of 80 F-14As was delivered to the Imperial Iranian Air Force in January 1976, these aircraft differing from those in US Navy service only in the standard of their ECM equipment. The F-14B version, which flew for the first time on 12 September 1973, is powered by two Pratt & Whitney F401 turbofans rated at 27,000lb thrust and is designed to accelerate from Mach 0.8 to Mach 1.6 in 1.38min. A further projected variant, the F-14C, with revised electronics and weapons, was shelved because of economic restrictions. Total planned Tomcat production (1978 figures) is 390 aircraft.

Grumman A-6 Intruder

USA

Role: Carrier-Borne Attack Bomber
Operational: 1963-
Data: A-6E

Engines: Two 9,300lb thrust Pratt & Whitney J52-P-8A turbojets
Span: 53ft
Length: 54ft 7in
Weight: 25,630lb (empty)
60,400lb (max loaded)
Crew: 2
Max speed: 643mph at sea level
Service ceiling: 47,000ft
Range: 2,700 miles, combat configuration with max fuel

Weapons: Underwing loads including 30 500lb bombs in clusters of six, or three 2,000lb GP bombs plus two 300 US gal drop tanks.

Designed specifically as a carrier-based low-level attack bomber with the ability to deliver both nuclear and conventional warloads with high accuracy and in all weathers, the Grumman A-6 Intruder was one of 11 competitors in a US Navy design contest of 1957, and was selected as the winner on 31 December that year. In March 1959 a contract was placed for four aircraft, followed by four more in 1960, and the A-6A prototype flew on 19 April 1960. The first operational aircraft entered service with Navy Squadron VA-42 on 1 February 1963 and the last A-6A delivery took place in December 1969,

by which time 469 had been built. The A-6A saw extensive action over Vietnam, providing the US 7th Fleet with a formidable strike force. Each aircraft could carry up to 15,000lb of bombs and employed a Digital Integrated Attack Navigation System, enabling the pilot to pre-select an attack pattern for his A-6A, which then approached the target, released its weapons and left the target area under automatic control. The next variant was the EA-6A, which — although retaining a reduced strike capability — had the primary task of supporting air and ground forces by detecting, locating, classifying, recording and jamming enemy transmissions, for which purpose it was fitted with over 30 different kinds of antenna. 27 EA-6As were produced for the US Marine Corps. The EA-6B Prowler was a development of the EA-6A with advanced electronics and a longer nose section to accommodate two extra ECM specialists. Ten US Navy countermeasures squadrons were equipped

with the Prowler by the end of 1977, with one US Marine squadron forming and two more planned for 1978-9.

Conversions of the basic A-6A were the A-6B, modified to carry the General Dynamics Standard ARM (Anti-Radiation Missile); the A-6C, with an under-fuselage turret housing forward-looking infra-red sensors and TV camera to increase night attack capability; the KA-6D, converted as a flight refuelling tanker but also able to act as an air-sea rescue co-ordinator and as a day bomber; and the A-6E, fitted with multi-mode radar and an IBM computer. The A-6E flew for the first time in February 1970 and first squadron delivery was made in 1972. Total procurement orders called for 318 A-6Es, including 119 converted from A-6As. The A-6E/TRAM (Target Recognition Attack Multisensor) was a further variant fitted with a highly advanced sensor package, flying for the first time in 1974.

Grumman E-2 Hawkeye   USA

Role: Carrier-Borne Early Warning
Operational: 1967-
Data: E-2A

Engines: Two 4,050eshp Allison T56-A-8/8A turboprops
Span: 80ft 7in
Length: 56ft 4in
Weight: 36,063lb (empty)
49,638lb (max loaded)
Crew: 5
Max speed: 368mph at sea level
Service ceiling: 31,700ft
Range: 1,905 miles (ferry)
Weapons: None

The Grumman E-2 Hawkeye was designed as a carrier-borne early warning aircraft capable also of operating from bases on land, including unprepared strips. The prototype flew on 20 October 1960 and the first production E-2A (formerly W2F-1) followed on 19 April 1961. The first 20 E-2As, which were completed by mid-1963, were used for service evaluation and carrier trials, and the type was formally accepted into US Navy service on 19 January 1964, when it began to equip Early Warning Squadron VAW-11 at San Diego. This unit went to sea with its Hawkeyes aboard the USS *Kitty Hawk* in 1966, by which time a second squadron — VAW-12 — had also formed. Sixty-two E-2As were built, including the prototypes, and construction

ended early in 1967. The E-2B, which flew for the first time on 20 February 1969, had a number of refinements including an L-304 microelectronic computer, and all operational E-2As were subsequently updated to E-2B standard. This variant served with Early Warning Squadrons RVAW-110, VAW-112, VAW-113, VAW-115, VAW-116 and VAW-117.

The latest Hawkeye variant was the E-2C, the first of two prototypes flying in January 1971. 47 E-2Cs had been delivered by the end of 1977 and there are plans to produce a further 36 by the end of 1984. Four have been supplied to Israel and four to Japan. The E-2C first entered service with VAW-123 at Norfolk, Virginia, in 1973, embarking for sea duty on the USS *Saratoga* late in 1974 and on the USS *John F. Kennedy* in June the following year. In 1978 this version was operational with RVAW-120, VAW-121, VAW-122, VAW-123, VAW-124, VAW-125 and VAW-126. The E-2C differs from earlier models in its use of the Grumman/General Dynamics AN/APS-111 radar, which can pick out air targets from ground 'clutter'.

Easily identifiable by its huge saucer-shaped radome, designed to develop enough lift in flight to offset its weight, and by its four-finned tail unit, the Hawkeye is able to give all-weather early warning coverage around a naval task force, and to detect and analyse any threat from high-speed, low-level aircraft. Two derivatives of the E-2C are also in use; the TE-2C trainer and the C-2A Greyhound Carrier On-Board Delivery transport.

Grumman OV-1 Mohawk

USA

Role: Battlefield Surveillance
Operational: 1961-
Data: OV-1D

Engines: Two 1,400shp Lycoming T53-L-701 turboprops
Span: 48ft
Length: 41ft
Weight: 12,054lb (empty) 18,109lb (max loaded)
Crew: 2
Max speed: 305mph at 5,000ft
Service ceiling: 25,000ft
Range: 1,011 miles with external tanks
Weapons: None

Designed in the mid-1950s to a US Army and Marine Corps requirement calling for a battlefield surveillance aircraft capable of operating round the clock in all weathers, the Grumman G-134 Mohawk was selected in 1957, a US Army contract ordering nine aircraft for evaluation under the designation YAO-1AF (later changed to YOV-1A). The prototype flew on 14 April 1959 and all nine aircraft were completed by the end of the year. By this time the Mohawk was purely a US Army venture, the USMC

having withdrawn from the project because of economy measures. The first production model, the OV-1A, was similar to the YOV-1A but with improved avionics, and entered service with the US Army in 1961. In July that year it was deployed with units of the 7th Army in Germany, and in July 1962 it arrived in Vietnam with the 23rd Special Warfare Aviation Detachment. Two years later an experimental armed version, the JOV-1A, was used operationally in Vietnam by the 11th Air Assault Division of the 1st Cavalry Division (Airmobile). Armed with 2.75in rocket pods and .5in gun pods, the JOV-1A was used by the 1st Cavalry until the spring of 1965, when it was allocated to the 73rd Aerial Surveillance Company. This unit had been formed in January 1965 by the amalgamation of the 23rd Special Warfare Aviation Detachment and the 4th Aerial Surveillance and Target Acquisition Detachment, which had arrived in Vietnam in 1964 with OV-1B and -1C Mohawks.

The OV-1B and -1C carried more advanced surveillance equipment than the earlier version, and the last Mohawk variant, the OV-1D, could be readily converted from infra-red to radar surveillance, combining the duties of the -1B and -1C. The last Mohawk was completed in December 1970, by which time 375 aircraft had been delivered.

Grumman S2F Tracker

USA

Role: Anti-Submarine Warfare
Operational: 1954-
Data: S-2E

Engines: Two 1,525hp Wright R-1820-82WA radials
Span: 72ft 7in
Length: 43ft 6in
Weight: 18,750lb (empty) 29,150lb (loaded)
Crew: 4
Max speed: 265mph at sea level
Service ceiling: 21,000ft
Range: 1,300 miles (ferry)

Weapons: Two homing torpedoes, two Mk 101 depth bombs or four 385lb depth charges internally, and six 250lb bombs, 5in HVARs or Zuni rockets on external pylons

One of the most important carrier-borne anti-submarine aircraft of the postwar years, the prototype Grumman XS2F-1 Tracker flew for the first time on 4 December 1952. First deliveries to the US Navy were made to VS-26 in February 1954, and at the end of that year the type embarked on the USS *Princeton* with VS-23. The initial production series of S2F-1s (later S-2As) were powered by two 1,525hp Wright R-1820-82 engines; 755 were built, and the type was also supplied to the Argentine, Japan, Italy,

Brazil, Taiwan, Thailand, Uruguay and the Netherlands. The S-2C (S2F-2), which was next on the assembly line, featured a larger torpedo bay capable of housing homing torpedoes. 60 were built, and most of these were later converted into US-2C utility aircraft. The S-2D (S2F-3) was a developed version with an increased wingspan and improved crew accommodation, as well as more advanced weaponry and avionics. It had twice the endurance of the S-2A when giving 'round the fleet' ASW coverage at a radius of 230 miles. The prototype flew on 20 May 1959, and 120 production aircraft were built. The S-2E (S2F-3S) was similar to the S-2D, but carried more advanced weaponry and ASW electronics. In addition to internal stores, this variant had provision for 5in rockets on underwing racks. The S-2E entered service with VS-41 in October 1962, and 241 were produced.

The S-2A Tracker was manufactured under licence in Canada by de Havilland Aircraft Ltd, the Canadian version being designated CS2F-1 and powered by Canadian-built Pratt & Whitney engines. Further variants were the CS2F-2 and -3, featuring improved electronics. The CS2F-1 and -2 were operated from shore bases by VU-32 and VU-33 Squadrons, RCN, while the CS2F-3 was used by VS-880 aboard the carrier HMCS *Bonaventure*. Of the 100 CS2F-1 Trackers built in Canada, 17 were supplied to the Royal Netherlands Navy and 12 to the Brazilian Navy, the latter batch operating from the carrier *Minas Gerais*. Variants of the basic Tracker design were the C-1A Trader general purpose transport and E-1B Tracer early warning and fighter direction aircraft, the latter fitted with triple fins and a large lenticular radome mounted above the fuselage and housing an APS-82 radar scanner sweeping through 360 degrees six times a minute.

Gloster Javelin

UK

Role: Two-Seat All-Weather Interceptor
Specification: F4/48
Operational: 1956-68
Data: FAW8

Engines: Two Bristol Siddeley Sapphire 203/204 (Sa7R) single-shaft turbojets rated at 11,000lb thrust (12,300lb with reheat)
Span: 52ft
Length: 56ft 4in
Weight: 29,000lb (empty)
42,930 (loaded)
Crew: 2
Max speed: 695mph at 10,000ft
Service ceiling: 55,000ft
Range: 1,200 miles
Weapons: 30mm Aden cannon and four DH (HS) Firestreak infra-red AAMs

The world's first twin-jet delta and an extremely radical design for its day, the Gloster Javelin was designed to meet the requirements of Specification F4/48 for a night and all-weather fighter for the RAF, in which it was in direct competition with the DH110. Construction of the prototype, designated GA5, began in April 1949, and the aircraft (WD804) flew for the first time on 26 November 1951, powered by two Armstrong Siddeley Sapphires of 7,000lb thrust each. The maiden flight was attended by a serious snag in the shape of rudder buffeting, and further flight testing was delayed while modifications were carried out. Then, on 29 June 1952, the prototype lost both elevators and was destroyed in a crash landing at Boscombe Down.

Tests continued with the second prototype (WD808), which flew on 21 August 1952, but this aircraft was also destroyed on 11 June 1953. Three more prototypes had been ordered in the meantime; the third aircraft (WT827) flew on 7 March 1953 and carried an armament of four 30mm cannon, while the fourth featured a modified wing shape and the fifth, which flew on 20 July 1954, was up to production standard.

As the Javelin FAW1, the new fighter was ordered into 'super-priority' production for the RAF. The first production aircraft flew on 22 July 1954 and deliveries began to No 46 Squadron at RAF Odiham in February 1956. Javelin FAW1s were also issued to No 87 Squadron, which formed part of 2nd TAF in Germany. In October 1955 a new variant, the Javelin FAW2, made its appearance; this was basically similar to the FAW1 apart from its radar and avionics, and replaced the earlier production model with No 46 Squadron. Next on the production line was the FAW4, the prototype of which was the 41st FAW1 with an all-moving tailplane. This variant entered service with No 141 Squadron early in 1957, and except for the tailplane was essentially similar to the FAW1. Later that year, No 151 Squadron received the first examples of the Javelin FAW5, which had a modified wing structure and increased internal fuel capacity, and in 1958 the Javelin FAW6 — which was basically an FAW5 with the same radar as the FAW2 — entered service with No 89 Squadron. By this time a dual-control training version, the Javelin T3, was also in service, the prototype having flown for the first time 20 August 1956.

In November 1956 the Javelin's already for-

midable combat potential was given an extra boost with the appearance of the FAW7, which was fitted with Sapphire ASSa7R turbojets developing 12,300lb thrust with reheat in place of the 8,300lb thrust Sapphire ASSa6 engines used in earlier marks. The Javelin FAW7, which incorporated further structural modifications, increased wing fuel tankage and advanced AI radar, had an armament of two 30mm Aden cannon and four Firestreak AAMs and entered service with No 33 Squadron. The FAW8, which flew on 9 May 1958, was externally similar to the FAW7, but incorporated US radar, a simplified afterburning system, a Sperry autopilot,

drooped wing leading edges and dampers on the yaw and pitch axes. The FAW8 was the last production model of the Javelin, the final aircraft being completed in June 1960 but a number of Javelin FAW7s were brought up to FAW8 standard (although retaining British AI radar) and designated FAW9.

During the 1960s the Javelin was progressively replaced by the Lightning in the air defence role. RAF squadrons using the Javelin during its 12-year career were Nos 3, 5, 11, 23, 25, 29, 33, 41, 46, 60, 64, 72, 85, 87, 89, 137, 141 and 151, as well as No 228 OCU.

Gloster Meteor F Mk 3 — U Mk 21   UK

Role: Fighter/PR/Ground-Attack
Specification: F9/40
Operational: 1945-65
Data: F Mk 8

Engines: Two 3,600lb thrust Rolls-Royce Derwent 8 turbojets
Span: 37ft 6in
Length: 43ft 6in
Weight: 10,626lb (empty)
17,350lb (loaded)
Crew: 1
Max speed: 592mph at sea level
Service ceiling: 44,000ft
Range: 520 miles at 20,000ft
Weapons: Four 20mm British Hispano Mk 5 cannon in nose; two 1,000lb bombs or 16 90lb rocket projectiles on underwing racks

First flown in 1943, the Gloster Meteor was the only Allied jet fighter to see action during World War II, first of all against the V-1 flying bomb in 1944. Early in 1945 the RAF's first two Meteor squadrons, Nos 616 and 504, went to Belgium and carried out

many ground-attack operations before the close of hostilities, although they never met the Luftwaffe in combat. Both squadrons were equipped with the Meteor F3, powered by two Rolls-Royce Derwent Series 1 turbojets; 210 were built between 1944 and 1946, and this mark equipped 15 squadrons of RAF Fighter Command in the immediate postwar years. It was also the first jet type to equip the fighter units of the Royal Auxiliary Air Force, and examples were sent for service evaluation to Australia, New Zealand and South Africa. One Mk 3, EE337, carried out deck landing trials on HMS *Illustrious* in September 1948, and several others were used for experimental purposes. On 7 August 1949 one of them, EE379, specially fitted with a nose probe, set up a jet endurance record of 12hr 3min, being refuelled by a Lancaster tanker.

The next variant was the Meteor F Mk 4, which first flew on 12 April 1945. Powered by two RR Derwent 5s, 489 were built by Gloster and 46 by Armstrong Whitworth. Two of them, EE454 and EE455, were allocated to the RAF High Speed Flight, and on 7 November 1945 Group Captain Wilson set up a new world air speed record of 606mph in EE454. Large numbers of F4s served with the RAF, and it was the first Meteor model to be exported in quantity. One hundred aircraft were supplied to Argentina in 1947-48, 50 of them ex-RAF machines; 38 were supplied to Holland in 1947, followed by a later batch of 27. 12 were purchased by Egypt, and Belgium ordered 48 in March 1949. 20 F4s also served with the Royal Danish Air Force, the first being delivered in October 1949. The Meteor Mk 5 was a photo-reconnaissance version of the F4; only a few were built, the prototype flying in June 1949. This later crashed, killing test pilot Rodney Dryland. The Mk 6 was a swept-wing Mk 4 project which never left the drawing board.

The Meteor T Mk 7, of which 640 were built, was a two-seat trainer version of the basic F4, the prototype flying on 19 March 1948. 43 were supplied to Holland between 1949 and 1956, 42 to Belgium between 1948 and 1952, three to Egypt, two to Syria, nine to Denmark, 10 to Brazil, 14 to France, four to Israel and three to Sweden.

To improve range and performance of the F4, Glosters designed a new high-speed tail unit, lengthened the forward fuselage, installed an extra 95gal internal fuel tank and introduced a one-piece sliding cockpit canopy over a Martin Baker ejection seat, the modified aircraft emerging as the Meteor F Mk 8 in October 1948, powered by two Derwent 8s. The F8 was the most prolific of the Meteor variants and formed the mainstay of RAF Fighter Command in the early 1950s, equipping 32 regular and 11 RAuxAF squadrons. Eight were exported to Egypt in 1955; 23 to Belgium, plus 67 licence-built by Fokker and assembled by Fairey-Gosselies; 20 to Denmark in 1951; 19 to Syria; five to Holland, plus 155 built by Fokker; 60 to Brazil in 1953; and 11 to Israel. The Egyptian and Israeli machines saw considerable action during the October 1956 war, and F8s equipped No 77 Squadron RAAF in Korea, where they proved excellent in the ground-attack role.

The Meteor FR9 fighter reconnaissance variant, which was a Mk8 with a redesigned nose, flew in March 1950. Deliveries to the RAF began in July 1950 and 126 were built, seven being delivered to Israel between 1954 and 1956, two to Syria in 1956; and 12 to Equador in May 1954. The Meteor PR10 was an unarmed photo-reconnaissance version of which 59 were produced, the first entering service with No 541 Squadron RAF (2nd TAF, Germany) in February 1951.

The 'long-nose' Meteor NF11 night fighter arose from specification F24/48, and, as Glosters were fully occupied in producing other marks, development was assigned to Armstrong Whitworth at Coventry. The nose was redesigned to take a large AI radar scanner and a two-seat cockpit with full night-fighting equipment. The Mk 8 tail was used, but 43ft Mk 3 wings were adopted with the four 20mm cannon armament transferred from the nose to just outboard of the engine nacelles. The prototype flew on 21 May 1950, and the type became the standard RAF night-fighter until the advent of the Gloster Javelin. Improved night-fighter variants were the NF12, NF13 — the latter a tropicalised version of the NF11, six of the 40 built being exported to Egypt, six to Israel, six to Syria and two to France — and the NF14, of which 100 were produced. The latter had a new clear-vision cockpit canopy, and deliveries to the RAF were completed in May 1955.

In October 1956 Flight Refuelling Ltd began the conversion of a number of ex-RAF F8s as target aircraft. Two hundred and thirty-three were subsequently converted between 1956 and 1969 with the designation U Mk 15 and U Mk 16, and a further batch was converted for use by the RAAF under the designation U Mk 21. The Meteor TT20, 30 of which were converted from the NF11, was a target tug.

Handley Page Victor

UK

Role: Strategic Bomber/Tanker
Specification: B35/46
Operational: 1958-
Data: B Mk 2

Engines: Four Rolls-Royce Conway RCo17 Mk 201 turbofans each rated at 19,750lb thrust
Span: 120ft
Length: 114ft 11in
Weight: 90,000lb (empty) 200,000lb (loaded)
Crew: 5
Max speed: 630mph at 40,000ft
Service ceiling: 55,000ft
Range: 6,000 miles with underwing and weapons bay tanks
Weapons: One HS Blue Steel ASM or up to 35 1,000lb conventional bombs

The last in a long line of Handley Page bombers, the HP80 Victor's design owed a great deal to research into the crescent wing carried out by the German Arado and Blohm und Voss firms during World War

II, their findings being investigated by the Handley Page design team late in 1945. A proposal for a high-speed bomber employing the crescent wing formula was submitted to the Air Ministry in June 1946, and a specification covering the project was issued on 1 January 1947. A scale model of the proposed bomber's crescent wing and tail surfaces was tested on the HP88 research aircraft in 1951, a prototype order for the full-size aircraft having been received on 1 January 1947. The completed HP80 Victor was sent to Boscombe Down in June 1952 for initial testing, but an accidental fire and bad weather delayed the first flight until 24 December 1952. Flight tests continued with the first prototype (WB771) until 14 July 1954, when the tailplane broke away in flight as a result of fatigue and the aircraft crashed. The second prototype (WB775) flew on 11 September 1954, and the first production Victor B Mk 1 followed on 1 February 1956. Production Victors differed from the prototypes in a number of respects, including the installation of Sapphire 200 Series engines instead of the 8,000lb thrust Sapphire 100.

Service deliveries of the B Mk 1 began in

November 1957, the first aircraft going to No 232 Operational Conversion Unit, and the first Victor Squadron, No 10, became operational in April 1958. Three more squadrons, Nos 15, 55 and 57, were formed by 1960, completing the planned total of Victor B Mk 1 units. The Victor B Mk 1A was an updated variant with more advanced equipment, including ECM in the tail. In 1964 Handley Page received a contract to convert a number of Victor B Mk 1s and 1As into three-point flight refuelling tankers, with a Mk 20B refuelling pod under each wing and a Mk 17 hose-drum unit in the rear of the bomb bay, which also contained extra fuel tanks. Designated B(K) Mk 1As, these aircraft entered service with No 55 Squadron in August 1965 and subsequently equipped Nos 57 and 214 Squadrons, forming the Victor Tanker Wing at RAF Marham, Norfolk.

The Victor B Mk 2, which first flew on 20 February 1959, was a much improved version with 17,250lb thrust Rolls-Royce Conway Mk 103 or 201 turbojets, featuring a larger span, enlarged intakes, a dorsal

fillet and a retractable scoop on either side of the rear fuselage to supply air to two alternators for the emergency power supply. A Bristol Siddeley Artouste turbine was housed in the starboard wing root to provide power for starting and other functions. The B Mk 2 was equipped to carry the HS Blue Steel thermonuclear ASM, and entered service with No 139 Squadron in February 1964. The other Victor Blue Steel squadron was No 100, both units operating in the high- and low-level strategic attack roles until 1968, when the British nuclear deterrent began to be taken over by the Royal Navy's Polaris submarines. Victor B Mk 2s were fitted with 'window' dispensers on the trailing edge of the wings, and with ECM in the tail cone. The Victor B(PR) Mk 1 and B(PR) Mk 2 were strategic reconnaissance variants, equipping No 543 Squadron at RAF Wyton until their role was taken over by the Vulcans of No 27 Squadron in the 1970s. A single Victor B(SR)2 was capable of radar-mapping the entire Mediterranean in one seven-hour sortie.

Hawker Fury/Sea Fury

Role: Fighter-Bomber
Specification: F6/42 and F2/43 (Fury) N7/43 and N22/43 (Sea Fury)
Operational: 1947-58 (Fury) 1947-62 (Sea Fury)
Photo: Sea Fury
Data: Sea Fury FB11

Engines: One 2,480hp Bristol Centaurus radial
Span: 38ft 4¾in
Length: 34ft 8in
Weight: 9,240lb (empty) 12,500lb (loaded)
Crew: 1
Max speed: 460mph at 18,000ft
Service ceiling: 35,800ft
Range: 1,040 miles (with 90gal auxiliary tanks)
Armament: Four 20mm British Hispano 20mm Mk 5 cannon in wings; provision for up to 2,000lb of bombs, mines, sonobuoys, RPs, napalm or fuel tanks

UK

In the autumn of 1942 Hawker Aircraft Ltd and the Air Ministry entered into discussions on the design of a new long-range fighter for operational use against the Japanese in the Pacific. Such a fighter had to be manoeuvrable enough to counter the latest Japanese combat aircraft, while having a superior performance and the necessary range to carry out escort missions over the ocean. The answer seemed to lie in a lightweight version of the Hawker Tempest fighter powered by the new Bristol Centaurus radial engine, since technical troubles with the latest British liquid-cooled engine, the Sabre, seemed to preclude its use in tropical climates.

The Air Ministry requirement crystallised in Specification F6/42, Hawker's design being known originally as the Tempest Light Fighter (Centaurus). The Royal Navy also showed an interest in the type, and it was proposed that the same design would fulfill the needs of both the RAF and RN. In January 1943, Specification F2/43 was raised to meet the RAF requirement, and N7/43 was raised for the Fleet Air Arm in February. The aircraft was to be put into full-scale production by Hawkers, and naval conversion would be undertaken by Boulton-Paul Aircraft Ltd.

Six F2/43 prototypes were ordered for the RAF in December 1943. Of these, two were to be equipped with the Bristol Centaurus XXII, two with the Rolls-Royce Griffon, and one with a Centaurus XII. The sixth was to be used for static tests. Early in 1944 the naval specification N7/43 was replaced by the revised N22/43, and in April that year the aircraft was ordered into series production, with 200 fighters for the RAF and 200 for the Fleet Air Arm. Four prototypes of the Fury Mk 1, as the RAF variant was named, were in fact built. The first, NX798, flew on 1 September 1944, powered by a Centaurus XII; it later received a Centaurus XVIII and was eventually sold to Egypt with the civil registration G-AKRY. The second prototype, LA610, flew on 27 November 1944 with a RR Griffon 85 engine; in 1946 this was replaced by a Napier Sabre VII, giving the aircraft a top speed in level flight of 485mph. The third prototype, which flew on 25 July 1945 with a Centaurus XV, was later re-engined with a Centaurus XVIII and delivered to Pakistan.

Then, with the war in Europe over and the Pacific conflict nearing its end, came the blow. The RAF cancelled all its Furies and the Admiralty half its order for the Sea Fury, as the naval version was known. As far as the land-based Fury was concerned, Hawker Aircraft made considerable efforts to exploit the export market, with some success; in December 1946 Iraq ordered 30 single-seat Fury fighters and fighter-bombers, and these were delivered in 1947-48 together with a pair of two-seat trainer conversions. 25 more single-seaters and three more trainers were ordered in 1951. 50 single-seat Fury Mk 60s (basically Sea Furies, but without naval equipment) were also delivered to Pakistan in 1950, followed by a further 37 in 1952-52. Pakistan also received five two-seaters and five ex-FAA Sea Furies. 12 new Furies were exported to Egypt in 1951; some of these were destroyed during the Anglo-French Suez operation five years later. Both Iraq and Pakistan were still using their surviving Furies in the late 1950s.

The Sea Fury prototype, meanwhile, had flown on 21 February 1945. This was a semi-navalised aircraft powered by a Centaurus XII (serial SR661), and was followed by the fully navalised second

prototype (SR666) with a Centaurus XV on 12 October that year. The first production Sea Fury F Mk X flew on 7 September 1946, powered by a Centaurus XVIII. During 1946 Hawker Aircraft Ltd received further Sea Fury orders, the Admiralty being anxious to fill the performance gap between the piston-engined Seafire 47 and the introduction of naval jet aircraft, and by the middle of 1950 Sea Fury production totalled 565 machines. The first Fleet Air Arm squadron to receive the Sea Fury X was No 807, in July 1947, followed by Nos 778, 802, 803 and 805 Squadrons.

In 1948 it was decided to modify the second 50 aircraft of the first Mk X production batch as fighter-bombers, with underwing points for a 2,000lb ordnance load, lengthened arrester hook and provision for RATOG. The new variant was designated Sea Fury FB11, first deliveries taking place to No 802 Squadron in May 1948. Nos 801, 803, 804, 805, 807 and 808 Squadrons also re-equipped with FB11s, serving aboard the Light Fleet Carriers Ocean, Theseus and Glory with the 1st, 17th and 21st Carrier Air Groups. The Sea Furies of No 807 Squadron (HMS Theseus), 802 (HMS Ocean), 801 and 804 (HMS Glory) and 805 and 808 (HMAS Sydney) saw considerable action during the Korean War, where they proved extremely effective in the ground attack role. Sea Fury pilots also claimed the destruction of two MiG-15 jets.

Twenty-five Sea Fury FB11s were transferred to the Royal Canadian Navy, operating from HMCS Magnificent. At home, the FB11 remained the standard FAA fighter and fighter bomber until 1953, when it was replaced by more modern types and allocated to RNVR units. RNVR Squadrons using the Sea Fury were Nos 1831, 1832, 1833, 1834, 1835 and 1836. These units also used the two-seat trainer version of the Sea Fury, the T20, of which 60 were produced.

Sea Furies were supplied to the air arms of several countries. The first customer, in October 1946, was the Royal Netherlands Naval Air Service, which ordered 24 aircraft. These served until 1959 aboard the Dutch carrier Karel Doorman. Burma received twelve reconditioned ex-FAA Sea Furies in 1957-58, 15 ex-FAA aircraft were sent to Cuba in 1957, together with two two-seaters, and 15 ex-FAA T20s were sold to Western Germany for target towing duties during 1957-62.

Hawker Hunter

UK

Role: Fighter/Ground-Attack
Specification: F3/48
Operational: 1954-
Photo: Mk 4s
Data: F6

Engines: One 10,050lb thrust Rolls-Royce Avon 203 turbojet
Span: 33ft 8in
Length: 45ft 10½in
Weight: 12,760lb (empty)
17,750lb (normal loaded)
Crew: 1
Max speed: 702mph at sea level
Service ceiling: 55,000ft
Range: 1,000 miles with external fuel
Weapons: Four 30mm Aden cannon in nose

Tracing its development history through the Hawker P1040 and the swept-wing P1052 prototypes, the P1067 Hunter's design was submitted to the Air Ministry in January 1947 in response to an urgent requirement for a short-range trans-sonic interceptor. Three prototypes were ordered in 1948, and the first of these (WB188) flew for the first time on 20 July 1951, powered by a Rolls-Royce Avon turbojet. The first production Hunter F Mk 1 flew on 16 May 1953, and the next 19 aircraft were used for trials and evaluation. All were powered by the 7,550lb thrust Rolls-Royce Avon RA7. A second variant, the Hunter F Mk 2, flew on 14 October 1953, powered by an 8,000lb thrust Sapphire 101 engine which gave it a marginally higher speed. A rear fuselage airbrake was fitted to both variants before their entry into service, and one of the machines used in the airbrake trials — WB188, the first prototype — captured the World Air Speed Record on 21 September 1953, reaching 721mph with the aid of an afterburning Avon RA7R. The first Hunter F1s entered service with the Central Fighter Establishment early in 1954, followed by deliveries to Nos 43, 54 and 222 Squadrons and Nos 229 and 233 OCUs, while the Mk 2 went to Nos 257 and 263 Squadrons. Total production of these initial variants was 113 Mk 1s and 45 Mk 2s, the latter built by Armstrong-Whitworth.

Engine surge problems during high-altitude gun firing trials led to some modifications to the Avon turbojet, and this — together with increased fuel capacity and provision for underwing tanks — led to the Hunter F4 and F5. As well as 365 F4s produced for the RAF, 120 were supplied to Sweden as the Mk 50 and 30 to Denmark as the Mk 51, and 16 ex-RAF machines were delivered to Peru as Mk 52s. The type was also built under licence in Belgium and the Netherlands. The Sapphire-engined F5 proved less popular and 105 were built, equipping five RAF squadrons (compared with 21 F4 squadrons). The F5s of Nos 1 and 34 Squadrons were used briefly during the Suez Crisis of 1956, operating from Cyprus, but had insufficient range to provide adequate air cover.

In 1953 Hawker equipped the Hunter with the large 10,000lb thrust Avon 203 engine, and this variant — designated Hunter F Mk 6 — flew for the first time in January 1954. 15 squadrons of RAF Fighter Command subsequently used the F6, deliveries beginning in 1956; 415 were built, 119 of them by Armstrong Whitworth. Many foreign countries showed an interest in the F6, the first overseas customer being India, which placed an order for 160 aircraft (designated Mk 56s) in 1957, the first 48 being ex-RAF machines. Switzerland also ordered 100 aircraft in January 1958 (Mk 58s), and 88 were in fact delivered. Like the F4, the F6 was built under licence in Belgium and Holland, equipping the Belgian Air Force's 7th Day Fighter Wing (7th and 8th Squadrons) and five squadrons of the Dutch Air Defence Command. Ex-RAF Hunters were also supplied to Iraq (15), Jordan (12) and the Lebanon (5). Total production of this variant in the UK was 383 aircraft.

The Hunter Mks 7, 8, 12, T52, T62, T66, T67 and T69 were all two-seat variants (see Trainers Section). Production of single-seat Hunters ended in September 1957, by which time 1,420 single-seaters had been built (excluding a further 445 aircraft produced under licence), but conversions were to go on for many more years. In 1958, 33 F6s were converted to FR Mk 10 standard by the installation of three nose cameras, the first aircraft entering service with Nos 2 and 4 Squadrons in Germany during 1959 and replacing the Swift FR5 in

the fighter-reconnaissance role. The Hunter FGA9 was basically an F6 with various modifications, including a tail braking parachute (first used on the Indian Mk 56s and Swiss Mk 58s) and cutaway flaps to make room for 230gal drop tanks. 88 were built for the RAF, and in the early 1960s 12 were supplied to Rhodesia, four to Kuwait and 18 to Iraq, the Kuwaiti and Iraqi aircraft being designated Mk 57s and Mk 59s. Other refurbished export Hunters include the Mk 70 for the Lebanon, the Mk 76 (FGA) and 76A (FR) for Abu Dhabi and the FGA74 and FR74A for Singapore. Six aircraft (ex-Danish) were supplied to the Kenya Air Force in 1974.

Hawker Sea Hawk

Role: Carrier-Borne Fighter-Bomber
Operational: 1953-
Specification: N7/46
Data: FGA6

Engines: One 5,400lb thrust Rolls-Royce Nene 103 (RN6) turbojet
Span: 39ft
Length: 40ft 3½in
Weight: 10,300lb (empty)
13,200lb (normal loaded)
Crew: 1
Max speed: 587mph at 20,000ft
Service ceiling: 44,000ft
Range: 800 miles with external fuel
Weapons: Four 20mm Hispano cannon in nose; two 500lb bombs or 20 3in rockets on underwing pylons

Towards the end of 1944 Hawker Aircraft Ltd began design studies of a single-seat land-based interceptor which eventually flew in prototype form as the P1040. By that time the RAF was committed to re-equipment with the Vampire and Meteor, but in December 1945 the Admiralty had invited tenders for a carrier-based interceptor and the Hawker design was considered highly suitable, its 'bifurcated trunk' jet exhaust system leaving the rear fuselage

Forty Hunter F4s were converted as operational trainers for the Royal Navy and redesignated GA11, the guns and gunsights being removed. These were still operational in the 1970s, as were the Hunter 6s and 9s of the RAF Strike Command Tactical Weapons Unit, comprising Nos 63, 79 and 324 Squadrons.

In a career spanning a quarter of a century the Hunter equipped 30 RAF Fighter squadrons, in addition to numerous units of foreign air forces. The grand total of Hunter production, including two-seaters, was 1,972 aircraft, and over 500 were subsequently rebuilt.

UK

free to house a large fuel tank and so provide a wide radius of action. Three prototypes were ordered, the first (VP401) flying on 2 September 1947, and the aircraft entered production as the Sea Hawk F1, powered by a 5,000lb thrust Rolls-Royce Nene 101 engine. As Hawkers were heavily committed to producing the Hunter for the RAF, Sea Hawk production was handed over to Sir W. G. Armstrong Whitworth Aircraft with the F Mk 2, which featured power-boosted ailerons. The third variant, the Sea Hawk FB3, had a strengthened wing enabling it to carry bombs, rockets or drop tanks, and the FGA4 was developed specifically for the ground attack role. In 1956 the Nene 101 engine gave way to the 5,400lb thrust Nene 103 engine, and with this new powerplant the Sea Hawks FB3 and FGA4 became the FB5 and FGA6.

Sea Hawks began re-equipping first-line squadrons of the Fleet Air Arm in 1953 and three years later the type saw action during the Suez Crisis with Nos 800, 802 and 810 Squadrons (HMS *Albion*), 804 and 897 Squadrons (HMS *Bulwark*), and 899 (HMS *Eagle*). These units were responsible for a major portion of the attacks on Egyptian airfields on 1 November 1956, and during the week that followed two Sea Hawks were lost.

Although the Sea Hawk was phased out of first-line service with the Royal Navy in 1960, the type continued in operational use in other parts of the

world. Twenty-two Sea Hawks — FGA6s, known by the export designation Mk 50 — were supplied to the Royal Netherlands Navy, in whose service they were modified to carry two Sidewinder missiles, and 68 — known as the Mk 100 and Mk 101 — were supplied to the Federal German Naval Air Arm. The Mk 100 was a close-support variant, basically an FGA6, while the Mk 101 was fitted with a radar pod under the starboard wing and used in the reconnaissance role. The German Seahawks were replaced by the F-104G Starfighter in 1963-4. The FGA6 Skyhawk was also delivered to the Indian Navy, two squadrons being formed with 30 aircraft and serving on the 16,000 ton carrier *Vikrant*. The Indian Sea Hawks were still in operational use in 1978.

Hawker Tempest II   UK

Role: Fighter-Bomber
Operational: 1945-51

Weapons: Four 20mm cannon; 2,000lb of bombs or rocket projectiles under wings

Engines: One 2,526bhp Bristol Centaurus V or VI radial
Span: 41ft
Length: 34ft 5in
Weight: 8,900lb (empty)
11,400lb (loaded)
Crew: 1
Max speed: 440mph at 14,000ft
Service ceiling: 37,000ft
Range: 1,640 miles (max with drop tanks)

First flown in September 1943 the radial-engined Tempest II was intended for operations against the Japanese, but the war ended before the type made its operational debut. The Tempest II entered service with No 54 Squadron RAF in November 1945 and subsequently equipped Nos 5, 16, 20, 26, 33, 152 and 247 Squadrons. No 33 Squadron used the type against terrorists in Malaya before converting to Hornets in 1951. Total production of the Tempest II was 472 aircraft.

Hawker Siddeley Harrier   UK

Role: Close Support/Reconnaissance
Operational: 1969-
Photo: FGR3
Data: GR3

Engines: One Rolls-Royce Bristol Pegasus Mk 103 vectored-thrust turbofan rated at 21,500lb thrust
Span: 25ft 3in
Length: 45ft 6in
Weight: 12,200lb (empty)
25,000+ (max loaded)

Crew: 1
Max speed: 737mph at sea level
Service ceiling: 50,000ft+
Range: 3,455 miles with one in-flight refuelling
Weapons: External combat load of up to 5,000lb, typically: two 30mm Aden gun pods, one 1,000lb bomb under fuselage, two 1,000lb bombs under wings, and one MATRA launcher with 19 68mm SNEB rockets. The AV-8A· can also carry Sidewinder AAMs

One of the most important and certainly the most revolutionary combat aircraft to emerge during the postwar years, the Hawker Siddeley Harrier V/STOL tactical fighter-bomber began its career as a private venture in 1957 following discussions between Hawker Aircraft Ltd and Bristol Aero-Engines Ltd, designers of the BS53 Pegasus turbofan engine. Development of this powerplant, which featured two pairs of connected rotating nozzles, one pair to provide jet lift, was partly financed with American funds, and in 1959-60 the Ministry of Aviation ordered two prototypes and four development aircraft under the designation P1127. The first prototype (XP831) made its first tethered hovering flight on 21 October 1960 and began conventional flight trials on 13 March 1961. Trials later included experimental operations from the carrier *Ark Royal*. In 1962 Britain, the United States and West Germany announced a joint order for nine Kestrels, as the aircraft was now known, for evaluation by a tripartite handling squadron at RAF West Raynham in 1965.

In its single-seat close-support and TacR version, the aircraft was ordered into production for the RAF as the Harrier GR1, the first of an initial order of 77 machines flying on 28 December 1967. On 1 April 1969 the GR1 entered service with the Harrier OCU at RAF Wittering, and the variant subsequently equipped No 1 Squadron at Wittering and Nos 3, 4 and 20 Squadrons in Germany. The first production Harriers were powered by 19,000lb thrust Pegasus 101 engines, but these were retrofitted with the Pegasus 102 (20,000lb thrust) and redesignated GR Mk 1A. Later production aircraft, using the 21,500lb thrust Pegasus 103, were designated GR Mk 3. Between 1973 and 1977 an additional 36 GR Mk 3s were ordered for the RAF, bringing the total Harrier strike force to 113. The Harrier trainer versions, however, also have a full combat capability.

These are the T Mks 2, 2A and 4, which use the same Pegasus variants as the GR types. The Harrier T Mk 2, which has two seats in tandem and a lengthened fuselage and tail cone, flew for the first time on 24 April 1969, and the first of 24 T2s, 2As and 4s entered RAF service in July 1970. In 1977-78, Harriers were deployed on a combat footing to Belize to meet an anticipated threat from Guatemala. All Harriers having flight refuelling capability and the GR3 version has a modified nose-cone housing a laser rangefinder.

During their service and pre-service career Harriers have operated from the decks of ships of some eight different nations, demonstrating the aircraft's capability in the seaborne strike role. In 1975 the British Government announced its intention to proceed with a variant for the Royal Navy, designated Sea Harrier FRS Mk 1 and designed to operate from the RN's 'through-deck' cruisers of the Invincible class from 1979. 24 FRS1s will equip Nos 800, 801 and 802 Squadrons of the Fleet Air Arm. Sea Harriers will also serve on the carrier HMS *Hermes*, which is being converted to the ASW role.

Six of the P1127 Kestrels evaluated in 1965 were subsequently shipped to the USA for further trials, and in 1969 the first 12 of 102 Harriers was ordered for the US Marine Corps. British designations of these aircraft are Mk 50 (GR3 equivalent) and Mk 54 (T Mk 4 equivalent), USMC designations being AV-8A and TAV-8A. These aircraft initially equipped three Marine Attack Squadrons, VMA-513, VMA-542 and VMA-231. Licensing rights to manufacture the Harrier in the USA are held by McDonnell Douglas, who are currently developing an 'Advanced Harrier' variant. Eleven AV-8As and two TAV-8As were supplied via the USA to the Spanish Navy. Known as Matadors, they equip the 8a Escudarilla.

Hawker Siddeley Nimrod

UK

Role: Long-Range Maritime Reconnaissance
Operational: 1969-
Photo: AEW version
Data: MR Mk 1

Engines: Four 11,500lb thrust Rolls-Royce Spey Mk 250 turbofans
Span: 114ft 10in
Length: 126ft 9in
Weight: 86,000lb (empty)
177,500lb (max take-off loaded)
Crew: 12
Max speed: 575mph at sea level
Service ceiling: 45,000ft
Range: 5,500 miles (ferry)
Weapons: Various ASW offensive stores internally; air-to-surface missiles, rocket or cannon pods, or mines on strengthened points under the wings outboard of mainwheel doors (Note: RAF Nimrods do not carry ASMs, although provision to do so is retained if required)

Derived from the Comet 4C, the Hawker Siddeley

Nimrod was designed to replace the Shackleton as RAF Strike Command's standard LRMP aircraft. Two prototypes were ordered, and the first — powered by four Rolls-Royce RB168 Spey turbofan engines — flew for the first time on 23 May 1967, followed by the second aircraft on 31 July. Both machines employed modified Comet 4C airframes, and the second was fitted with the Comet's original Avon engines. The Nimrod's fuselage was $6\frac{1}{2}$ft shorter than the Comet's and was fitted with a long, underslung pannier housing operational equipment and weapons. The tail unit was modified, with ESM and MAD equipment in a fairing on top of the fin and in an extended tail cone.

The aircraft entered production for RAF Strike Command as the Nimrod MR Mk 1, first deliveries being made to No 236 OCU at RAF St Mawgan, Cornwall, in October 1969. Nos 42, 120, 201, 203 and 206 Squadrons subsequently equipped with the type. The first 38 Nimrods were delivered between 1969 and 1972, and the first of eight more aircraft was delivered in 1975. Three more aircraft, designated Nimrod R Mk 1, were delivered to No 51 Squadron at RAF Wyton, Huntingdonshire, in 1971, for use in the electronic reconnaissance role. In

1975, the RAF's Nimrod fleet began to be refitted with new communications equipment, tactical and navigation systems, and aircraft undergoing this modernisation programme are scheduled to re-enter service with Strike Command in 1978-80 under the designation Nimrod MR Mk 2.

Three of the follow-on order for eight Nimrod MR Mk 1s have been used in the development of an airborne early warning version, the Nimrod AEW Mk 3, which is capable of detecting, tracking and classifying aircraft, missiles and ships at long range and any altitude. The AEW3 can also control interceptors, direct strike aircraft and act as a search and rescue co-ordinator. The Nimrod is also suitable for fishery protection and as a flight refuelling tanker, and can carry 45 passengers in the emergency transport role. In its primary role of maritime reconnaissance and ASW, the Nimrod combines the advantages of fast transit speed with good low speed manoeuvrability in the search area, and if required two of its Spey engines can be shut down to increase endurance.

Hindustan HF-24 Marut

India

Role: Ground-Attack Fighter
Operational: 1968-
Data: HF-24 Mk 1

Engines: Two 4,850lb thrust Rolls-Royce Orpheus 703 turbojets
Span: 29ft 6½in
Length: 52ft 0¾in
Weight: 13,658lb (empty)
19,734lb (normal loaded)
Crew: 1
Max speed: Mach 1.02 at 40,000ft

Service ceiling: 50,000ft
Range: 800 miles
Weapons: Four 30mm Aden cannon in nose; pack of 48 air-to-air rockets in lower fuselage aft of nosewheel; four 1,000lb bombs or other stores under wings

Designed by a team under the leadership of Dr Kurt Tank, architect of Germany's wartime Focke-Wulf aircraft, the HAL HF-24 Marut (Wind Spirit) underwent a protracted development history, over a decade elapsing between design work starting in 1956 and the first fully operational examples entering service with the Indian Air Force. Flight trials were carried out with a full-scale glider model beginning in March 1959, but the project ran into serious difficulties soon afterwards when it was learned that the afterburning Bristol Orpheus B Or 12 turbojet, around which the HF-24 was designed, was to be shelved through lack of a British operational requirement. The prototype HF-24 Mk 1, therefore, was re-engined with the Russian RD-9F engine (the type used in the MiG-19) and flew for the first time with this powerplant on 17 June 1961, followed by a second aircraft on 4 October 1962. In 1963 because of snags with the RD-9F, it was decided to employ the 4,850lb thrust Orpheus 703, and the first of 18 pre-production Maruts flew with this engine in March 1963. As a prestige exercise two Mk 1s were

handed over to the Indian Air Force on 10 May 1964, followed by 12 more, one of which served as a test-bed in 1966 for the planned Mk 1A variant with a locally-designed afterburner. The first series production Marut flew in November 1967 and deliveries to the Indian Air Force commenced the following year, the type eventually equipping Nos 10, 31 and 220 Squadrons. The IAF's Maruts saw action during the 1971 war between India and Pakistan, operating in the ground attack role without loss. Some 150 Maruts had been delivered to the IAF by the end of 1977, together with about 20 examples of a two-seat combat trainer designated Mk 1T. The HF-25 is a single-engined strike fighter variant, still in the mock-up stage in 1978.

Hispano HA-1112

Data: HA-1109-K1L

Engines: One 1,300hp Hispano-Suiza HS12-Z-17 in-line
Span: 32ft 8½in
Length: 29ft 4in
Weight: 4,872lb (empty)
6,058lb (loaded)
Crew: 1
Max speed: 404mph at 13,780ft
Service ceiling: 32,800ft
Range: 360miles
Weapons: Two 12.7mm BREDA-SAFAT machine guns in fairings under wings

In 1942, the Spanish Air Ministry selected the Messerschmitt Bf109G-2 for licence production by Hispano-Aviacion, but by 1944 it became apparent that little assistance could be expected from Germany, so work began on the adaptation of the airframe to take the Hispano-Suza 12-Z-89 engine instead of the DB605. The first aircraft so converted flew on 2 March 1945 and was designated

(Spanish-built)

HA-1109-J1L, and 23 further aircraft were completed despite the fact that the powerplant proved generally unsatisfactory. In 1951 a new variant, the HA-1109-K1L, made its appearance powered by a French-built HS-12-Z-17 engine, and production deliveries to the Spanish Air Force began in 1952. Other variants were the HA-1109-K2L, with the Breda-SAFAT machine-guns transferred from under the wings to the engine cowling and provision for eight 80mm Oerlikon rockets under the wings; the HA-1109-K3L which carried rockets only, the gun armament being deleted; and the HA-1112-K1L, with two wing-mounted HS-404 or -804 wing-mounted cannon plus rocket racks. In Spanish Air Force Service, this variant was known as the C4J. A two-seat trainer version, the HA-1110-K1L, was also built in small numbers.

In 1953 work began on re-fitting most HA-1109s with the Rolls-Royce Merlin 500-45 engine, and these aircraft were designated HA-1109-M1L. A few examples of Spain's 109s were still flying in the 1960s, and the surviving aircraft were used in the filming of *The Battle of Britain*.

IAe24 Calquin

Role: Attack Bomber
Operational: 1947-60

Engines: Two 1,050hp Pratt & Whitney R-1830-SC-G radials
Span: 53ft 5¾in
Length: 39ft 4½in
Weight: 11,772lb (empty)
15,873lb (loaded)
Crew: 2
Max speed: 273mph
Service ceiling: 28,000ft
Range: 746 miles
Weapons: Four 20mm Hispano 804 cannon in fuselage nose (Note: some aircraft had four .5in machine guns); up to 1,650lb of bombs internally, and 12 75mm rockets on underwing racks

Designed and built by the Instituto Aerotecnico at Cordoba, the IAe24 Calquin (Royal Eagle) closely resembled the de Havilland Mosquito and was

Argentina

clearly inspired by the British aircraft. In fact, it was originally intended to power the Calquin with two Rolls-Royce Merlin liquid-cooled engines, but none was available for export to Argentina and the lower-powered Pratt & Whitney R-1830-SC-G radial was used instead. The prototype flew for the first time in June 1946 and an order was placed for 200 production aircraft, the first of these flying on 4 July 1947. Together with a small number of Avro Lancasters, the Calquin remained the mainstay of the Argentine Air Force's bomber arm until 1960, when it was finally withdrawn from the squadrons. The aircraft was built mainly of wood, like the Mosquito, a similar 'balsa sandwich' being used in the construction of the fuselage.

IAe58 Pucara

Role: Counter-Insurgency
Operational: 1976-

Engines: Two 1,022ehp Turbomeca Astazou XV1G turboprops
Span: 47ft 6¾in
Length: 45ft 7¼in
Weight: 7,826lb (empty)
13,668lb (max loaded)
Crew: 2
Max speed: 323mph at 9,840ft
Service ceiling: 27,165ft
Range: 1,890 miles (max fuel)
Weapons: Two 20mm Hispano and four 7.62mm

FN machine guns in fuselage; up to 3,307lb of external stores

Originally known as the Delfin, the IAe58 Pucara twin-turboprop COIN aircraft flew for the first time on 20 August 1969, powered by two AiResearch TPE331 engines. Production aircraft are fitted with Turbomeca Astazous. An initial batch of 30 Pucaras was ordered for the Argentine Air Force, and eight of these had been delivered to the II Escuadron de Exploration y Ataque by the end of June 1978. It is expected that about 70 Pucaras will eventually be delivered to the Argentine Air Force.

Ikarus S-49

Role: Fighter/Ground-Attack
Operational: 1951-57
Data: S-49C

Engines: One 1,500hp Hispano-Suiza 12Z-11Y in-line
Span: 33ft 9½in
Length: 29ft 8¾in
Weight: 7,055lb (normal loaded)
7,646lb (max loaded)
Crew: 1
Max speed: 398mph at 5,000ft
Service ceiling: 32,810ft
Range: 497 miles
Weapons: One 20mm Mauser MG 151 cannon; two 12.7mm machine guns; four 82mm or 110mm rocket missiles, four 55lb or 110lb bombs on underwing racks

The first postwar fighter to be designed in Yugoslavia, the S-49 was a development of the prewar Ikarus IK-3. The prototype flew in 1948, powered by a 1,222hp Klimov VK-105PF-2 liquid-cooled engine, and the type was ordered into production for the Yugoslav Air Force, the first examples entering service as the S-49A in 1951. Maximum speed was only 360mph at 16,400ft and service ceiling 31,170ft, but when Yugoslavia broke off relations with the Soviet Union in 1948 the aircraft was re-engined with the Hispano-Suiza 12Z-11Y engine, 80 of which were purchased from France. Developing 1,500hp, this powerplant offered a better all-round performance, and, with other refinements including a revised cockpit canopy and undercarriage the aircraft emerged in 1952 as the S-49C. It was eventually replaced in first-line service by the F84G Thunderjet, but served as an operational trainer until the late 1950s.

Ilyushin Il-10

Role: Tactical Support
Operational: 1944-58
NATO Code-Name: Beast
Engines: One 2,000hp Mikulin AM-42
Span: 45ft 6in
Length: 40ft
Weight: 9,921lb (empty)
13,968lb (normal loaded)
Crew: 2
Max speed: 315mph at sea level
Service ceiling: 13,123ft
Range: 528 miles with eight RPs and 882lb of bombs
Weapons: Two NS-23 cannon in wings and one 20mm ShVAK cannon in rear cockpit; four 500lb bombs or eight 56lb rockets and two 500lb bombs (Note: some late production Il-10s carried a modified armament of two extra 7.62mm MGs in the wings and a 12.7mm UBT gun in the rear cockpit instead of the ShVAK)

An improved version of the Ilyushin Il-2 assault aircraft, the Il-10 flew for the first time in 1943 and deliveries of operational aircraft to Soviet Air Force units began in the autumn of 1944. Aerodynamically, the new aircraft was much more refined than its predecessor, and was powered by a Mikulin AM-42 engine housed under a streamlined cowling. The Il-10 saw action over Germany during the closing weeks of World War II, but it was in the postwar years that it assumed real importance, forming the mainstay of the Soviet satellite air forces' assault squadrons. The first recipients outside the Soviet Union were Poland and Czechoslovakia, followed by Bulgaria and Hungary, and Hungarian AF Il-10s were used against Soviet forces during the uprising of 1956. The aircraft was manufactured under licence in Czechoslovakia as the Avia B33 and BS33, the latter being a dual control trainer; between 1950 and 1954, some 2,000 were built. Substantial numbers of Il-10s were also delivered to the Chinese Communists in 1948-49 and 62 were supplied to North Korea, many of these being destroyed during the Korean War. Surprisingly, the Il-10 remained in first-line operational service with the Soviet Frontovaia Aviatsiya until 1956, the last unit to use it being the 200th Ground Attack Division, which was disbanded at Brandenburg, East Germany, in June that year. The type remained operational with Russia's satellites until 1958, and a few were still airworthy in 1978, being used as flying 'museum pieces'.

Ilyushin Il-28

USSR

Role: Light Bomber
Operational: 1949-
NATO Code-Name: Beagle

Engines: Two 5,950lb thrust Klimov VK-1 turbojets
Span: 64ft
Length: 58ft
Weight: 28,350lb (empty)
46,640lb (normal loaded)
Crew: 3
Max speed: 530mph at sea level
Service ceiling: 41,500ft
Range: 1,560 miles
Weapons: Two fixed forward-firing 23mm Nudelman-Suranov cannon in nose; two Nudelman-Rikhter 23mm cannon in rear turret; up to 2,500lb of bombs internally

Designed as a tactical light bomber to replace the piston-engined Tupolev Tu-2, Ilyushin's Il-28 formed the mainstay of the Soviet Bloc's tactical air striking forces during the 1950s and was subsequently widely exported to countries within the Soviet sphere of influence. The first prototype Il-28 was fitted with RD-10 (Jumo 004) turbojets, but these failed to provide sufficient power and the second and subsequent machines employed the Klimov VK-1, a Russian copy of the Rolls-Royce Nene 1 turbojet. The first VK-1-powered Il-28 flew for the first time on 20 September 1948 and first deliveries to units of the Frontovaia Aviatsiya, Russia's tactical air arm, began the following year, the aircraft's simple and robust construction facilitating mass production. Some examples of the Il-28 appeared on bases in Manchuria during the Korean War, although these never ventured over the Yalu River and may have been Soviet Air Force machines. By 1955 some 800 Il-28s were serving with Eastern Bloc air forces, excluding those in Soviet service. Early recipients were Poland, Czechoslovakia and China, followed by Rumania and Hungary. Il-28s in Czech Air Force service were designated B228. In 1955-56 60 were delivered to Egypt, some 20 being destroyed at Luxor in an attack by French Air Force F-84F Thunderstreaks during the Suez Crisis. 40 more were delivered in 1957. Most of these deliveries involved ex-Czech aircraft, and in 1958 Indonesia received 35 aircraft from a similar source, a nucleus of pilots being trained in Egypt. Some Egyptian Il-28s, flown by Egyptian crews, operated with the Federal Nigerian Air Force during the civil war with Biafra in 1969. Other countries using the Il-28 were Algeria (24), Afganistan (48), North Vietnam (10), North Korea (50) and Cuba. The latter's Il-28 deliveries were a leading factor in the crisis of October 1962, which brought the world to the brink of war, and in fact several shipments were turned back by US warships.

The Il-28 has been produced under licence in China since 1960 and was still serving operationally in that country in 1978. Two aircraft, with guns removed and fitted with target towing equipment, were also in use in Finland. A two-seat trainer version, the Il-28U (NATO code-name Mascot) was also produced, and a transport version — the Il-20 — served in some numbers with Aeroflot.

Ilyushin Il-38

USSR

Role: Long-Range Maritime Reconnaissance
Operational: 1973-
NATO Code-Name: May

Engines: Four Ivchenko AI-20 turboprops rated at 4,000ehp
Span: 122ft 8½in

Length: 129ft 10in
Weight: 63,000lb (approx empty)
Loaded: Not known
Crew: 12+
Max speed: 400mph at 26,250ft
Service ceiling: 28,000ft
Range: 4,500 miles max
Weapons: Variety of ASW stores

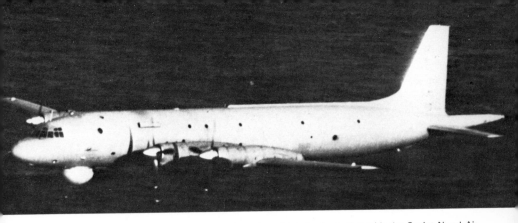

The Ilyushin Il-38 is a long-range maritime patrol development of the Il-18 civil airliner, the Soviet equivalent of Lockheed's P-3 Orion. The fuselage is longer than that of the Il-18 and has a sting-type tail housing MAD equipment. An ASW radome is also fitted under the nose. Between 60 and 70 Il-79s are thought to be in service with the Soviet Naval Air Arm, and the type has been identified over the Atlantic and Mediterranean. Some Il-38s operating in the Mediterranean area carried Egyptian markings, but are believed to have been manned by Soviet crews.

Israel Aircraft Industries Kfir

Israel

Role: Multi-Role Combat
Operational: 1975-

Engines: One General Electric J79 turbojet rated at 11,870lb thrust (17,900lb with reheat)
Span: 26ft 11½in
Length: 51ft 0¼in
Weight: 16,060lb (empty)
32,188lb (max loaded)
Crew: 1
Max speed: 1,450 mph at 36,100ft
Service ceiling: 50,000ft+
Range: 1,000 + miles
Weapons: Two IAI-built DEFA 30mm cannon; two Rafael Shafrir infra-red AAMs; Shrike, Maverick or Hobo ASMs; two 1,000lb bombs or a Luz-1 ASM; four 500lb bombs

Developed from the Dassault Mirage 5, following France's embargo on the supply of these aircraft to Israel, the IAI Kfir (Lion Cub) employs a basic Mirage 5 airframe but with a shorter, larger diameter rear fuselage housing a General Electric J79 turbojet in place of the SNECMA Atar. Two squadrons of the Israeli Air Force were equipped with the Kfir, beginning in 1975. The Kfir C2 is a modified version featuring swept canard surfaces mounted just aft of the air intakes, similar to those of the SAAB Viggen. The C2 is the principal production version for the Israeli Air Force and is also offered for export. A potential customer was Ecuador, but the sale of 24 Kfirs to this country was vetoed by the US Government in 1977. US approval was, however, obtained to sell 50 Kfirs to Taiwan in July 1978.

Lavochkin La-9/La-11

USSR

Role: Single-Seat Fighter
Operational: 1945-55
NATO Code-Name: Fritz (La-9)
Fang (La-11)

	La-9	La-11
Engines: (both)	One 1,870lb Ash-82 FN radial	
Span:	34ft 9¼in	31ft 10in
Length:	30ft 2¼in	28ft 6½in
Weight: (empty)	6,500lb	6,900lb
(Loaded)	8,000lb	8,790lb
Crew:	1	1
Max speed:	430mph at sea level	420mph at sea level
Service ceiling:	35,600ft	33,800ft
Range:	1,084 miles	1,430 miles (external tanks)
Weapons:	Four SLVAK 20mm cannon	Three SLVAK 20mm cannon

La-9

The last piston-engined fighters to serve with the Soviet Air Force, the La-9 and La-11 were logical developments of Lavochkin's famous La-7 of World War II. Design of the La-9 began in 1944 and its development continued during the last months of the war, although it arrived too late to see action against the Germans. It was slightly larger than the La-7 and differed from its predecessor in having an all-metal construction, a redesigned cockpit canopy and square-cut wingtips. In first-line service with the Soviet Air Force until 1948-49, when it was replaced by jet fighters, the La-9 served for some years after that as an operational trainer and was also supplied to several satellite air forces, including North Korea and China. It was frequently encountered during the early months of the Korean War by UN pilots. Some La-9s were experimentally fitted with rocket motors in the tail, and one experimental version, the La-9RD, was equipped with two RD-13 pulse jets under the wings. Four of these aircraft were publicly displayed at the Tushino Air Show on 18 August 1946.

La-11

The La-11, also of all-metal construction, was delivered to Soviet Air Force units in early 1946, and Western experts had an opportunity to examine the type in detail when a Russian pilot defected in one to Tullinge, in Sweden, on 18 May 1949. The La-11 had a slightly smaller wing area than the LA-9 and carried a reduced armament. Some aircraft were equipped with a gun camera unusually mounted externally above the forward cockpit. Like the La-9, the La-11 was encountered over Korea in both Chinese and North Korean markings.

Lavochkin La-15

USSR

Role: Interceptor
Operational: 1949-57
NATO Code-Name: Fantail
Engines: One 3,527lb thrust RD-500 (Rolls-Royce Derwent) turbojet
Span: 28ft 11½in
Length: 34ft 5⅓in
Weight: 6,200lb (empty)
8,488lb (normal loaded)
Crew: 1
Max speed: 637mph at 16,400ft
Service ceiling: 42,880ft
Range: 737 miles (max on internal fuel)
Weapons: Two 23mm NR-23 cannon
Originally designated La-174, the Lavochkin La-15 was a refined version of the La-168 experimental interceptor. Powered by the Soviet copy of the Rolls-Royce Derwent, the RD-500, the aircraft flew for the first time early in 1948 and was ordered into production for the Soviet Air Force in August that year. The type entered service with the IA-PVO in 1949, but its performance was inadequate for the interceptor role and only a few units were equipped with it, the MiG-15 becoming the standard Soviet Air Force jet fighter. Nevertheless, the La-15 continued in service in the ground attack role until the late 1950s and was also used as a combat trainer. The La-15UTI trainer version had a second seat inserted aft of the main cockpit in what had previously been the main fuel bay, and this variant was fitted with drop tanks.

Lockheed F-80 Shooting Star

USA

Role: Fighter-Bomber
Operational: 1945-63
Data: F-80C

Engines: One 5,400lb thrust Allison J33-A-35 turbojet
Span: 38ft 10½in
Length: 34ft 6in
Weight: 8,240lb (empty)
15,335lb (loaded)
Crew: 1
Max speed: 543mph at 25,000ft
Service ceiling: 44,100ft
Range: 1,345 miles (max with drop tanks)
Weapons: Six .5in machine guns in fuselage nose; up to 2,000lb of bombs and rockets

The first jet-propelled combat aircraft to enter service with the USAF, the Lockheed F-80 Shooting Star remained the workhorse of America's tactical fighter-bomber and fighter-interceptor squadrons for five years after the end of World War II, until it was replaced in 1950-51 by more modern types such as the F-84 Thunderjet and the F-86 Sabre. The prototype XP-80 was designed around a de Havilland H-1 turbojet which was supplied to the United States in July 1943 and the aircraft was completed in just 143 days, making its first flight on 9 January 1944. In April 1945, two P-80s were shipped to Italy for evaluation under operational conditions, being the only US jet aircraft to see front-line service during the war, but apart from a few short day reconnaissance flights they saw no action. Early production P-80As entered USAF service late in 1945 with the 412th Fighter Group, which became the 1st Fighter Group in July 1946 and comprised the 27th, 71st and 94th Fighter Squadrons. The P-80A was replaced by the P-80B in 1947 in most first line Shooting Star units, and began to be replaced by the F-86 Sabre in 1949.

The major production version was the F-80C, powered by an Allison J33 turbojet, and this was still first-line equipment in the summer of 1950, at the outbreak of the war in Korea. Units using the F-80C in the Pacific at that time were the 8th, 9th and 49th Fighter Bomber Groups and the 35th Fighter Interceptor Group in Japan, the 18th Fighter Bomber

Group in the Philippines and the 51st Fighter Interceptor Group on Okinawa. RF-80A unarmed reconnaissance aircraft were also in service with the 8th Tactical Reconnaissance Squadron in Japan. The F-80s of the 35th Fighter Bomber Squadron, 8th Fighter Bomber Wing, were the first to see combat destroying four Ilyushin Il-10s on 27 June 1950. During the months that followed the Shooting Stars were in the forefront of the fighting, flying escort missions for B-29s as well as carrying out ground-attack work on a large scale, and on 7 November 1950 Shooting Stars of the 51st Fighter Interceptor Wing fought MiG-15s over the Yalu in history's first jet-versus-jet battle, destroying one of the Soviet aircraft. Nevertheless, it was clear that the F-80 was no match for the MiG, and losses grew steadily until Sabres began to take over the fighter escort role in December. After that, the Shooting Stars were gradually phased out, until by the end of hostilities in July 1953 only the RF-80Cs of the 67th Tactical Reconnaissance Wing were operational in Korea.

Further development of the basic F-80 design resulted in the two-seat T-33 trainer, which was subsequently supplied to every US-equipped air force, and its naval counterpart, the T-1A. The Shooting Star was supplied to some Latin American air forces in small numbers, and was used as first-line equipment by Ecuador and Uruguay until the early 1960s.

Lockheed F-94 Starfire   USA

Role: All-Weather Interceptor
Operational: 1950-58
Data: F94C

Engines: One Pratt & Whitney J48-P-5 turbojet of 6,350lbst (8,750lb with reheat)
Span: 37ft 6in
Length: 41ft 5in
Weight: 13,000lb (empty)
23,000lb (loaded)
Crew: 2

Max speed: 646mph at sea level, 585mph at 35,000ft
Service ceiling: 55,000ft
Max range: 1,900 miles
Weapons: 48 70mm Mighty Mouse rockets in nose and wing pods

The Lockheed F-94 Starfire was developed from the T33A trainer to meet the need for an interim two-seat all-weather interceptor, two production T-33-1-LO airframes being converted as YF-94s. The first of these flew on 16 April 1949, and four months later

77

the USAF placed contracts for 17 F-94A-1-LO and 92 F-94A-5-LO fighters, together with one YF-94B — the latter aircraft having centrally-mounted wingtip tanks instead of underslung tanks.

The F-94A, which incorporated 75% of the components used in the T-33 and F-80 Shooting Star, had 940lb of radar equipment in the nose and an armament of four 0.5in Colt-Browning machine guns. The aircraft was powered by an Allison J33-A-33 centrifugal-type turbojet with a normal maximum thrust of 4,600lb, boosted to 5,400lb with water injection and 6,000lb with reheat. In service, F-94As were fitted with 191.5 imp gal Fletcher wingtip tanks. The F-94A went into production in 1949; 200 were built, the first entering service in June 1950 with the 319th All-Weather Fighter Squadron.

The YF-94B was converted from the 19th F94-A in 1950, and a total of 357 F-94Bs were built. Apart from the revised wingtip tanks, they differed from the F-94A mainly in having a modified hydraulics system and avionics, including a Sperry Zero-Reader flight director. The next variant, the F-94C, differed so extensively from its predecessors that it was originally known as the YF-97A. This designation remained in force from the aircraft's maiden flight on 16 January 1950 until 12 September that year, when the designation YF-94C was officially adopted.

The F-94C was fitted with a 6,350lb thrust (8,750lb with reheat) Pratt & Whitney J48-P-5, and other changes included an increase in wing dihedral and a reduction in thickness/chord ratio from 13% to 10%, the introduction of a swept tailplane, and the replacement of the gun armament by 24 unguided folding-fin rockets in a ring of tubes around the nose-cone. Later, provision was also made for a further 24 rockets in wing pods. The F-94C carried 1,200lb of electronics, and two 1,000lb thrust RATOG packs could be fitted under the fuselage. Total production of the F-94C came to 387 aircraft before the series was completed in 1954.

F-94Cs saw limited service during the Korean War with the 68th Fighter Interceptor Squadron, when they were used mainly to combat North Korean PO-2 'intruder' biplanes. One F-94 did manage to shoot down a PO-2 by throttling right back and lowering gear and flaps to reduce its speed, but the fighter stalled immediately afterwards and spun in, killing its crew. Another F-94 was lost when it collided with a PO-2.

The F-94D was a proposed single-seat ground-attack and long-range escort variant; a prototype was built in 1951 and 112 examples were ordered, but the contract was later cancelled.

Lockheed F-104 Starfighter

Role: Supersonic Interceptor
Operational: 1958–
Data: F-104S

Engines: One General Electric J79-GE-19 turbojet rated at 11,870lb thrust (17,900lb with reheat)
Span: 21ft 11in
Length: 54ft 9in
Weight: 14,573lb (empty)
31,000lb (max loaded)
Crew: 1
Max speed: 1,450mph at 40,000ft
Service ceiling: 57,000ft
Range: 2,200miles (ferry)

USA

Weapons: One 20mm Vulcan rotary cannon, two AIM-7 Sparrow III semi-active radar homing and two AIM-9 Sidewinder infra-red homing AAMs

Development of Lockheed's radical F-104 Starfighter was begun in 1951, when the lessons of the Korean air war were already bringing about profound changes in combat aircraft design on both sides of the Iron Curtain. A contract for two XF-104 prototypes was placed in 1953 and the first of these flew on 7 February 1954, only 11 months later. The two XF-104s were followed by 15 YF-104s for service evaluation, most of these, like the prototypes, being powered by the Wright J65-W-6 turbojet (10,500lb thrust with reheat). The aircraft was

ordered into full production as the F-104A, this being basically similar to the XF-104 but with a more powerful General Electric J79-GE-3B engine and other refinements, including air intake shock cones. The first production F-104A flew on 17 February 1956 and deliveries to the US Air Defense Command began in January 1958. 153 were built, 25 being supplied to Nationalist China and 12 to Pakistan. Because of its lack of all-weather capability the F-104A saw only limited service with Air Defense Command, equipping two Fighter Interceptor Squadrons the 319th and 331st. During the Indo-Pakistan conflict of 1969, the Pakistan Air Force's F-104As destroyed five Indian aircraft, but lost six of their own number. In 1967 18 ex-Chinese F-104As and four two-seat F-104Bs were supplied to Jordan.

The NF-104A was a special variant used to train USAF pilots for flight at altitudes up to 130,000ft, attaining this height with the aid of a 6,000lb thrust Rocketdyne AR-2 rocket motor. Only three were built, the first flying in July 1963. The F-104B was a tandem two-seat version with a larger fin area, the prototype flying on 7 February 1957. 26 were built, serving as operational trainers and combat aircraft with Air Defense Command. One was delivered to Nationalist China. The QF-104 was a remotely controlled, recoverable target conversion of the F-104A, 24 being produced, while the RF-104A was a cancelled reconnaissance variant.

The next Starfighter version, the F-104C, was a tactical fighter-bomber, deliveries to USAF Tactical Air Command beginning in October 1958. Seventy-seven were built, equipping a single tactical fighter wing, the 479th. The F-104D, 22 of which were built, was a two-seat variant. 20 F-104DJs were built for the Japan Air Self-Defence Force. Another two-seater, the F-104F, was basically similar to the F-104D apart from some equipment changes. 30 were delivered to the Luftwaffe, beginning in 1960. Numerically the most important variant, the Lockheed F-104G Starfighter was a single-seat multi-mission aircraft based on the F-104C and powered by a J79-GE-11A turbojet developing 15,800lb thrust with reheat. This variant had a strengthened structure and many equipment changes, including an upwards-ejecting Lockheed C-2 seat (earlier variants had downward-ejecting seats). The first F-104G flew on 5 October 1960 and 1,266 examples were produced up to February 1966, 977 by the European Starfighter consortium and the remainder by Lockheed. 750 were supplied to the Luftwaffe, 154 to the Italian Air Force, 120 to the Royal Netherlands Air Force and 99 to the Belgian Air Force. The basically similar CF-104 was a strike-reconnaissance aircraft, 200 of which were built by Canadair for the RCAF. Canadair also built 110 more F-104Gs for delivery to the air forces of Norway, Nationalist China, Spain, Denmark, Greece and Turkey. Further variants of the F-104G were the FR-104G, which was fitted with an internal camera pack, and the TF-104G, a two-seat conversion trainer. A total of 137 TF-104Gs were ordered for the Luftwaffe, 14 for the Netherlands and 29 for other air forces. Also similar to the F-104G was the F-104J for the Japan Air Self-Defence Force; the first one flew on 30 June 1961 and 207 were produced by Mitsubishi. The F-104S was an interceptor development of the F-104G, with provision for external stores. Equipped with a J79-GE-19 turbojet developing 17,900lb thrust, the aircraft attained a maximum speed of Mach 2.4. A total of 165 were built under licence in Italy. The F104N was an astronaut proficiency trainer, three of which were built on behalf of NASA.

Lockheed P2V Neptune

USA

Role: Long-Range Maritime Patrol
Operational: 1945-
Data: P2V-7

Engines: Two Wright R-3350-32W Turbo Compound engines rated at 3,500shp and two Westinghouse J34-WE-36 turbojets rated at 3,400lb thrust each
Span: 103ft 10in
Length: 91ft 8in
Weight: 49,935lb (empty)
79,895lb (loaded)
Crew: 10+
Max speed: 403mph (all engines operating)
356mph (piston engines only)
Service ceiling: 22,000ft

Range: 3,695 miles (max)
Weapons: Two .5in machine guns in dorsal turret (later deleted); four 20mm cannon in nose (some aircraft only); full range of maritime offensive stores internally; provision for air-to-surface missiles on underwing racks

The first land-based aircraft designed specifically for the long-range maritime reconnaissance role, the Lockheed Neptune was destined to be one of the longest-serving military aircraft ever built, variants of the basic type still equipping first-line maritime units 30 years after the two XP2V-1 prototypes were ordered on 4 April 1944. The first of these flew on 17 May 1945. Fifteen pre-production P2V-1s had also been ordered in April 1944, and a further order for 151 examples was placed the following

December. Production P2V-1s were powered by Wright R-3350-8A engines of 2,300hp. The third production P2V-1, named *Truculent Turtle*, stripped of its armament and fitted with long-range tanks, flew non-stop from Perth, Australia to Columbus, Ohio — a distance of 11,236 miles — on 29-30 September 1946.

Deliveries of the P2V-1 to the US Navy (Patrol Squadron VP-ML-2) began in March 1947, by which time another variant, the P2V-2, had also flown. The P2V-2 had a longer nose housing extra search and tactical radar equipment and a battery of six 20mm cannon, and was powered by 2,800hp R-3350-24W engines. Eighty-one were built. Conversions were the P2V-2N with an experimental ski undercarriage (two built) and the P2V-2S with a ventral radome (one built). Next variant was the P2V-3 with R-3350-26WA engines; 83 were built, including two P2V-3Z special armoured transports, two P2V-3Cs modified for carrier operations, and 30 P2V-3W early warning aircraft. On 7 March 1949 one of the P2V-3Cs took off from the carrier USS *Coral Sea* at a weight of 74,000lb, flew 2,000 miles and released a dummy 10,000lb nuclear weapon, then flew another 2,000 miles to a land base. Yet another engine change (R-3350-30W) resulted in the P2V-4, which carried underwing fuel tanks. Its designation was later changed to P-2D.

The P2V-5 Neptune, which flew on 29 December 1950, had the same engines as its predecessor and was the first to be fitted with MAD equipment in an extended tail cone in place of the rear gun turret. It was also the first Neptune variant to be supplied to foreign air arms, 36 P2V-5Fs (P-2Es) being delivered to RAF Coastal Command and serving with Nos 36, 203, 210 and 207 Squadrons as the Neptune MR1, six to the Argentine, 14 to Brazil and 12 to Portugal. In addition to its two piston engines, the P2V-5F was fitted with two Westinghouse J34-WE-36 turbojets in underwing pods outboard of the main engine nacelles. In the course of production the nose gun turret was replaced by a transparent observation blister and the dorsal turret was deleted.

The last of 424 P2V-5s was delivered to the US Navy in September 1954. Other variants included the P2V-5FE (EP-2E) and the P2V-5FS (SP-2E), which were fitted with 'Julie' and 'Jezebel' anti-submarine detection equipment.

The P2V-6 Neptune (P-2F) had a minelaying capability in addition to its anti-submarine role and was not fitted with auxiliary turbojets. Eighty-three were delivered to the US Navy and 12 to France's Aeronavale, where it equipped Flotille 22F. Variants were the P2V-6M (MP-2F), equipped to carry two Fairchild AUM-N-2 missiles; the P2V-6T (TP-2F) trainer; and the P2V-6F (P-2G), which was to have been fitted with auxiliary turbojets but which never entered service. The last production version was the P2V-7 (P-2H), which flew for the first time on 26 April 1954 and was produced both with and without auxiliary turbojets. Twenty-five P2V-7s were supplied to the RCAF, 12 to the RAAF, 15 to the RNethAF and 24 to the Aeronavale, equipping Flotilles 23F, 24F and 25F. The P2V-7S (SP-2H) was fitted with the 'Julie/Jezebel' ASW detection system and equipped US Navy Squadrons VP-1, 2, 9, 11, 17, 18, 23, 24, 31 and 56, and 16 examples were delivered to the Japan Maritime Self-Defence Force. The P2V-7LP (LP-2J) was a 'one-off' conversion adapted for Antarctic survey operations.

The P2V-7 was produced under licence in Japan by Kawasaki, 42 being built in 1958 and a further six in 1962. The Japanese also produced a variant of the P2V-7 with a lengthened fuselage and two 2,850shp General Electric T64-IHI-10 turboprops. Designated P-2J in JMSDF service, the type flew for the first time on 21 July 1966 and the first of a batch of 46 was delivered in November that year. Total production of all Neptune variants, excluding the Japanese-built aircraft, was 1,099, of which 838 went to the US Navy.

Lockheed P-3 Orion

Role: Long-Range Maritime Reconnaissance
Operational: 1962–
Data: P-3C

Engines: Four 4,910ehp Allison T56-A-14 turboprops
Span: 99ft 8in
Length: 116ft 10in
Weight: 61,491lb (empty)
135,000lb (max take-off loaded)
Crew: 10
Max speed: 476mph at 15,000ft
Service ceiling: 28,300ft
Range: 3hr on station at 1,500ft, 1,550 miles
Weapons: Two Mk 101 nuclear depth bombs and four Mk 43, 44 or 46 torpedoes, or eight Mk 54 bombs internally; torpedoes, mines or rockets on 10 external pylons

A variant of the Lockheed Electra airliner, the P-3 (formerly P3V-1) Orion was Lockheed's winning submission in a 1958 US Navy contest for a new off-the-shelf' ASW aircraft which could be brought into service very rapidly by modifying an existing type. Two YP3V-1 prototypes were ordered, the first flying on 19 August 1958 and the second on 25 November 1959. The initial production version was the P-3A, which first flew in April 1961 powered by four 4,500ehp Allison T65-A-10W turboprops, and the first deliveries to the US Navy took place in August 1962, replacing the P-2 Neptunes of Navy Patrol

USA

Squadron VP-8. The 110th and subsequent production aircraft were fitted with the Deltic tactical display, search and detection system and known as Deltic P-3As. Three aircraft of this type were delivered to the Spanish Air Force. The WP-3A was a weather reconnaissance version, four of which were delivered to the USN in 1970 to replace the WC-121N. The next patrol version was the P-3B, fitted with 4,910ehp T56-A-14 engines. Total P-3A/B production ran to 286 aircraft for the US Navy, plus five for the RNZAF (delivered in 1966), ten to the RAAF (1968) and five to Norway (1969). The P-3C, which appeared in 1969, was equipped with a Univac digital computer, the nerve centre of a fully integrated search, analysis and attack system. Further improvements were incorporated in 1974-75, and in addition to the 132 P-3Cs delivered to the US Navy 10 aircraft were ordered by the RAAF for delivery to No 10 Squadron in 1977-78.

Further variants of the basic Orion were the RP-3D, a solitary P-3C converted for use by the US Navy Oceanographic Office to survey the Earth's magnetic field and operated by Oceanographic Development Squadron VXN-8; the WP-3D, two of which are in use as atmospheric research aircraft; the EP-3A electronic intelligence aircraft, 10 of which replaced the elderly Lockheed EC-121s in service with squadrons VQ-1 and VQ-2; the P-3F, six of which (similar to the P-3C) were delivered to the Imperial Iranian Air Force in 1975; and the CP-140 Aurora, a variant for the Canadian Armed Forces which is scheduled to begin replacing the CL-28 Argus in 1980.

Lockheed S-3A Viking

Role: Anti-Submarine Warfare
Operational: 1975–

Engines: Two 9,275lb thrust General Electric TF34-GE-2 turbofans
Span: 68ft 8in
Length: 53ft 4in
Weight: 26,650lb (empty)
42,500lb (normal loaded)

USA

Crew: 4
Max speed: 518mph
Service ceiling: 35,000ft +
Range: 3,454 miles (ferry)
Weapons: Various internal and external loads of bombs, rockets, torpedoes, mines, depth bombs, cluster bombs, flare launchers etc

The Lockheed S-3A Viking was designed in response

to a 1969 US Navy requirement for a carrier-borne anti-submarine weapons system built around a Univac digital computer. The aircraft and weapon systems were designed by Lockheed, while the wings, tail unit, undercarriage and engine pods were the work of the Vought Division of LTV. The prototype flew for the first time on 21 January 1972, by which time Lockheed had received a contract to build eight research and development aircraft. The following May, the US Navy ordered an initial production batch of 13 S-3As, and 80 more were ordered by the end of 1973. The first US Navy squadron to re-equip with the Viking was VS-41, an operational training unit, which received its first S-3As in March 1974. Other units operating the Viking since that time are VS-21, VS-22, VS-24, VS-28, VS-29, VS-30, VS-31, VS-32, VS-33, VS-37, VS-38 and VS-41, these units serving with carriers in the Atlantic and Pacific Fleets on a rotation basis. The last of 187 Vikings was delivered to the USN in the Spring of 1978.

The US-3A, which flew for the first time in July 1976, is an on-board delivery transport variant, and other versions under study in 1978 are the KS-3A tanker and the ES-3 electronic surveillance aircraft.

Lockheed SR-71   USA

Role: Strategic Reconnaissance
Operational: 1966-
Data: SR-71A

Engines: Two Pratt & Whitney J58 turbojets each rated at 32,500lb thrust
Span: 55ft 7in

Length: 107ft 5in
Weight: 170,000lb (loaded)
Crew: 2
Max speed: Mach 3.5
Absolute ceiling: 88,600ft
Range: 2,980 miles at Mach 3.0 and 78,740ft
Weapons: None

In 1959 a team led by Clarence L. Johnson, Lockheed's Vice-President for Advanced Development Projects, began work on the design of a radical new aircraft to supersede the Lockheed U-2 in the strategic reconnaissance role. Designated A-11, the new machine took shape in conditions of the utmost secrecy in a highly restricted section of the Lockheed plant at Burbank known as the 'Skunk Works', and seven aircraft were produced up to February 1964, when the A-11s existence was revealed to the world for the first time by President Lyndon B. Johnson. By that time, the A-11 had already been extensively tested at Edwards AFB, reaching speed of over 2,000mph at heights of over 70,000ft. Early flight tests were aimed at assessing the A-11's suitability as a long-range interceptor, and the experimental interceptor version was shown to the public at Edwards AFB in September 1964, bearing the designation YF-12A. Two YF-12As were built, equipped with Hughes AN/ASG-18 pulse Doppler fire control radar in a nose radome, infra-red sensors and weapon bays in the front section of the fuselage side fairings, these housing an armament of eight Hughes AIM-47A AAMs. On 1 May 1965 the YF-12A set up three world records and six international class records, achieving 2,070.102mph over a 15/25km course, 1,643.042mph over a 500km closed circuit, 1,688,891mph over a 1,000km closed circuit with a 2,000kg payload, and a sustained height of 80,257.91ft in horizontal flight.

The major production version of the A-11 was the SR-71A strategic reconnaissance aircraft, which carried equipment ranging from battlefield surveillance systems to long-range strategic systems capable of surveying up to 60,000 square miles of territory in one hour. The SR-71A made its first flight on 22 December 1964, and deliveries of operational aircraft began in January 1966 to the 9th and 4200th Strategic Reconnaissance Wings at Beale AFB, California. the SR-71B was a tandem two-seat training version; only one was built and was later destroyed in an accident, being replaced by the SR-71C with revised systems.

Only 20 YF-12s/SR-71s are thought to have been built, and several of these have been accidentally destroyed.

Lockheed U-2

Role: Electronic and Photo-Reconnaissance
Operational: 1956–
Data: U-2B

Engines: One Pratt & Whitney J-75-P-13 two-spool turbojet rated at 15,000lb + thrust
Span: 80ft
Length: 49ft 7in
Weight: 11,000lb (empty)
15,850lb (loaded)
Crew: 1
Max speed: 495mph at 40,000ft
Service ceiling: 65,000-70,000ft
Range: 2,600 miles at 460mph (with auxiliary tanks)
Weapons: None

Probably the most controversial and politically-

USA

explosive aircraft of all time, the Lockheed U-2 originated in an urgent USAF requirement for a high-level deep penetration reconnaissance aircraft, the Korean War having shown that existing types had a low survival factor in hostile airspace. Its specification emerged after lengthy consultation between Lockheed's chief designer, Clarence L. Johnson, the USAF and the Central Intelligence Agency, and Lockheeds were ordered to build a prototype in October 1954. The aircraft was hand-built at the company's Burbank, California plant, and made its first flight from Watertown Strip in Nevada in August 1955, an order for 52 production aircraft following quickly.

The U-2's design was essentially simple and conventional, the aircraft being basically a highly streamlined powered glider with a wingspan of 80ft against a length of less than 50, the wing having an aspect ratio of 14.3:1 and a loading of only

25lb sq ft. The engine was a single 11,200lb thrust Pratt & Whitney J-57, housed in a slender fuselage whose maximum diameter was 5ft. Because of the extreme altitudes at which the U-2 had to fly, a special fuel known as MIL-F-25524A was developed, with a boiling point of 300°F at sea level. Early U-2As had a range of about 2,000 miles and later U-2Bs 4,000 miles thanks to the addition of slipper tanks, but range could be extended considerably under operational conditions by flaming-out the engine and gliding for lengthy distances. Most U-2s were later fitted with a 15,000lb thrust J-57-P-13 turbojet, bringing them up to U-2B standard, and the small number retaining the original engine were re-designated WU-2A.

Training of early U-2 pilots (mainly ex-USAF Lockheed employees) for the aircraft's intelligence-gathering role took place at Watertown, Nevada, within a unit known as the 1st Weather Observation Squadron (Provisional). Most operational U-2 flights were undertaken from either Japan or Turkey, with detachments sent to Pakistan, West Germany, Norway and England. In Western Europe, the main U-2 unit was the 2nd Weather Observation Wing (Provisional), based at Wiesbaden. By 1960 U-2s had made a least 100 overflights across Soviet and Warsaw Pact territories, as well as about 200 legitimate research flights involving tasks such as radiation sampling. Clandestine flights across the Soviet Union continued until 1 May 1960, when U-

2B 566689 of the 2nd Weather Observation Squadron (P), operating out of Incirlik in Turkey and flown by Lt Gary Powers, was shot down by Soviet air defences south of Sverdlovsk.

Although the political implications of the Powers incident brought a halt to deep-penetration flights over the Soviet Union, short overflights of communist territory continued from Alaska and Japan, while radiation-sampling and other research flights continued from RAF Upper Heyford and from Victoria, Australia. In September and October 1962 two U-2s were shot down over Red China, one by a fighter and the other by a SA-2 missile. Meanwhile, U-2s had also been active over Cuba, and after CIA aircraft had detected the initial build-up of Soviet missiles there the reconnaissance task was taken over by Strategic Air Command U-2s. On 27 October 1962, a U-2 of the 4028th Strategic Reconnaissance Squadron was shot down over the island, and another U-2 crashed in Cuba in November 1963. Four U-2s were acquired by the Chinese Nationalist Air Force in 1963, and all of them were subsequently lost. U-2s also operated over North Vietnam during 1965-66. In addition to the losses on operations, at least 17 U-2s were lost accidentally. Although no longer used for reconnaissance purposes, a handful of U-2s still carry out research flights on behalf of various US Government organisations.

Lockheed WV-2/EC-121

USA

Role: Early Warning/Electronic Reconnaissance
Operational: 1952-
Data: EC-121J

Engines: Four 3,250hp Wright R-3350-C18 Turbo-Cyclones
Span: 123ft
Length: 13ft 7in
Weight: 100,000lb (empty) 160,000lb (loaded)
Crew: Up to 31
Max speed: 340mph at 22,600ft
Service ceiling: 28,000ft
Range: 5,600 miles
Weapons: None

In 1950-51, the United States Navy acquired two Lockheed Model 749 Constellations and, under the designation WV-1, modified them to test advanced electronic surveillance systems. These trials proved satisfactory, and the US Navy ordered into production a version of the Model 0149 Super

Constellation to serve as a high-altitude reconnaissance and early warning radar intelligence aircraft, designated WV-2. Powered by four 3,250hp Wright Turbo Compound engines, the WV-2 carried some $5\frac{1}{2}$ tons of electronic equipment, including General Electric height-finding radar in a 7ft high upper fuselage radome, and surveillance radar in a large radome under the fuselage. The fuselage interior housed a complete Combat Information Centre for coordination and transmission of all intelligence data, and five radar consoles/plotting stations permitted full analysis of incoming data. The WV-2 normally carried a 30-strong double crew on long-range early warning missions, or one crew of 19 on shorter electronic reconnaissance sorties. The WV-2E was an improved variant with a very large radar scanner in a lenticular housing mounted on a pylon above the fuselage, while the WV-3 was a weather reconnaissance variant. The first delivery of the WV-2 took place in July 1952 to Early Warning Squadron VW-2. The EC-121C and EC-121D were variants of the WV-2 for the USAF, and in fact the USN's WV-2s were redesignated EC-121 in the early 1960s. Between 1955 and 1965, the US Navy's

WV-2s/EC-121s were responsible for early warning coverage of the North Atlantic, this being taken over by ground radar units in August 1965. The last AEW patrol in this connection was flown by an EC-121J Warning Star of VW-11 (Keflavik, Iceland) on 26 August 1965.

On 14 April 1969 an EC-121 was shot down by North Korean fighters while carrying out a routine electronic surveillance mission from Atsugi, Japan, over the Sea of Japan. All 31 crew members were killed. In USAF service, EC-121s equipped the 551st and 552nd AEW and Countermeasures Wings of Air Defense Command, one covering the Atlantic seaboard of the USA and the other the Pacific.

LTV (Vought) A-7 Corsair II USA

Role: Carrier-Borne Attack
Operational: 1966-
Photo: A-7D
Data: A-7E

Engines: One Allison TF41-A-2 (Rolls-Royce Spey) turbofan rated at 15,000lb thrust
Span: 38ft 9in
Length: 46ft 1½in
Weight: 19,403lb (empty)
42,000lb (max loaded)
Crew: 1
Max speed: 691mph at sea level
Service ceiling: 45,000ft
Range: 3,224 miles (max ferry)
Weapons: Up to 15,000lb of bombs, rockets, AAMs and ASMs on underwing pylons

The A-7A Corsair II was designed in response to a US Navy requirement for a subsonic attack aircraft capable of carrying a greater load of conventional weapons than the A-4 Skyhawk, and in March 1964 Ling-Temco-Vought Inc was awarded a contract to build three prototypes. Based on the design of the F-8 Crusader, the Corsair II flew for the first time on 27 September 1965, and several versions of the basic type were subsequently produced for the US Navy and the USAF by the Vought Corporation, a subsidiary of LTV. The first attack version was the A-7A, which was powered by an 11,350lb thrust Pratt & Whitney TF30-P-6 turbofan engine and entered service with Attack Squadron VA-174 in October 1966. In December 1967 the type made its combat debut over Vietnam, operating with VA-147 from the USS *Ranger* in the Gulf of Tonkin. The last of 199 A-7As was delivered to the USN early in 1968. The next variant was the A-7B, 196 of which were built. This version was powered by an uprated TF30-P-8, and joined the air war over Vietnam in March 1969. The A-7D was a tactical fighter version for the USAF, capable of delivering its bomb load in all weathers, and was powered by an Allison TF-41-A1 (Rolls-Royce Spey) engine. The first unit to equip with the A-7D was the 54th Tactical Fighter Wing, at the end of 1968, and in October 1972 the aircraft went into action in Vietnam with the 354th Tactical Fighter Wing. Many of the 459 A-7Ds built before production ended in December 1976 were delivered to Air National Guard units.

The A-7E was a close support/interdiction variant developed for the US Navy. The first 67 aircraft, fitted with TF30-P-8 engines, were designated A-7C, but subsequent machines (A-7Es) were powered by the TF41-AS-2. First delivered to the USN in July 1969, the A-7E was deployed to South-East Asia with Attack Squadrons VA-146 and -147 (USS *America*) in May the following year. By the end of the conflict in Vietnam A-7s had flown more than 100,000 combat missions.

Other variants of the A-7 are the TA-7C (65 A-7Bs and -7Cs converted to the two-seat trainer role, retaining attack cabability); the RA-7E, which carries a reconnaissance pod; and the A-7H, 60 of which were ordered by the Royal Hellenic Air Force in 1975. The KA-7F was a proposed carrier-borne tanker, and the A-7G a proposed Swiss Air Force version. Neither was built.

Martin AM-1 Mauler

USA

Role: Carrier-Borne Attack
Operational: 1948-50

Engine: One 3,000hp Pratt & Whitney R-4360-4 Wasp Major radial
Span: 50ft 1in
Length: 41ft 8in
Weight: 12,500lb (empty)
19,500lb (loaded)
Crew: 1/2
Max speed: 350mph at sea level
Service ceiling: 28,000ft
Range: 1,700 miles
Armament: Four 20mm cannon; up to 4,000lb of bombs, rockets or a torpedo

Originally designated BTM-1, the Martin AM-1 Mauler was designed in 1944 to meet a US Navy requirement for a single-seat dive-bomber. The type flew for the first time in August 1944, but changing requirements and the end of the war in the Pacific delayed its entry into service and only 152 were produced, the first being delivered to Attack Squadron VA-17A in March 1948. The AM-1 was of all-metal construction, with intermeshing finger-type dive brakes on upper and lower wing surfaces and a perforated air brake under the fuselage, allowing a diving speed of less than 350mph. The Mauler's weapons load was carried externally, a crutch under the fuselage enabling a single bomb (of up to 4,000lb) to swing clear of the propeller when released. Some AM-1s were converted to the electronic surveillance role under the designation AM-1Q, this variant carrying a two-man crew, and the last examples were retired from squadron VC-4 in October 1950.

Martin B-57/RB-57

USA

Role: Tactical Bomber/Reconnaissance
Operational: 1955-

Engines: Two 7,220lb thrust Wright J65-W-5 turbojets
Span: 63ft 11½in
Length: 65ft 6in
Weight: 30,000lb (empty)
49,500lb (loaded with wingtip tanks)
Crew: 2
Max speed: 520mph at sea level
Service ceiling: 48,000ft
Range: 2,300 miles (normal)
Weapons: Eight .5in machine guns and four 20mm cannon in wings; 5,000lb of offensive stores in bomb bay and 3,000lb on underwing pylons

In 1953, the Glenn L. Martin Company began licence production of the English Electric Canberra B2 under the company designation Model 272 and the USAF designation B-57. The B-57A, which flew for the first time on 20 July 1953, was externally similar to the B2 but was powered by two Wright J65-W-1 turbojets and featured many internal changes. Only eight B-57As had been produced when production changed to the RB-57A photo-reconnaissance variant, the first of which was delivered to the USAF in March 1954. 67 RB-57As were built.

The next US Canberra variant, the B-57B, incorporated much redesign, including a tandem two-seat cockpit under a one-piece jettisonable canopy, a pre-loaded revolving bomb bay which rotated through 180 degrees, a wing-mounted armament of cannon and machine guns and underwing points for rockets or napalm tanks. The B-57B, in fact, accounted for the bulk of American Canberra production, the B-57C was basically similar but had dual controls for the additional role of conversion trainer. 26 B-57Bs and Cs were supplied to Pakistan and saw action during that country's disputes with India in 1965 and 1971. The B-57E was a development of the B-57C for target towing duties as well as the tactical role, carrying up to four high-speed targets. The B-57B/C was retired from first-line USAF service in the early 1960s and most examples converted to the reconnaissance role with the Air National Guard, but in 1964 it was withdrawn from the ANG and restored to full combat configuration for service in Vietnam, where it saw continuous action until the middle of 1968. The type later reverted to the ANG.

The RB-57D reconnaissance variant featured an entirely new wing, with a span increased to over 109ft, and was powered by two 9,700lb thrust Pratt & Whitney J75-P-5 turbojets. The fuselage was also redesigned internally to house cameras, radar and electronic reconnaissance equipment. The B-57F was a further reconnaissance variant converted by General Dynamics; its span was extended to 122ft. Power was supplied by two 18,000lb thrust Pratt & Whitney TF-33 turbofans and two auxiliary 3,300lb thrust Pratt & Whitney J-60 turbojets in pods under

wings. The first RB-57F was delivered to the 58th Weather Reconnaissance Squadron in June 1964, and the type — with a reported range of 4,000 miles and a maximum ceiling in the order of 100,000ft — is known to have made incursions into communist air-space. At least two RB-57s, operating with the Chinese Nationalist Air Force, were shot down over Red China in 1961, although these were the earlier RB-57A variant.

Martin P4M Mercator
USA

Role: Long-Range Maritime Patrol
Operational: 1950-60

Engines: Two 2,500hp Pratt & Whitney R-4360-20 Wasp Major radials and two Allison J33-A-23 turbojets rated at 4,600lb thrust each
Span: 114ft
Length: 84ft
Weight: 48,536lb (empty)
81,463lb (normal loaded)
Crew: 10-13
Max speed: 379mph at sea level (all four engines)
Service ceiling: 34,600ft ·
Range: 2,840 miles
Weapons: Twin 20mm cannon in nose and tail positions; .5in machine guns in dorsal and waist positions; various ASW stores internally, including two torpedoes.

The Martin P4M Mercator was designed to meet a US Navy requirement for a long-range maritime reconnaissance bomber, issued in July 1944. Two XP4M-1 prototypes were built, each powered by two 2,975hp Pratt & Whitney R-4360-4 Wasp Major piston engines and two 3,825lb thrust Allison J33-A-17 turbojets, the latter housed in the rear of the main engine nacelles. The XP4M-1 flew for the first time on 20 September 1946 and a contract was placed for 19 production P4M-1s, the last being completed in 1950. The first operational P4Ms entered service with Patrol Squadron VP-21 on 28 June that year, and a second Mercator unit was formed on 1 June 1955. This was Electronic Countermeasures Squadron VQ-1, the first of its type in the US Navy, which commissioned at Iwakuni, Japan, and equipped with P4M-1Q aircraft fitted with ECM gear. The unit's task was to probe Soviet and Red Chinese radar defences in the Far East, and had an eventful career. On 22 August 1956 one of its Mercators was shot down 32 miles off the China coast, the crew being killed, and on 16 June 1959 another P4M was attacked by two MiG-15s off Korea, suffering severe damage but making a successful emergency landing in Japan. The last of VQ-1's Mercators was finally retired in May 1960.

Martin P5M Marlin
USA

Role: Long-Range Maritime Patrol
Operational: 1952-67
Data: P5M-2

Engines: Two 3,400hp Wright R-3350-32WA Turbo-Cyclone radials
Span: 118ft 2½in
Length: 100ft 7¼in
Weight: 50,485lb (empty)
76,635lb (loaded)
Crew: 11
Max speed: 245mph at sea level
Service ceiling: 22,400ft
Range: 2,880 miles
Weapons: Bomb bay in lower portion of each engine nacelle housing two torpedoes or two 2,000lb bombs; eight 1,000lb bombs or eight depth charges on external racks; two 20mm cannon in tail position

Developed from the Martin PBM Mariner, the prototype XP-5M-1 Marlin flying boat flew for the first time on 30 April 1948, and deliveries of the first production aircraft were made on 23 April 1952 to Patrol Squadron VP-44. One of the most comprehensively-equipped patrol aircraft in the world when it entered service, the P5M-1 had a conventional tail unit, with tailplane set at the base of the fin, but the P5M-2 featured a 'T' tail. 239 Marlins were built, the last aircraft being delivered in December 1960. The P5M-2 entered service with US Navy and Coast Guard in 1954, and in 1958-59 80 of the earlier P5M-1s were brought up to P5M-2 standard with the installation of Magnetic Anomaly Detection and other ASW equipment. 10 P5M-2s were supplied to France's Aeronavale, equipping Flottille 27F at Dakar from 1959 until the late 1960s. Marlins served with the US Navy until 1967; on 6 November that year an SP-5B of VP-40, Naval Air Station North Island made the last operational flight of a US Navy flying boat, marking the final phase of the conversion of American ASW units to landplanes.

McDonnell F2H Banshee
USA

Role: Carrier-Borne Fighter-Bomber
Operational: 1949-64
Data: F2H-2

Engines: Two 3,250lb thrust Westinghouse J34-WE-34 turbojets
Span: 41ft 7½in
Length: 40ft 2in
Weight: 10,000lb (empty)
14,000lb (loaded)
Crew: 1
Max speed: 590mph at sea level
Service ceiling: 40,000ft
Range: 2,250 miles max
Weapons: Four 20mm cannon in nose

On 2 March 1945 the United States Navy placed a contract with the McDonnell Aircraft Corporation for two prototypes of a new naval fighter-bomber design. Designated XF2D-1, the first prototype flew on 11 January 1947, powered by two 3,000lb thrust Westinghouse J34-WE-22 turbojets. The series production version, designated F2H-1 Banshee, was armed with four 20mm cannon; 56 were produced, the first being delivered to Navy Squadron VF-171 in March 1949. In August that year, Lt J. L. Fruin of VF-171 made the first use in the United States of an ejection seat in a real emergency, ejecting from a Banshee at a speed of over 500knots.

The F2H-2 was an improved version with 3,250lb Westinghouse J34-WE-34 turbojets and an additional fuselage section to accommodate a further 147 imp gal fuel tank. Wingtip tanks were also fitted. An initial order for 188 F2H-2s, including 14 F2H-2N night fighters, was placed in 1949, and this was followed by a further contract for 146 aircraft in April 1952. By this time, the Banshee had been blooded in action in the Korean War, serving with several operational squadrons of Task Force 77. The type went into combat for the first time on 23 August 1951, when the F2H-2s of VF-172 (USS Essex) struck at targets in north-eastern Korea. Two days later, Banshees of the same unit undertook their first fighter escort mission, accompanying B-29s in a high altitude bombing attack on enemy marshalling yards at Rashin on Korea's extreme north-east border. The F2H-2 Banshee still equipped Marine Squadrons VMF-133, VMF-141, VMF-233 and VMF-441 in 1958. The F2H-2P, of which 58 were built, was a photo-reconnaissance version with a lengthened nose to accommodate cameras. In December 1952 F2H-2Ps from the USS Princeton played a major part in the firing trials of the Regulus guided missile, their pilots controlling it in flight for long distances over the Navy's Sea Test Range.

The F2H-3 (redesignated F2-C in 1962) was a long-range limited all-weather development embodying a further increase in fuselage length. 250 were built, and the type equipped two squadrons of the Royal Canadian Navy, VF-870 in November 1955 and VF-871 in October 1956, both units operating from the carrier HMCS Bonaventure. The F2H-4 was externally similar to the F2H-3, but with more powerful J34-WE-38 engines; 150 were delivered, beginning in 1953. An all-weather fighter equipped for flight refuelling, the F2H-4 was later redesignated F2-D.

The Banshee was retired from first-line US Navy service in September 1959, the last unit to be equipped with it (F2H-3/4) being VAW-11. The Canadian Navy's Banshees remained in use until the mid-1960s.

McDonnell F3H Demon   USA

Role: Carrier-Borne Interceptor
Operational: 1956-64
Data: F3H-2M/F3B

Engines: One Allison J71-A-2 turbojet rated at 9,700lb thrust (14,000lb with reheat)
Span: 35ft 4in
Length: 58ft 11in
Weight: 22,133lb (empty)
33,900lb (max loaded)
Crew: 1
Max speed: 700mph at sea level
Service ceiling: 48,000ft
Range: 1,500 miles max
Weapons: Four 20mm cannon; four Sparrow III AAMs

Designed in response to a US Navy requirement for a carrier-based fighter with a performance comparable to that of land-based aircraft, the McDonnell XF3H-1 Demon flew for the first time on 7 August 1951, powered by the new Westinghouse XJ40-WE-6 turbojet. This aircraft was subsequently destroyed, but the test programme continued with the second prototype and the US Navy placed substantial production orders for two variants: the F3H-1N, built by McDonnell and powered by a 7,500lb thrust J40-WE-8, and the F3H-3, built by Temco and powered by the J40-WE-22. Problems with the J40 engine, however, and the eventual decision to abandon it altogether, caused serious disruption of the whole Demon programme; the F3H-1N order was drastically reduced and the F3H-3 was cancelled altogether. The whole production line was held up until the Allison J71 turbojet became available, and although a few J40-powered Demons were delivered to the US Navy for evaluation in January 1954, it was with the Allison engine that the type became fully operational with Navy Fighter Squadron VF-14 in March 1956. The first Demons to be assigned to the Fleet were the F3H-2N night and all-weather fighter variant; further variants were the F3H-2M day fighter, armed with Sparrow missiles, and the F3H-2P photo-reconnaissance aircraft. The first Sparrow-armed F3H-2Ms were deployed with the Seventh Fleet in the Pacific late in 1958, the squadrons involved being VF-64 (USS Midway) and VF-193 (USS Bon Homme Richard). 29 of the F3H-

2s delivered to the US Navy were in fact F3H-1s, updated and equipped with the J71 engine. 119 F3H-2 Demons were built before production ended in 1959 and the type remained in service until August 1964, the last F2H-3Ms (F-3Bs) retiring from VF-161.

McDonnell F-101 Voodoo

USA

Role: Long-Range Interceptor
Operational: 1956-
Photo: F-101F
Data: F-101B

Engines: Two Pratt & Whitney J57-P-55 turbojets each rated at 13,000lb thrust (16,900lb with reheat)
Span: 39ft 8½in
Length: 67ft 4¾in
Weight: 28,000lb (empty) 40,000lb (loaded)
Crew: 2
Max speed: 1,220mph at 40,000ft
Service ceiling: 52,000ft
Range: 2,800 miles (max, with external fuel)
Weapons: Two Genie or three Super Falcon AAMs

In 1946 in response to an urgent USAF requirement for a long-range 'penetration' fighter capable of escorting the Convair B-36, which was about to enter service with Strategic Air Command, the McDonnell Aircraft Company embarked on the design of a heavy twin-engined jet fighter designated XF-88, the prototype of which flew in October 1948. Although the XF-88 successfully completed its USAF acceptance trials, however, a change in tactical requirements resulted in the development contract

being cancelled in August 1950. The design was resurrected the following year and subjected to a number of changes, including the lengthening of the fuselage by over 13ft to accommodate extra fuel tankage, and redesignated YF-101A. The prototype flew on 29 December 1954, and although SAC had by this time abandoned the long-range escort fighter idea, the programme was taken over by Tactical Air Command, which saw the F-101 as a potential replacement for the Northrop F-89 Scorpion. The aircraft went into series production as the F-101A, powered by two 11,700lb thrust Pratt & Whitney J57-P-13 turbojets. Armament consisted of four 20mm M-39E cannon, plus three Hughes GAR-1D or GAR-2A Falcon missiles and 12 HVAR. 75 F-101As were built, and these equipped three squadrons of Tactical Air Command. In 1956, two prototypes of the YRF-101A reconnaissance variant were built, the first flying on 10 May, and deliveries of production RF-101As began in May 1957 to the 63rd Tactical Reconnaissance Wing. Thirty-three were built.

The next Voodoo variant was the F-101B, a two-seat all-weather interceptor which made its first flight on 27 March 1957. Powered by two Pratt & Whitney J57-P-53/55s and armed with two AIR-2A Genie or three AIM-4E/F Super Falcon missiles, the F-101B subsequently equipped 16 squadrons of Air Defense Command: the 2nd, 13th,

15th, 18th, 29th, 49th, 60th, 62nd, 75th, 84th, 87th, 98th, 322nd, 437th, 444th, and 445th. Total F-101B production ran to 359 aircraft. In June 1961, 56 F-101Bs were sold to Canada and, as the CF-101B, equipped three squadrons of the RCAF's Air Defense Command. The TF-101B was a dual-control trainer version, retaining the F-101B's interception capability.

The F-101C was a single-seat fighter-bomber version for TAC, entering service with the 523rd Tactical Fighter Squadron of the 27th Fighter

Bomber Wing in May 1957. It equipped nine squadrons, but its operational career was relatively short, the type being replaced by the F-105 Thunderchief and F-4 Phantom in the early 1960s. The reconnaissance version, the RF-101C, saw much operational service over Vietnam, and aircraft in service with the Chinese Nationalist Air Force made frequent reconnaissance flights over the Chinese mainland. The RF-101C carried a nose-mounted battery of up to six cameras. 219 F- and RF-101Cs were built.

McDonnell FH-1 Phantom

Role: Carrier-Borne Fighter
Operational: 1947-50

Engines: Two 1,600lb thrust Westinghouse J30-WE-20 turbojets
Span: 40ft 9in
Length: 38ft 9in
Weight: 6,683lb (empty)
10,035lb (loaded)
Crew: 1
Max speed: 505mph
Service ceiling: 43,000ft
Range: 1,400 miles with ventral tank
Weapons: Four 20mm cannon

USA

The first American jet aircraft designed to operate from carriers, the FH-1 Phantom originated in 1943. Designated XFD-1, the prototype flew for the first time on 25 January 1945, powered by two 1,365lb thrust Westinghouse J30 turbojets. On 21 July the following year a pre-series FD-1 Phantom carried out the first US jet aircraft carrier trials aboard the USS *Franklin D. Roosevelt*. An order was placed for 100 production aircraft under the designation FH-1, but this was later cut to 60. On 5 May 1948 Fighter Squadron 17-A, equipped with 16 FH-1s, became the first carrier-qualified jet squadron in the US Navy, operating from the USS *Saipan*. The type remained in first-line service until July 1950, the last unit to use it being Marine Fighter Squadron VMF-122.

McDonnell F-4 Phantom

Role: Multi-Role Combat
Operational: 1960-
Data: F-4E

Engines: Two 17,900lb thrust (with reheat) General Electric J79-GE-17A turbojets
Span: 38ft 4¾in
Length: 62ft 10in
Weight: 30,328lb (empty)
61,795lb (max loaded)
Crew: 2
Max speed: 1,498mph at 40,000ft
Serivce ceiling: 71,000ft
Range: 1,978 miles (ferry)

USA

Weapons: One 20mm M61A1 rotary cannon; four/six AIM-7E Sparrow IIIB plus four AIM-9D Sidewinder AAMs; up to 16,000lb of conventional or nuclear stores

One of the most potent and versatile combat aircraft ever built, the McDonnell F-4 Phantom stemmed from a 1954 project for an advanced naval fighter designated F3H-G/H. A mock-up was built and in October 1954 the US Navy ordered two prototypes for evaluation under the designation YAH-1. This aircraft was to have been a single-seater, armed with four 20mm cannon and powered by two Wright J65 turbojets, but when the Navy finalised its re-

90

quirement in April 1955 the design was changed substantially, the aircraft being fitted with two General Electric J79s, two seats and an armament of four Sparrow missiles instead of the cannon. The designation was changed to F4H-1, and the XF4H-1 prototype flew for the first time on 27 May 1958. 23 development aircraft were procured, followed by 45 production machines for the US Navy. These were originally designated F4H-1F, but this was later changed to F-4A. The F-4B was a slightly improved version with J79-GE-8 engines, and between them the F-4A and F-4B captured many world records over a four-year period. On 25 September 1960, for example, an F-4A established a 100km closed circuit record of 1,390mph, and in 1962 the F-4B set up no fewer than eight time-to-height records.

Carrier trials were carried out in 1960 and in December that year the first Phantoms were delivered to training squadron VF-121. The first fully operational Phantom squadron, VF-114, commissioned with F-4Bs in October 1961, and in June 1962 the first USMC deliveries were made to VMF(AW)-314. Total F-4B production was 649 aircraft. The RF-4B was an unarmed reconnaissance version for the USMC, 46 being delivered between 1965 and 1970, while the QF-4B, of which 44 were produced, was a drone conversion for the Pacific Missile Test Center.

Twenty-nine F-4Bs were loaned to the USAF for evaluation in 1962 and proved superior to any Air Force fighter-bomber. A production order was quickly placed for a USAF variant; this was originally designated F-110A, but later changed to F-4C. Deliveries to the USAF began in 1963, 583 aircraft being built. The first units to use the type were the 8th, 12th and 15th Tactical Fighter Wings. The RF-4C, of which 505 were produced (originally as the RF-110A) was a multi-sensor reconnaissance variant, delivered to the USAF between September 1964 and January 1974, and the F-4D (825 built) was basically an F-4C with improved systems and redesigned radome. The major production version was the F-4E, 913 of which were delivered to the USAF between October 1967 and December 1976. F-4E export orders totalled 558, 138 being built under licence in Japan. The RF-4E was the tactical reconnaissance version, of which 157 had been produced by the Spring of 1978. The F-4F (175 built) was a version for the Luftwaffe, intended primarily for the air superiority role but retaining multi-role capability, while F-4G was the designation applied to 12 F-4B Phantoms modified to test automatic carrier landing systems. The F-4G Wild Weasel is the F-4E modified for the suppression of hostile missile guidance systems, fitted with a nose radome containing ECM equipment; first deliveries of 116 aircraft began in the spring of 1978. The successor to the F-4B in USN/USMC service was the F-4J, which possessed greater ground attack capability. The first of 522 production aircraft was delivered in June 1976. Updated F-4Js for the USN (260 ordered) carry the designation F-4S, while 178 F-4Bs which were updated during 1972-73 were designated F-4N.

The first foreign country to order the Phantom was Great Britain, the British aircraft being powered by Rolls-Royce RB168-25R Spey 201 engines. Versions for the Royal Navy and the RAF were designated F-4K and F-4M respectively. The F-4K was delivered to No 700P Squadron for service trials in April 1968; this unit was disbanded in January 1969 and replaced by No 767 Squadron, which disbanded in turn in August 1972. This left No 892 Squadron as the Fleet Air Arm's only Phantom unit, alternating between HMS *Ark Royal* and RAF Leuchars, in Scotland. 52 F-4Ks were delivered in 1968/69 and these were progressively handed over to the RAF with the run-down of the Fleet Air Arm's fixed-wing units, becoming the Phantom FG1 in RAF service. In 1978 the RAF's only Phantom FG1 squadron was No 43, but No 74 was reportedly scheduled to form with No 892 Squadron's surplus aircraft at the end of the year. The RAF's own version, the F-4M Phantom FGR2, entered service with No 228 OCU in July 1970, and FGR2s subsequently equipped Nos 2, 6, 14, 17, 19, 23, 29, 31, 41, 54, 56, 92 and 111 Squadrons. Several of these subsequently disbanded and re-formed with Jaguars. 118 F-4Ms were built for the RAF, all of them used for air defence by 1978 as the Jaguar undertook the ground-attack role.

The Imperial Iranian Air Force acquired the first of some 200 F-4Es between 1968 and 1977, deliveries beginning to the 360th Fighter Squadron in September 1968, and 29 RF-4Es were also delivered in 1971. Israel also received 204 F-4Es between 1969 and 1976, and these saw considerable action during the Yom Kippur War of 1973. Israel has also received at least six RF-4Es. 18 F-4D Phantoms were delivered to the Republic of Korea Air Force in 1969, followed by a further 18 on lease until the arrival of F-5As in 1975 and by 37 F-4Es, the last of which will be delivered in 1979. As the F-4EJ, the Phantom serves with the Japanese Air Self-Defence Force (Nos 301, 302, 303, 304 and 305 Squadrons), most of the 140 Japanese aircraft being licence-built by Mitsubishi and Kawasaki. 14 RF-4EJs were also supplied to Japan in 1974/75. The RAAF leased 24

F-4Es in 1970, these equipping Nos 1 and 6 Squadrons until the arrival (long delayed) of the F-111C, when the Phantoms were returned to the USA in June 1973.

Eighty-eight RF-4Es were delivered to the Luftwaffe in 1971, equipping Aufklärungs-geschwader 51 and 52, while 175 F-4Fs replaced the F-104s of JG 71, JG 74 and JBG 36, as well as the Fiat G-91s of JBG 36. The last German F-4F was delivered in April 1976. 36 F-4Cs were transferred to the Spanish Air Force in 1971-72, equipping Escaudrones 121 and 122, with four more F-4Cs and four RF-4Cs being delivered in 1978; 38 F-4Es were supplied to the Greek Air Force in 1974-76, followed by 18 more plus six RF-4Es in 1977-78; and the Turkish Air Force received 40 F-4Es between 1974 and 1976.

The Phantom will undoubtedly be best remembered for its combat career in Vietnam, where it proved extremely efficient as an interdictor and defence suppression aircraft. In the air superiority role, it accounted for the majority of MiG-21 'kills' achieved by the Americans. In June 1978 the number of Phantoms built or on order totalled 5,300.

McDonnell Douglas F-15 Eagle   USA

Role: Air Superiority Fighter
Operational: 1975-
Data: F-15A

Engines: Two 25,000lb thrust Pratt & Whitney F100-PW-100 turbofans.
Span: 42ft 9¾in
Length: 63ft 9in
Weight: Empty not available
56,000lb (max take-off)
Crew: 1
Max speed: Mach 2.5+
Absolute ceiling: 100,000ft
Range: 3,450miles (ferry, with FAST pack)
Weapons: One 20mm M61A-1 six barrel cannon; four AIM-9L Sidewinders; four AIM-7F Sparrow AAMs.

In 1965 the USAF requested funds for the development of a new air superiority fighter, and over the next four years designs were submitted by Fairchild Hiller, McDonnell Douglas and North American Rockwell. By this time the development programme had assumed great urgency, for the USAF possessed no operational aircraft capable of meeting the Soviet Air Force's MiG-25 interceptor on equal terms. In December 1969 McDonnell Douglas was selected as the prime airframe contractor and an order was placed for 20 development aircraft, comprising 18 single-seat F-15As and two TF-15A two-seat trainers. The first F-15A flew on 27 July 1972, and in March the following year McDonnell Douglas was authorised to build the first 30 operational aircraft. Over the next four years, annual Defense Procurement Bills authorised the production of further numbers of 62, 72, 135 and 108 aircraft, including 13 TF-15A trainers. The first F-15A Eagle was delivered to the USAF in November 1974 and deliveries of fully operational aircraft began the following year to the 57th and 58th Tactical Fighter Training Wings. By the end of 1977 Eagles also equipped the 1st, 49th and 36th Tactical Fighter Wings, the latter becoming the first F-15 unit to be deployed overseas (to Bitburg, Germany, in April 1977). The F-15 is also scheduled to equip the 33rd TFW in 1979. Four F-15As (refurbished development aircraft) were supplied to the Israeli Air Force in April 1977, and Israel subsequently ordered 25 more. In the Spring of 1978 plans were being made to build the F-15 under licence in Japan, with production envisaged of 109 F-15As and 14 TF-15As.

Although designed primarily as an air superiority fighter, the F-15 also has a substantial ground attack capability. Thanks to the use of two Fuel and Sensor Tactical Packs, each containing some 5,000lb of fuel, the aircraft has a ferry range of over 3,000 miles without the need for flight refuelling facilities, aiding rapid long-range deployment. In January/February 1975 the F-15 'Streak Eagle' captured eight time-to-height records, although some were later recaptured by the Russian E-266M (MiG-25).

Messerschmitt 109 (postwar)

Germany (Czech-built)

AVIA S199

Role: Single-Seat Fighter
Operational: 1945-57
Data: S199

Engines: One 1,350hp Junkers Jumo 211F
Span: 32ft 8½in
Length: 29ft 6in
Weight: 4,500lb (empty)
7,850lb (loaded)
Crew: 1
Max speed: 330mph at 24,250ft
Service ceiling: 31,170ft
Range: 350 miles
Weapons: Two 20mm MG 151 cannon in underwing gondolas; two 13mm machine guns above engine

In 1944 following heavy air attacks on Germany's aircraft production centres, it was decided to allocate part of the Messerschmitt Bf109G-14 production to the Prague-Cakovice plant, in Czechoslavakia, and enough parts were assembled to build 500 machines. Production continued after the collapse of

Germany, the fighter being given the Czech designation C10. Because of a shortage of Daimler-Benz engines only 20 single-seaters and two C110 two-seat trainers were completed, these entering service with the Czech Air Force as the S-99 and CS-99. The 1,350hp Junkers Jumo 211F engine was selected as an alternative powerplant, and with this engine the aircraft was redesignated S-199. The type equipped most Czech fighter units until the arrival of the first Soviet-built jet fighters, and was highly unpopular with its pilots, who dubbed it 'Mezec' (Mule). Its wing loading was 35lb st compared with 33.97lb sq ft for less than 330mph in level flight. Service ceiling was only 31,170ft, and maximum range was a hard-earned 528 miles with auxiliary fuel tank. In 1948 the newly-formed Israeli Air Force purchased 26 S199s, and these equipped No 101 Squadron until eventually replaced by Meteor F8s. The type saw combat during Israel's war of independence, but was generally inferior to the Spitfire LF16e used by the Egyptians. In Czechoslovakia, the S199 and the two-seater trainer version, the CS199, equipped National Security Guard units in small numbers until 1957.

MiG-9

USSR

Role: Single-Seat Day Fighter
Operational: 1946-49
NATO Code-Name: Fargo

Engines: Two 1,760lb thrust RD-20 (BMW 003) turbojets
Span: 40ft 1¾in
Length: 38ft 0¾in
Weight: 7,500lb (empty)
11,200lb (loaded)
Crew: 1
Max speed: 570mph at 16,000ft
Service ceiling: 40,500ft
Range: 680 miles (900 miles with underwing tanks)
Weapons: One 37mm Nudelman cannon mounted

on air intake central pylon; two Nudelmann-Suranov NS-23 23mm cannon on underside of nose

When the Soviet Union initiated a crash programme to develop jet fighters with the aid of captured German turbojet engines at the end of World War II the Soviet design bureaux produced only two viable projects. The first was Yakovlev's Yak-15; the second was the MiG-9, designed by Artem I. Mikoyan. Although the Yakovlev design was to be produced in much greater quantity, the MiG-9 was in fact the first type to reach squadron service, so becoming the first jet aircraft to be operated by the Soviet Air Force. Development was initiated in February 1945, the aircraft being initially known as the I-300. An all-metal mid-wing monoplane, it was powered by two 1,760lb thrust BMW 003 turbojets mounted side by side and exhausting under the rear fuselage. Mikoyan adopted the twin-jet arrangement in a bid to raise the aircraft's maximum speed to something in the order of 560mph; Yakovlev, on the other hand, chose a single installation, and early models of the Yak-15 suffered accordingly from being underpowered.

Construction of the prototype MiG-9 proceeded very quickly, the aircraft making its first flight on 24 April 1946 only 15 months after work was started. It made its first public appearance at Tushino only a week later, with test pilot A. N. Grinchik at the controls. During its early flights, the MiG-9 reached a maximum of 570mph at 16,000ft and climbed to

42,000ft. Unfortunately, Grinchik was killed in unknown circumstances on 11 July 1946, the flight test programme being taken over by M. L. Gallai and G. M. Shianov. On the whole, the flight tests revealed few serious problems, although there was some early trouble with nosewheel shimmy.

Production of a small series of MiG-9s was begun in the autumn of 1946 and first deliveries to squadrons of the IA-PVO began in December. Early in 1947, production MiG-9s were fitted with the uprated RD-21 engine and redesignated MiG-9F. The last batch of production aircraft had pressurised cockpits and carried the designation MiG-9FR. Some service MiG-9s carried drop tanks under the wingtips.

MiG-15

Role: Single-Seat Fighter
Operational: 1948-
NATO Code-Name: Fagot
Data: MiG-15B

Engines: One Klimov VK-1 turbojet rated at 5,935lb thrust (dry)
Span: 33ft 1in
Length: 36ft 4in
Weight: 8,320lb (empty)
11,268lb (normal loaded)
Crew: 1
Max speed: 683mph at sea level
Service ceiling: 51,000ft
Range: 1,200 miles with underwing tanks
Weapons: One Nudelman 37mm N-37 cannon (400rpm), two 23mm Nudelman-Rikhter NR-23 cannon (800rpm); two 500lb or two 1,000lb bombs carried underwing in the ground attack role

One of the most outstanding combat aircraft of the postwar years, Russia's famous MiG-15 fighter was also produced in greater numbers than any other machine of its type, some 18,000 having been built. Designed by a Russo-German team headed by Artem I. Mikoyan and Mikhail A. Gurevitch, it flew for the first time on 30 December 1947 and entered series production the following year. The first MiG-15s were powered by a 4,850lb thrust RD-45 turbojet (a Soviet copy of the Rolls-Royce Nene, 25 of which were purchased from Britain early in 1947). The first prototype crashed during testing, killing its pilot, and the second aircraft was extensively modified, with a strengthened wing featuring slight anhedral and boundary layer fences. Many first-line fighter units of the IA-PVO had re-equipped with the type by the end of 1948, and a number of improvements were made to the basic design. Airframe design progress, in fact, went hand-in-hand with engine development, and from November 1948 the MiG-15's fuselage was modified to accommodate an uprated version of the basic Nene designated VK-1 after the engine design bureau led by Vladimir Klimov. This engine had re-designed turbine blades, larger combustion chambers and developed 5,953lb thrust (6,750lb with water injection). This variant, designated MiG-15B, was serving in large numbers with the IA-PVO by the end of 1950, and deliveries to Russia's

USSR

satellite air forces began early in 1952.

The Korean War gave the Russians a golden opportunity to evaluate the MiG-15 under combat conditions. The fighter made its combat debut on 1 November 1950, when a flight of six MiG-15s attacked USAF Mustangs south of the Yalu River without doing any damage. Throughout the war — or at least to the beginning of 1953 — Soviet MiG-15 units undertook regular tours of combat duty over Korea, flying in conjunction with Chinese Communist and North Korean formations. In action, the MiG-15 proved to have a better acceleration, rate of climb and ceiling than its main opponent the F-86 Sabre, but it was a poor gun platform at high speed and it could be out-turned by the American fighter. Moreover, its armament of two 23mm and one 37mm cannon, intended for bomber interception, placed it at a disadvantage in action against other fighters, the guns having a slow rate of fire and lacking sufficient ammunition capacity. Nevertheless, in the hands of a skilled pilot the MiG-15 was a formidable opponent, and had more of its pilots over Korea enjoyed the same standard of training and experience as some of the Soviet formation leaders, the 14-to-1 kill ratio established by the UN Sabres would have been drastically reduced.

In 1949 a tandem two-seat trainer version, the MiG-15UTI, made its appearance. Powered by a RD-45F turbojet, this variant had all armament deleted. Since the installation of a second cockpit reduced internal fuel tankage, the MiG-15UTI was fitted with underwing fuel tanks, which were also standard on later models of the MiG-15B. During the Korean War, MiG-15s with auxiliary tanks occasionally penetrated as far south as the 38th Parallel.

Compared with its western contemporaries the MiG-15 was a robust and rudimentary aircraft, and this was reflected in its cockpit layout and equipment. The gunsight was a mechanical type with a maximum range setting of 2,650ft, radar ranging equipment only being included in models built after the autumn of 1952. The MiG-15s avionics were updated as a result of the lessons learned over Korea; standard equipment on the MiG-15B included a RSIU-3M VHF transceiver, and ARK-5 radio compass, and RV-2 or RV-10 radio altimeter, and an RSO IFF transponder.

The MiG-15 was built under licence in Communist China under the designation Shenyang F-2, and in Poland and Czechoslovakia, the Polish and Czech machines being designated LIM-1 and S-102. The two-seat MiG-15UTI was also built in Czechoslovakia under the designation CS-102. The fighter served with all Soviet satellite air forces and from 1955 was widely exported to countries within the Soviet sphere of influence. MiG-15s saw considerable action in the Middle East during the various Arab-Israeli conflicts, and were also used operationally over North Vietnam and in the Nigerian civil war.

MiG-17 USSR

Role: Fighter/Ground-Attack
Operational: 1952-
NATO Code-Name: Fresco
Data: Fresco-C

Engines: One 5,950lb thrust Klimov VK-1A turbojet (6,990lb with reheat)
Span: 36ft
Length: 40ft
Weight: 9,850lb (empty)
15,500lb (max loaded)
Crew: 1
Max speed: 656mph at 35,000ft
Service ceiling: 58,000ft
Range: 1,600 miles with max external fuel
Weapons: Three 23mm Nudelman-Rikhter cannon (Fresco-D: Eight 55mm unguided rockets in four underwing pods)

In 1949, the Mikoyan Design Bureau began work on a more refined version of the basic MiG-15bis design with the object of achieving a substantial all-round performance increase. Powered by a Klimov VK-1 turbojet, the modified aircraft (designated SI) flew in prototype form towards the end of 1949. It had a longer fuselage and greater sweepback than the MiG-15, its wings featuring a thinner section to improve compressibility characteristics. Initial flight testing was carried out by test Pilot I. T. Ivashchenko, and the Russians claimed that this pilot exceeded Mach 1 in level flight in the SI in February 1950, although in view of the available power and the aircraft's aerodynamic characteristics this seems unlikely. Service testing was carried out by test pilot G. A. Sedov, and several armament and equipment changes were made (as a result of Korean War experience with the MiG-15) before the type entered service as a day fighter with the IA-PVO in 1952 under the designation MiG-17, still powered by a VK-1 engine. This version was known as the Fresco-A under the NATO reporting system; the Fresco-B was similar, but with fuselage dive-brakes positioned further forward.

Known as the MiG-17P in Soviet AF service, the initial production version was replaced on the assembly line in 1954 by the MiG-17F (Fresco-C), which employed an afterburning VK-1A engine. The MiG-17F was built in larger numbers than any other variant and was widely exported, being supplied to Afghanistan, Albania, Bulgaria, Cuba, Egypt, Hungary, Indonesia, Iraq, Morocco, North Korea, North Vietnam, Rumania and Syria. It was also built under licence in Communist China, where it was known as the Shenyang F-4, in Poland as the LIM-5 and in Czechoslovakia as the S104. The version saw combat in the Middle East against Israel, in North Vietnam, and in Nigeria during the civil war with Biafra, the aircraft used in the latter instance belonging to the Egyptian Air Force. The next variant on the production line was the MiG-17PF (Fresco-D) all-weather fighter, with AI radar in a bullet-type fairing in the centre of the air intake and radar ranging equipment in an extended 'lip' above the intake. The MiG-17PFU (Fresco-E) was similar to the -D, but was not fitted with an afterburner and had provision for unguided rocket packs under the wings.

With the entry into service of more advanced types such as the MiG-19, the MiG-17 was progressively relegated to the ground-attack role, replacing the MiG-15 from 1955 onwards, and some Polish LIM-5s were fitted with twin-wheel main undercarriages and low pressure tyres for grass strip operation. Other modifications included thickened inboard wing sections housing the wheel wells and additional fuel tankage.

In the early 1960s the MiG-17 was serving in greater numbers than any other jet fighter in the world, and many are still in use in the 1970s as combat proficiency trainers.

MiG-19   USSR

Role: Fighter/Ground-Attack
Operational: 1955-
NATO Code-Name: Farmer
Data: Farmer-B

Engines: Two Klimov RD-6 (VK-9) rated at 6,170lb
thrust (7,850lb with reheat)
Span: 29ft 6in
Length: 41ft 4¾in
Weight: 12,132lb (empty)
18,630lb (normal loaded)
Crew: 1
Max speed: 902mph at 32,810ft
Service ceiling: 55,775ft
Range: 1,365 miles with external fuel
Weapons: Three 23mm Nudelman-Rikhter cannon;
four pods each containing eight 55mm air-to-air
rockets or two pods each with 19 55mm rockets;
two 220mm or 325mm air-to-air missiles; 210mm
rocket packs, bombs etc in the ground-attack role

In 1951 the Mikoyan Design Bureau began
construction of a prototype interceptor, a successor
to the MiG-15/-17 series, designed to exceed
Mach 1 in level flight. The new aircraft, designated
MiG-19, featured sharply-swept (55 degree) wings
and flew for the first time early in 1953, powered by
two 4,800lb thrust RD-5 engines with afterburners.
It was first seen publicly at Tushino in 1955, the year
of its service debut with the Soviet Air Force's
IA-PVO interceptor force. Apart from its more
advanced aerodynamic qualities, the first production
MiG-19 (Farmer-A) showed a number of other
improvements over earlier MiG jet fighters, including
a slab-type tailplane. The characteristic MiG
armament of two 23mm and one 37mm cannon,
however, was retained, together with an optical
gunsight. The next variant, Farmer-B, had two
uprated Klimov VK-9 turbojets and an armament of
three 23mm cannon; this was the major production
version, serving widely with the IA-PVO, the Tactical
Air Force and the Naval Air Arm. It was also built
under licence in Poland, Czechoslovakia and China,
where it was designated F-6. Some Chinese-built
aircraft were supplied to Pakistan and saw combat in
the conflict with India in December 1971.

The final production version, the Farmer-C, was
fitted with single-barrel 30mm revolver type cannon
in the wing roots, these proving more effective than
the earlier 23mm weapons. Its engines were
improved yet again, and it incorporated more
advanced AI radar. With the entry into service of the
MiG-21, the MiG-19 was progressively relegated to
the ground-attack role. A very versatile aircraft, the
MiG-19 introduced many Eastern Bloc air forces to
supersonic flight and enabled the Soviet Air Force to
retain parity with the USAF, being very narrowly
beaten into service by its American counterpart, the
F-100 Super Sabre.

MiG-21   USSR

Role: Interceptor
Operational: 1959-
NATO Code-Name: Fishbed
Data: Fishbed-J

Engines: One Tumansky R-13-300 turbojet rated at
11,240lb thrust (14,450lb with reheat)
Span: 23ft 5½in
Length: 44ft 2in
Weight: 14,500lb (empty)
20,500lb (max loaded)

Crew: 1
Max speed: 1,325mph at 36,000ft
Service ceiling: 57,400ft
Range: 1,150 miles with external fuel
Weapons: One 30mm NR-30 cannon; GP-9 pack
with two GSh-23 twin-barrel cannon under the
fuselage; two to four K-13A Atoll or Advanced Atoll
AAMs; variety of offensive external stores, including
ASMs, free-falling bombs and rocket packs

One of the most successful combat aircraft to
emerge since 1945, and a major export success

story for Russia's aviation industry, the MiG-21 was born on the drawing boards of the Mikoyan Design Bureau in 1953. Air combat experience of the Korean War had shown a need for a light, single-seat target defence interceptor with high supersonic manoeuvrability, and to meet this requirement Mikoyan built two prototypes, both of which were demonstrated at Tushino in June 1956. One, with sharply swept wings (NATO: Faceplate) did not proceed beyond the evaluation stage, the other aircraft, featuring a delta wing and designated E-5, being ordered into production instead. The initial production versions (Fishbed-A and -B) were built only in limited numbers, being short-range day fighters with a comparatively light armament of two 30mm NR-30 cannon, but the next variant, the MiG-21F Fishbed-C, carried two K-13 Atoll infra-red homing AAMs, and had an uprated Tumansky R-11 turbojet as well as improved avionics.

The MiG-21F which was the first major production version, entered service with the IA-PVO in 1960 and was progressively modified and updated over the years that followed. The MiG-21PF Fishbed-D was basically similar, but had an enlarged air intake to accommodate R1L (NATO: Spin Scan-A) centrebody search/track radar, providing limited all-weather interception capability. The MiG-21PF was the first variant to be fitted with rocket-assisted take-off gear, and late production aircraft (Fishbed-E) were fitted with a twin-barrel 23mm cannon in a GP-9 underbelly pack. Both Fishbed-D and -E were in large scale service with the Soviet Air Force, and some foreign air forces, by the middle of 1964. The MiG-21FL, which appeared in 1966, was the first export version of the MiG-21PF. Some 200 were either assembled or built under licence in India by Hindustan Aeronautics Ltd; the first example was delivered to the Indian Air Force in October 1970. The MiG-21PFS was similar to the Fishbed-D but with a flap-blowing system known as SPS, while the MiG-21PFM (Fishbed-F) embodied all the improvements incorporated in the PF and PFS. The Fishbed-G was an experimental VTOL aircraft, with a modified fuselage housing two vertically-mounted jet lift engines; another experimental 'one-off' MiG-21 was fitted with a scaled-down replica of the wing of the Tu-144 supersonic transport and had no tailplane.

The MiG-21PFMA Fishbed-J was the first multi-role version of the basic design, with four underwing pylons for offensive stores, a GP-9 gun pack and other refinements such as a zero-speed, zero-altitude ejection seat. The MiG-21M was similar, replacing the MiG-21FL on the HAL production line in India and entering service with the Indian Air Force in February 1973. The MiG-21R Fishbed-H was a tactical reconnaissance version of the -21PFMA, with cameras, sensors or ECM equipment in an external pod, while the MiG-21MF was a lighter version of the -21PFMA with a Tumansky R-13-300 turbojet. The MiG-21RF was the tactical reconnaissance version of the MiG-21MF. Also similar to the -21MF was the MiG-21SMT Fishbed-K, the main difference being the -K's deep dorsal spine. This variant was in widespread service with the Soviet and Warsaw Pack Air Forces in 1972.

In the early 1970s, the MiG-21 was virtually-redesigned, re-emerging as the MiG-21bis (Fishbed-L) multi-role air superiority fighter/ground-attack aircraft. The Fishbed-N was even further improved, with advanced electronics and a 16,535lb thrust Tumansky R-25 engine, and was standard Soviet Air Force equipment in 1978, replacing several earlier models.

The MiG-21U (NATO: Mongol) is a two-seat trainer version. A record-breaking version of this type, which set up several women's records in 1965, was designated E-33, while other aircraft in the MiG-21F series, specially modified for record attempts, were designated E-66 and E-76. In the 1960s, the E-33/66/76 established a dozen FAI-recognised international speed and height records.

In 1978 the MiG-21 was the most widely-used jet fighter in service anywhere, equipping some 25 air forces. Apart from India, the type is built in Czechoslovakia and China, where it is designated F-8. Egypt and Syria have over 200 MiG-21s each, while Iraq has more than 100. The type has seen considerable action, mainly in the Middle East and India, and has been used in various African guerilla conflicts in the 1970s. Apart from those listed above, countries using the MiG-21 include Afghanistan, Algeria, Bangladesh, Bulgaria, Cuba, Finland, East Germany, Hungary, Indonesia, North Korea, Poland, Romania, South Yemen, Tanzania (Chinese-built F-8s), North Vietnam, Yemen Arab Republic and Yugoslavia.

MiG-23/27   USSR

Role: Air Superiority Fighter
Operational: 1972-
NATO Code-Name: Flogger
Photo: MiG-2BB
Data: MiG-23 (estimated)

Engines: One unidentified turbojet developing an estimated 14,330lb thrust (20,500lb with reheat)
Span: 46ft 9in (spread)
26ft 9$\frac{1}{2}$in (fully swept)
Length: 55ft 1$\frac{1}{2}$in
Weight: 33,000lb (max loaded)
Crew: 1
Max speed: Mach 2.3 at height
Service ceiling: 59,000ft
Range: 1,300 miles with external fuel
Weapons: One 23mm GSh-23 twin-barrel cannon in belly pack; four 'Apex' or 'Aphid' AAMs on underwing pylons

First seen publicly in July 1967 when it flew in prototype form at Domodedovo, Mikoyan's MiG-23 variable-geometry fighter underwent considerable redesign before the production version entered service with first-line units of the IA-PVO in 1971,

and even then it was the Spring of 1972 before the type became fully operational. Code-named Flogger-B, the first production variant was identified in service with two Soviet IA-PVO regiments in East Germany in 1973/74 and about 1,000 are thought to have been delivered by the autumn of 1977. Soviet designation for the Flogger-B is MiG-23S, and an export version (Flogger-E) has been supplied to the Egyptian, Iraqi, Libyan and Syrian Air Forces. The MiG-23U Flogger-C is a tandem two-seat trainer version retaining full combat capability.

A ground-attack version, designated MiG-27 and code-named Flogger-D, has an uprated engine developing an estimated 24,250lb thrust with reheat and features a redesigned forward fuselage, with a sharply tapered nose housing a laser rangefinder in place of the MiG-23's ogival radome. An under-fuselage pack houses a six-barrel 23mm cannon, and there are five underwing points for external tactical stores. The export version of the MiG-27, code-named Flogger-F, has been supplied to the Egyptian Air Force, but this retains the engine and fixed armament of the MiG-23.

In the Spring of 1978, a MiG-23 interceptor of the IA-PVO forced down a South Korean Boeing 707 airliner which had strayed off course over North Russia.

MiG-25   USSR

Role: Interceptor/Strike Fighter
Operational: 1967-
Nato Code-Name: Foxbat
Photo and Data: Foxbat-A

Engines: Two Tumansky R-31 single-shaft turbojets rated at 24,250lb thrust each with reheat
Span: 45ft 9in
Length: 73ft 2in
Weight: 44,100lb (normal)
79,800lb (max take-off)
Crew: 1
Max speed: 2,110mph (Mach 3.2) at 45,000ft
Service ceiling: 80,000ft
Range: 1,400 miles (normal)
Weapons: Four 'Acrid' AAMs on underwing pylons

In the late 1950s, the Soviet Union placed considerable emphasis on the development of a new interceptor to counter the potential threat posed by

the North American B-70 Valkyrie Mach 3 strategic bomber. The design selected was the MiG-25, and work on it continued unchecked — with emphasis on its development as a strike and reconnaissance aircraft as well as an interceptor — even after the B-70 bomber project was cancelled in March 1961. In April 1965 one of the MiG-25 prototypes — carrying the designation E-266 and flown by test pilot Alexander Fedotov—set up a 1,000km closed circuit speed record of 1,441.5mph carrying a 2,000kg payload at a height of 69,000-72,000ft, and on 5 October 1967 Fedotov set up a payload-to-height record of 98,349ft with a 2,000kg payload in the same aircraft following a rocket-assisted take-off. The E-266 was now identified with a twin-engined, twin-finned fighter first seen publicly at the Domodedovo air display in July 1967 and was allocated the NATO reporting name Foxbat. The official designation MiG-25 was confirmed some time later.

More records fell to the E-266 in October 1967, when M. Komarov set a speed record of 1,852mph over a 500km closed circuit and P. Ostapenko raised the 1,000km closed circuit record to 1,814.81mph while carrying a 2,000kg payload. More indications of the E-266/MiG-25's performance were to follow over the next few years. On 8 April 1973, Fedotov set up a new 100km closed circuit record of 1,618.734mph, and on 25 July that year he established a new World absolute height record of 118,898ft. Later that same day he also climbed to 115,584ft with a 2,000kg payload. Three time-to-height records were also set up by the E-266 on 4 June 1973; 20,000m in 2min 49.8sec, 25,000m in 3min 12.6sec, and 30,000m in 4min 3.86sec. These three records were recaptured by the McDonnell Douglas F-15 Streak Eagle early in 1975, but two were recaptured by an E-266M — a development with uprated engines — in May 1975.

In September 1976, Western experts gained a unique opportunity to study the basic interceptor version of the MiG-25 (Foxbat-A) when Lt Viktor Belenko defected to Japan in one. The Foxbat-A's equipment included Fox Fire nose radar and underwing attachments for four 'Acrid' AAMs, with target illuminating radar in the nose or the wingtip anti-flutter bodies. Although bulky, the fire control system (with a 600kW power source) had a limited range, the emphasis being on counter-ECM. The aircraft's own ECM was of a high standard, although the electronics featured suprisingly little solid-state circuitry. Cockpit layout was good, with instrumentation kept to a minimum.

The basic reconnaissance version of the MiG-25 is the MiG-25R (Foxbat-B), with five camera ports and side looking airborne radar. This version carries no armament and has a slightly reduced span. A further reconnaissance variant, the Foxbat-D, carries surveillance radar only. In 1971-72, four MiG-25Rs — which had been airlifted to Egypt in Antonov An-22 transports in April 1971 — carried out high-speed, high-level reconnaissance missions over the Sinai Peninsula, and Israeli Air Force Phantoms failed to intercept them. The aircraft remained in Egypt until September 1975. Since that time, MiG-25Rs have been reported in Eastern Germany and Syria.

The MiG-25U is a trainer version, with a redesigned nose accommodating a second cockpit forward of the original. It is thought that the MiG-25U was the aircraft, designated E-133, in which Svetlana Savitskaya established a women's world speed record of 1,667.412mph on 2 June 1975.

Mitsubishi F-1   Japan

Role: Close Support Fighter
Operational: 1978-

Engines: Two Rolls-Royce Turbomeca Adour turbofans rated at 4,710lb thrust (7,070lb with reheat)
Span: 25ft 10¾in
Length: 58ft 6¾in
Weight: 14,017lb (empty)
30,146lb (max loaded)
Crew: 1

Max speed: Mach 1.6 at 36,000ft
Service ceiling: 50,000ft
Range: 1,610 miles (ferry, with external tanks)
Weapons: One JM-61 multi-barrel 20mm cannon; four points underwing and one under fuselage for bombs, rockets and fuel tanks

Designed to replace the F-86 Sabre in the Japanese Air Self-Defence Force, the F-1 strike fighter was developed from the T-2 supersonic trainer. The second and third production T-2s were converted as

prototypes, flying in June 1975, and the aircraft was officially designated F-1 in November 1976. Orders for 59 F-1s had been placed by mid-1978, and, with plans to equip three squadrons with the type, this total will probably rise to 70 in the early 1980s. The

first production F-1 was delivered to the JASDF in September 1977, and the first operational F-1 unit — No 3 Squadron of the 3rd Air Wing — formed in March 1978 with 18 aircraft.

Myasishchev M-4 Molot USSR

Role: Strategic Bomber/Reconnaissance
Operational: 1955-
NATO Code-Name: Bison
Data: Bison-A

Engines: Four 19,180lb thrust Mikulin AM-3D turbojets
Span: 165ft 7½in
Length: 154ft 10in
Weight: Empty not known
350,000lb (loaded max take-off)
Crew: 6-13, depending on mission
Max speed: 560mph at 36,000ft
Service ceiling: 45,000ft
Range: 7,000 miles at 520mph with 10,000lb bomb load
Weapons: Ten 23mm cannon in five twin-gun turrets; up to 20,000lb of conventional or nuclear bombs

Contemporary with the turboprop-engined Tu-95 Bear, Vladimir M. Myasishchev's four-jet M-4 Molot (Hammer) was never an outstanding success in the long-range strategic bombing role for which it was designed, and it was Tupolev's Tu-16 and Tu-95 which formed the mainstay of the Soviet Air Force's strategic bombing squadrons in the 1950s and 1960s. Nevertheless, it was the Soviet Union's first (and only) operational four-jet bomber, and was comparable with early versions of the B-52

Stratofortress. First seen publicly at Tushino in May 1954, the Bison entered service with the Soviet Air Force a year later and appears to have fallen short of performance requirements, only about 150 having been produced. The first variant, the Bison-A, had a ceiling of only 45,000ft, calling for a heavy defensive armament of 10 23mm cannon. According to US Intelligence sources, 85 Bison-As were still serving with the Soviet long-range bomber force in 1975, and these aircraft were being progressively converted to the long-range tanker role in support of the new 'Backfire' supersonic bomber force. About 50 Bisons are known to have been so converted, equipped with a hose-reel unit in the bomb bay.

The Bison-B maritime reconnaissance version entered service with the Soviet Naval Air Arm in 1963-64, and has a solid nose radome instead of the Bison-A's glazed bomb-aimer's position, together with many fuselage blisters housing electronic surveillance and intelligence-gathering equipment. Armament is six 23mm cannon. The Bison-C is similar, but has a longer nose housing built-in search radar and a prone visual bomb-aiming/observation station is retained aft of the radar installation. A stripped-down Bison-C, with the designation 201-M, established seven payload-to-height records in 1959. About 50 Bison-Bs and -Cs are thought to be operational with the Soviet Naval Air Arm (1978). A few other aircraft, mostly early-model Bison-As, are reported to be in use as test-beds for engines and other equipment.

North American AJ Savage USA

Role: Carrier-Borne Attack
Operational: 1949-60
Photo: AJ-1
Data: AJ-2

Engines: Two Pratt & Whitney Double Wasp R-2800-48 radials rated at 2,400hp each, and one Allison J33-A-10 turbojet rated at 4,600lb thrust
Span: 71ft 5in
Length: 63ft 1in
Weight: 27,558lb (empty)
55,000lb (loaded)
Crew: 3
Max speed: 425mph at sea level
Service ceiling: 37,000ft
Range: 3,000 miles (max)
Weapons: Two 20mm cannon and up to 12,000lb of bombs

The world's first heavy carrier-borne attack aircraft, the North American Savage was also the first naval aircraft designed to carry nuclear weapons. North American Aviation, Inc, received a contract to build three XAJ-1 prototypes in June 1946 and the first of these flew on 2 July 1948. 28 production aircraft were ordered by the US Navy as the AJ-1 in 1949, followed by an additional 15 the following year. Service deliveries began in September 1949 to Composite Squadron VC-5, and on 21 April 1950 the commanding officer of this unit made the first carrier take-off by a Savage from the USS *Coral Sea*. Carrier qualifications were completed in August and the type was declared fully operational. The AJ-2 was a developed version with increased power, while the AJ-2P photographic reconnaissance variant carried 18 cameras and electronic surveillance equipment. The XA2J-1 was an experimental version with two Allison T40-A-6 turboprops. The AJ-1/2 Savage, production of which reached 143 aircraft, was powered by two Pratt & Whitney R-2800 piston engines under the wings and a single Allison J33 turbojet in the rear fuselage. In the turboprop-powered XA2J-1, the J33 was removed and replaced by a gun turret with radar direction. The Savage remained in first-line US Navy service until January 1960, the last units to use it (AJ2-P) being VAP-62 and VCP-61. After retirement, some Savages were converted to fire-fighting duties, with a bomb-bay tank housing 2,000gal of chemical.

North American B-45 Tornado USA

Role: Tactical Light Bomber
Operational: 1948-59
Data: B-45C

Engines: Four General Electric J47-GE-15 turbojets rated at 5,200lb thrust each
Span: 89ft 6in
Length: 74ft
Weight: 66,000lb (empty)
82,600lb (loaded)
Crew: 3
Max speed: 550mph
Service ceiling: 40,000ft
Range: 1,200 miles

Weapons: Two .5in machine guns in tail position; up to 18,000lb of bombs

Flown for the first time on 17 March 1947, the XB-45 Tornado was the first American multi-jet bomber to be ordered into production. The initial production version was the B-45A and 96 examples were built. The B-45C was an updated version of the B-45A and the RB-45C, which was equipped for in-flight refuelling, was a high altitude photo-reconnaissance variant with five camera stations. The first unit to re-equip with the Tornado was the 47th Bombardment Wing, which exchanged its B-26s for the new type in 1948. The 47th Wing was deployed to the United Kingdom in 1952, forming part of the US Third Air Force's 49th Air Division.

North American F-51 Mustang (postwar)　　USA

Role: Fighter-Bomber
Operational: 1942-65
Data: F-51D

Engines: One 1,490hp Packard Merlin V-1650-7 in-line
Span: 37ft
Length: 32ft 3in
Weight: 7,125lb (empty)
11,600lb (loaded)
Crew: 1
Max speed: 437mph at 25,000ft
Service ceiling: 41,900ft
Range: 2,080 miles (max)
Weapons: Four or six .5in machine guns; up to 2,000lb of bombs or ten 5inch RPs

At the end of World War II, the principal variant of the famous Mustang fighter-bomber was the P-51D, of which 7,965 were built. Two further variants, the P-51H (555 built) and the P-51K (1,337 built) were too late to see operational service. Mustang production continued in Australia, where the Commonwealth Aircraft Corporation assembled 80 P-51Ds under the designation CA-17 Mustang Mk 20, the first of which flew in May 1945; other Australian variants were the Mustang Mk 21 (15 built), the Mk 22, a Mk 21 converted to the photo-reconnaissance role (13 built) and the Mk 23, which was powered by a R-R Merlin 66 or 70 engine (67 built). The RAF Mustangs were replaced by Vampires in 1949-51.

Canada also purchased 100 P-51Ds in 1945, and these served with the RCAF until 1956; Nationalist China equipped three squadrons with the type in 1946-47; Cuba received some F-51Ds in 1947 and these served until they were replaced by Soviet equipment in 1960; the Republic of Dominica bought 32 examples from Sweden in October 1952 and these remained in service until 1962; between 30 and 40 ex-Dutch East Indies AF machines were turned over to Indonesia in 1950, being replaced by Russian aircraft from 1959; Guatemala, Haiti and Honduras used small numbers of F-51Ds until the mid-1960s; Israel purchased 25 ex-Swedish AF machines in 1952, and these performed valuable service in the ground-attack role during the Sinai Campaign of 1956; 48 were used by the Italian Air Force between 1948 and 1953; South Korea used the type from 1950 to 1960; 30 were delivered to the RNZAF in 1945-6; Nicaragua and the Philippines used the F-51D between 1947 and 1964, and 1946 and 1960 respectively; Sweden bought 50 examples in 1945 and 90 the following year; 100 were acquired in Switzerland in 1945, serving until 1956; and Uruguay used the Mustang until 1960.

The F-51D served valiantly during the early months of the Korean War, serving with the 18th Fighter Bomber Group, the 35th Fighter Interceptor Group, No 77 Squadron RAAF and No 2 Squadron South African AF, as well as with the Republic of Korea AF Combat Wing.

North American F-82 Twin Mustang　　USA

Role: Long-Range Escort Fighter
Operational: 1946-52
Data: F-82G

Engines: Two Allison V-1710-143/145 engines of 1,600hp
Span: 51ft 3in
Length: 42ft 5in
Weight: 14,105lb (empty)
25,891lb (loaded)
Crew: 2
Max speed: 461mph at 21,000ft
Service ceiling: 38,900ft
Range : 2,240 miles
Weapons: Six 0.5in machine guns, with provision for 25 5in rockets, four 1,000lb or two 2,000lb bombs in wing racks

The North American F-82 Twin Mustang, conceived in 1943 to meet a requirement for a long-range escort fighter to serve in the Pacific theatre of war, was destined to become the last propeller-driven fighter ordered by the USAF. Design was begun in January 1944, the aircraft consisting basically of two P-51H Mustang fuselages joined together by a constant chord wing centre section and a rectangular tailplane. The pilot was housed in the port fuselage, the co-pilot in the starboard.

The first of two prototypes, designated XP-82, flew on 15 April 1945, powered by two Packard Merlin V-1650-23/25 engines developing 1,860hp. The third prototype, the XP-82A, had Allison V-1710-119s, with the propellers rotating in the same direction. 500 production aircraft were ordered, armed with six 0.5in (12.7mm) machine guns and wing racks for four 1,000lb or two 2,000lb bombs, 25 5in rockets or a central pod with eight more machine-guns, but this order was cut back to only 20 machines following the end of the Pacific war. One of these, named Betty Jo (44-65168) established several distance records after the war, and two others were completed as experimental night-fighters, the P-82C with SCR-720 AI radar and the P-82D with APS-4, housed in a large nacelle attached to the wing centre section and projecting forward of the engines. Other equipment included an APN-1 radar altimeter and APS-13 tail warning radar, and the radar operator was housed in the starboard cockpit.

In March 1947 orders were placed for an additional 250 Twin Mustangs. The first 100 of these (46-255 to 354) were P-82E (F-82E) escort and ground-attack fighters. Of the remainder, 91 were completed as P-82F night-fighters with APS-4

radar and 59 as P-82Gs with SCR-720 radar, all three variants being powered by Allison V-1710-143/145 engines.

The F-82 Twin Mustang (the 'F' replacing the 'P' prefix in June 1948) replaced the P-61 Black Widow with the USAF Air Defense Command, and several squadrons were deployed overseas with the 5th Air Force in Japan. When the Korean War broke out in June 1950, the 4th Fighter Squadron (All-Weather) was operational at Naha on Okinawa, the 68th Fighter Squadron (All-Weather) at Itazuke on Kyushu, and the 339th Fighter Squadron (All-Weather) at Yokota, near Tokyo. During the first days of the war, these units covered the air evacuation of US civilians from Korea, the 4th and 339th Squadrons forming the 347th (Provisional) Fighter Group at Itazuke. On 27 June 1950, an F-82G of the 68th Fighter Squadron was credited with the destruction of the first enemy aircraft in the Korean hostilities.

Following their withdrawal from the Far East, 14 F-82F and F-82G Twin Mustangs were winterised, redesignated F-82H, and assigned to Air Defense Command in Alaska. In addition to those listed above, USAF units operating the various marks of F-82 were: the 27th Fighter Escort Group, Strategic Air Command (comprising the 522nd, 523rd and 524th Squadrons;) the 51st Fighter Interceptor Group (comprising the 16th, 25th and 26th Squadrons); the 52nd All-Weather Fighter Group (2nd and 5th Squadrons); the 325th All-Weather Fighter Group (317th, 318th and 319th Squadrons); the 449th Fighter Interceptor Squadron in Alaska; and the 84th Reserve Fighter Group (496th, 497th and 498th Squadrons).

North American F-86 Sabre — USA

Role: Interceptor
Operational: 1948-
Photo: F-86H
Data: F-86K

Engines: One 5,425lb thrust (7,450lb with reheat) General Electric J47-GE-17B turbojet
Span: 37ft 1in
Length: 41ft
Weight: 12,000lb (empty)
18,500lb (loaded)
Crew: 1
Max speed: 680mph at 10,000ft
Service ceiling: 48,000ft
Range: 900 miles
Weapons: Four 20mm M-39 cannon and two sidewinder AAMs

Without doubt one of the greatest combat aircraft of all time, North American's thoroughbred F-86 Sabre had its origin in a 1944 USAF requirement for a medium range day fighter. At that time, North American were working on the design of the XFJ-1 Fury carrier-borne jet fighter, and a version of this was offered to the USAF, minus its naval equipment. Three prototypes were ordered in May 1945 under the designation XP-86. Like its naval counterpart, the XP-86 had had a straight wing, but with the availability of captured German aerodynamic research material it was decided to adopt swept flying surfaces, and this called for substantial redesign. In December 1946 the USAF placed a contract for 33 P-86-1-NA Sabres, and the prototype swept-wing XP-86 flew for the first time on 1 October 1947, powered by a 3,750lb thrust General Electric J35-C-3 turbojet. The second prototype, fitted with a more powerful J47-GE-1, flew on 18 May 1948 and was in fact the first Sabre off the production line, deliveries of production aircraft to the USAF beginning 10 days later. The first operational Sabre unit was the 94th Squadron of the 1st Fighter Wing, which equipped with the F-86A-5-NA in January 1949. By this time, the initial production order for 188 Sabres had been supplemented by further orders for 333 F-86As, and the USAF re-equipment programme was accelerated following the news that the Sabre's Soviet counterpart, the MiG-15, had arrived in China in July 1950, the month after the outbreak of the Korean War. In November, the 4th Fighter Interceptor Group arrived in Japan with its F-86As and was soon operating from Kimpo in South Korea. On 17 December the Sabres scored their first kill when

Lt-Col Bruce Hinton of the 336th Fighter Interceptor Squadron destroyed a MiG-15 over Sinuiju, and during the next $2\frac{1}{2}$ years the Sabres destroyed 810 enemy aircraft in combat, 792 of them MiG-15s, for the loss of 78 of their own number.

In December 1950, production of the F-86A Sabre ended with the 554th aircraft, and development of the basic design was well under way. The next two variants were the F-86C heavy penetration fighter and the F-86D all-weather interceptor (the F-86B having been a proposed variant with larger wheels). In fact, the F-86C which was powered by a P&W XJ48-P-1 turbojet was so extensively redesigned that it was redesignated YF-93A. The USAF ordered 118 production F-93As, but this was cancelled and only two prototypes flew. The F-86D Sabre was also greatly modified, having a large nose radome, a strengthened wing and larger fuselage and vertical tail surfaces. The first of two YF-86D prototypes flew on 22 December 1949 and an initial order for 122 production aircraft was placed early in 1950. During its development, this variant was briefly designated F-95A. The F-86D was fitted with the Hughes AN/APX-6 radar and E-4 fire control system, which computed the collision course intercept and automatically lowered the pack housing 24 2.75in Mighty Mouse rockets, firing the missiles at the correct range. 2,201 F-86Ds were subsequently built.

While the F-86D was still under development, North American fitted power-operated controls and an all-flying tail to two F-86As, and the modified aircraft entered production as the F-86E. It was externally similar to the late production F-86A and 396 aircraft were built, the type being replaced on the production line by the F-86F in April 1952. This variant, which saw action in Korea, was fitted with a 6,100lb thrust J47-GE-27 turbojet and had a modified wing leading edge to increase combat efficiency. Production ran to 2,247 examples. The F-86G was a proposed version of the F-86D with a J47-GE-33 turbojet, subsequently abandoned, and the next variant on the production line was the F-86H, a specialised fighter-bomber which was heavier than previous models and which was developed alongside the US Navy's FJ-3 Fury. The first of two YF-86H prototypes flew on 30 April 1953, and 450 production aircraft were subsequently delivered to the USAF. The F-86H was the first American-built Sabre variant to be armed with four 20mm M-39 cannon in place of the more usual armament of six .5in machine guns, although the latter were retained on the first production batch.

The next version was the F-86K; the designation F-86I was never allocated and F-86J was applied to the Canadair-built Sabre Mk 3. The F-86K was essentially a simplified F-86D intended primarily for the NATO air forces and was fitted with four 20mm cannon in place of the rocket pack. In the early 1960s the F-86K was probably the most effective single-seat all-weather fighter in the world. A total of 296 was built by North American and a further 231 under licence by Fiat. F-86Ks equipped two Luftwaffe wings, the Armee de l'Air's 13e Escadre, the Italian Air Force's 1° Stormo, Nos 700, 701 and 702 Squadrons of the RNethAF, and Nos 334, 337 and 339 Squadrons of the Norwegian Air Force. The F-86L was an updated version of the F-86D with a modifed wing and Data Link equipment.

On 9 August 1950, the first flight took place of an F-86A Sabre assembled by Canadair and designated CL-13 Sabre Mk 1. The production model, the Sabre Mk 2, featured the same modifications as the F-86E. 350 were built, of which 60 were acquired by the USAF and three by the RAF. Most of the RCAF Mk 2s were transferred to Greece and Turkey in 1954-55, each country receiving 107 aircraft. The Sabre Mk 3 was powered by a 6,000lb thrust Orenda 1 turbojet and served as a test-bed for the Mk 5 development programme, while the Sabre Mk 4 was an F-86E with a modified cockpit layout. Beginning in late 1952 the RAF received 427 Mk 4s and these equipped Nos 3, 4, 20, 26, 66, 67, 71, 92, 93, 112, 130 and 234 Squadrons for some three years until

they were replaced by the Hunter, when 188 were transferred to Italy and 121 to Yugoslavia. The Orenda-powered Sabre Mk 5, which showed a substantial performance increase over earlier variants, flew in July 1953; 370 were built, of which 76 were supplied to the Luftwaffe in 1957. The Sabre Mk 6, which flew in November 1954, was also powered by an Orenda. The RCAF received 390. Six were supplied to Colombia, 34 to South Africa and 225 to West Germany, 90 of the latter being transferred to Pakistan in 1966. Various other Sabre projects were studied by Canadair, but the Mk 6 was the last series production variant.

The Sabre was also built under licence in Australia by the Commonwealth Aircraft Corporation, a 7,500lb thrust Rolls-Royce Avon RA7 turbojet being installed in an F-86F airframe. The prototype Avon-powered Sabre flew for the first time on 3 August 1953, and the first production CA-27 Sabre Mk 30 was delivered to the RAAF on 30 August 1954. 20 Mk 30s were built, followed by 19 Mk 31s with Avon 20 engines. The major Australian production version was the Mk 32, powered by an Avon 26, and this equipped Nos 3, 75 and 77 Squadrons until replaced by the Mirage III. Armament was two 30mm Aden cannon and two Sidewinder AAMs, and an underwing load of up to 1,200lb of bombs or rockets could be carried in the close support role.

The TF-86F was a two-seat transonic trainer version which flew in August 1954, but which did not enter production.

North American FJ-1 Fury

Role: Carrier-Borne Single-Seat Fighter
Operational: 1947-49

Engines: One 4,000lb thrust J35-A-4 turbojet
Span: 38ft 1in
Length: 33ft 7in
Weight: 8,843lb (empty)
15,115 (normal loaded)
Crew: 1
Max speed: 547mph at 9,000ft
Service ceiling: 47,000ft
Range: 1,400 miles max at 348mph
Weapons: Six 0.5inch machine guns in forward fuselage

Although its operational career was short, the North American FJ-1 Fury has an assured place in aviation history not only as the first American jet fighter to operate from a carrier in squadron strength, but also as the parent of one of the most famous jet fighters of all time — the F-86 Sabre. The basic design of the Fury was conceived in 1944 before German data on sweepback became available, and the North American project — bearing the company designation NA-134 — featured conventional straight flying surfaces. Three prototypes were ordered in January 1945 under the designation XFJ-1, and 100 production aircraft — subsequently reduced to 30 — were ordered on 18 May 1945 for the United States Navy. On that same day, the USAAF ordered three prototypes of the basically similar NA-140, a projected medium-range day fighter which could

USA

also be used for escort and dive bombing, under the service designation XP-86. This, substantially redesigned and with swept surfaces, was to become the Sabre.

The Navy's XFJ-1 flew for the first time on 27 November 1946, powered by a 3,820lb thrust General Electric J35-GE-2 turbojet. Early the following year one of the Fury prototypes attained Mach 0.87 in a dive, the highest speed attained by an American fighter up to that time. Production FJ-1 Furies, the first of which was delivered to Navy Squadron VF-51 at San Diego, California, towards the end of 1947, differed from the prototype aircraft in having an Allison-built J35-A-4 turbojet rated at 4,000lb thrust and leading edge extensions at the wing root.

On 29 February 1948, FJ-1 Furies of VF-51 set up three records, flying the 1,025 miles from Seattle to Los Angeles in 1hr 58min 7 sec at an average speed of 521mph, the 1,135 miles from Seattle to San Diego in 2hr 12min 54sec at an average of 511.8mph and the 690 miles from Seattle to San Diego in 1hr 24min, an average speed of 492.6mph. The following month, the Furies of VF-51 completed their carrier trials aboard the USS *Boxer*. The FJ-1 remained in first-line service until 1949, when it was replaced by more advanced types such as the Grumman Panther.

North American FJ-2/FJ-4 Fury
USA

Role: Carrier-Borne Fighter-Bomber
Operational: 1954-62
Photo: AF-IE
Data: FJ-4B

Engines: One 7,700lb Wright J65-W-16A turbojet
Span: 39ft 1in
Length: 37ft 6in
Weight: 12,000lb (empty)
19,000lb (normal loaded)
Crew: 1
Max speed: 715mph at sea level
Service ceiling: 45,000ft
Range: 2,770 miles with max external fuel
Weapons: Four 20mm Mk 12 cannon; up to
7,000lb of underwing offensive stores

In 1951, the US Navy Bureau of Aeronautics asked North American Aviation to 'navalise' two F-86E Sabre airframes for carrier trials, as the Korean War was proving that existing carrier fighters were inferior to the MiG-15. Designated XFJ-2, the first navalised aircraft flew on 19 February 1952, and the second aircraft carried an armament of four 20mm cannon in place of the F-86's .5in machine guns. Carrier trials aboard the USS *Midway* were completed in August 1952 and the type entered full

production for the US Navy. The first unit to receive the FJ-2 was VMF-122 Marine Fighter Squadron, in January 1954. Production FJ-2s differed from the prototypes in several respects, having a modified wing structure and hydraulic wing folding gear. In the spring of 1954 the FJ-2 gave way on the production line to the FJ-3, powered by a 7,220lb thrust Wright J65-W-3 turbojet and later by the J65-W-16. The last variant was the FJ-4, which incorporated so many new design features that it was virtually a new aircraft. The fuselage was deeper than that of the FJ-3, with a prominent dorsal spine, and the main undercarriage was similar to that of the F-100 Super Sabre. The wing planform had a greater chord and embodied a number of refinements, including large-chord flaps and inboard 'flaperons'. The FJ-4 had provision for a wide variety of underwing stores and a further variant, the FJ-4B — which flew for the first time on 4 December 1956 — was developed specifically for low-level attack operations, featuring a good deal of structural strengthening and a low-altitude bombing system. The last of 1,115 Furies was delivered to the US Navy in May 1958 and the FJ-4B remained in first-line service until September 1962, the last unit to use it being Attack Squadron VA-216. In April 1959 an FJ-4B unit, VA-212 (USS *Lexington*) became the first to deploy overseas with Bullpup ASMs.

North American F-100 Super Sabre
USA

Role: Tactical Fighter-Bomber
Operational: 1954-
Data: F-100D

Engines: One Pratt & Whitney J57-P-21A turbojet rated at 11,700lb thrust (19,950lb with reheat)
Span: 38ft 9½in
Length: 54ft 3in
Weight: 14,000lb (empty)
29,762lb (normal loaded)
Crew: 1
Max speed: 924mph at 36,000ft
Service ceiling: 51,000ft
Range: 1,500 miles max with external fuel
Weapons: One Mk 7, Mk 38 or Mk 43 nuclear weapon, or six 1,000lb bombs, or two Bullpup missiles, or 24 HVAR rockets. Interceptor version: Four Pontiac M-39E cannon

In February 1949 the North American design team began work on redesigning the F-86 Sabre with the aim of evolving a fighter that could reach and sustain supersonic speeds in level flight. Originally known as the Sabre 45, the new aircraft bore little resemblance to its predecessor, having a contoured, low-drag fuselage and wings and tail surfaces swept at an angle of 45 degrees. On 1 November 1951 the USAF awarded a contract for two YF-100A prototypes and 110 F-100A production aircraft; the first prototype flew on 25 May 1953 and exceeded Mach 1 on its maiden flight, powered by a Pratt & Whitney XJ57-P-7 turbojet. On 29 October this aircraft raised the World Speed Record to 755.149mph.

The first F-100A Super Sabres were delivered to the 479th Fighter Day Wing at George AFB, California, in September 1954, but were grounded in November following a series of unexplained crashes. It was established that the vertical tail surfaces were too small to maintain control during certain manoeuvres and so they were redesigned with 27% more area, the wingspan also being increased by just over 2ft. With these modifications the F-100A began flying operationally again in February 1955 and 203 were subsequently built, of which 45 (brought up to F-100D standard) were later delivered to the Nationalist Chinese Air Force.

The F-100B was an all-weather fighter project, later redesignated F-107, and the next series production variant was the F-100C, which flew for the first time in January 1955. Capable of carrying out both ground-attack and interception missions, the F-100C began to equip the 322nd Fighter Day Group in July 1955, and on 20 August the first production F-100C raised the World Speed Record to 822.135mph. The F-100C underwent various equipment changes during its career, variants being designated F-100C-1-NA to F-100C-25-NA. Total production was 451, of which 260 were supplied to the Turkish Air Force. The F-100C-10-NH, of which 25 were produced at North American's Columbus plant, was a special aerobatic version which equipped the 'Thunderbirds' aerobatic team.

The F-100D, of which 940 were built at Los Angeles and 334 at Columbus, differed from the F-100C in having an automatic pilot, jettisonable underwing pylons and modified vertical tail surfaces. In addition to USAF Tactical Air Command, the F-100D was assigned to the Royal Danish Air Force, the Armee de l'Air and the Royal Hellenic AF. The TF-100C was a two-seat trainer variant which served as the prototype of the F-100F, the latter flying for the first time on 3 July 1957. 339 were built before production ended in 1959, and the variant was supplied to Taiwan, Denmark, France and Turkey. The Super Sabre, principally the F-100D saw extensive service in Vietnam, and in addition to first-line service with Tactical Air Command equipped nine Air National Guard units. Total production of all variants was 2,294, of which 359 were built at Columbus.

North American A-5 Vigilante USA

Role: Carrier-Borne Attack Bomber
Operational: 1961-
Photo and Data: RA-5C

Engines: Two General Electric J79-GE-10 turbojets each rated at 11,870lb thrust (17,860lb with reheat)
Span: 53ft
Length: 75ft 10in
Weight: 61,730lb (loaded)
80,000lb (max overload)
Crew: 2
Max speed: 1,385mph (Mach 2.1) at 40,000ft
Service ceiling: 64,000ft
Range: 2,995 miles max

Weapons: Conventional or nuclear/thermonuclear stores on underwing pylons

In September 1956 following a US Navy design competition to find a successor to the Douglas Skywarrior, North American Aviation Inc received a contract to build a small number of prototypes of a two-seat all-weather attack bomber designated A3J, this designation being later changed to A-5. The first of two prototype YA-5As flew on 31 August 1958, and carrier trials of the A-5A, now named Vigilante, were completed in July 1960 on the USS *Saratoga*. The A-5A was designed to carry either conventional or nuclear weapons in a linear bomb bay, consisting of a tunnel inside the fuselage, the bombs being

ejected rearwards between the two turbojet tail pipes. This arrangement gave the Vigilante, which had an over-target speed of Mach 2, additional seconds in which to clear the burst of its own nuclear weapons when operating in the low-level role. The aircraft also carried a variety of external weapons and could be fitted with a flight refuelling pack. The first delivery of production A-5As was made in 1961 to Heavy Attack Squadron 7 at Sanford, Florida, and this unit embarked in the USS *Enterprise* in 1962. 59 A-5As were delivered to the US Navy.

An interim long-range version, the A-5B (formerly A3J-2), flew on 29 April 1962. This had an extra fuel tank, a raised rear cockpit and modified flying control surfaces. 20 were built, and all of them were later converted to RA-5C standard, as were a number of A-5As.

The RA-5C, which first flew on 30 June 1962, was basically a reconnaissance version with cameras and sensory equipment, but it retained an attack capability with externally-mounted nuclear or conventional weapons. The aircraft was, in fact, the airborne unit of the carrier- or shore-based Integrated Operational Intelligence System (IOIS). First service deliveries were made in January 1964 to VAH-3, the training squadron for Heavy Attack Wing One, and Reconnaissance Attack Squadron 5 became operational with the RA-5C on USS *Ranger* in the South China Sea later that year. Reconnaissance Attack Squadron 7 also equipped with the type in June 1965, completing the phasing out of the A-5A from operational carrier-borne units. Heavy Attack Wing One was later redesignated Reconnaissance Attack Wing One, and seven more Reconnaissance Attack Squadrons also received the RA-5C at a later date. All the early production RA-5Cs were converted to A-5As and A-5Bs, production of 46 new RA-5Cs was begun early in 1969. The Vigilante saw extensive operational service during the Vietnam War, providing much of the reconnaissance data needed for the American naval air strikes on North Vietnamese targets.

North American OV-10 Bronco   USA

Role: Armed Reconnaissance/COIN
Operational: 1968-
Photo and Data: OV-10A

Engines: Two 715ehp AiResearch T76-G-416/417 turboprops
Span: 40ft
Length: 41ft 7in
Weight: 6,969lb (empty)
14,466lb (max loaded)
Crew: 2
Max speed: 281mph at sea level
Service ceiling: 14,000ft
Range: 1,428 miles (ferry)
Weapons: Two 7.62mm machine guns in sponsons on lower fuselage; one Sidewinder AAM under each wing; up to 3,600lb of rockets, bombs or flares under wings

In August 1964 it was announced that North American Aviation had won a US Navy competition for a light armed reconnaissance and counter-insurgency aircraft. Originally designated NA-300, the first of seven prototypes flew on 16 July 1965 as the YOV-10A Bronco, powered by two AiResearch T76 turboprop engines. The first production

OV-10As entered service with the US Marine Corps and the USAF in 1968 and by the end of the following year 270 were in service, many being employed in Vietnam for light armed reconnaissance, helicopter escort and forward air control. The type could also act in the ground-support role as a stop-gap until the arrival of tactical fighters. OV-10A production for the US forces ended in 1969, but 15 aircraft were modified by LTV Electrosystems in 1971 for night forward air control and strike under the USAF 'Pave Nail' programme. Equipment in these aircraft included a laser rangefinder/target illuminator. The OV-10B was similar to the OV-10A, six being supplied to Federal Germany as target tugs, and the OV-10B(Z), 18 of which were also supplied to Federal Germany for the target towing role, had a 2,950lb thrust J85-GE-4 turbojet mounted in a pod above the wing to increase performance.

The OV-10C was a version for the Royal Thai Air Force, 32 delivered in 1973, while the OV-10D is a night observation and ground attack variant for the US Marine Corps, possessing additional weapons capability. Other variants are the OV-10E, 16 of which have been delivered to the Venezuelan Air Force, and the OV-10F, 16 of which were also delivered to Indonesia in 1976.

Northrop F-89 Scorpion

Role: All-Weather Interceptor
Operational: 1950-68
Data: F-89H

Engines: Two Allison J35-A-35 turbojets rated at 5,450lb thrust each (7,200lb with reheat)
Span: 59ft 8in
Length: 53ft 10in
Weight: 28,000lb (empty)
40,000lb (normal loaded)
Crew: 2
Max speed: 595mph at sea level
Service ceiling: 40,000ft
Range: 1,200 miles max
Weapons: Six Hughes GAR-1 Falcon AAMs and 42 FFARs in wingtip pods; one MB-1 Genie nuclear AAM

USA

The most potent all-weather interceptor in the world at the time of its service debut with the USAF, the F-89 Scorpion was one of two contenders for a USAF contract in May 1946, the other being the Curtiss F-87 Nighthawk. Two XF-89 prototypes were ordered, the first flying on 16 August 1948, and after USAF evaluation Northrop received an order for an initial batch of 48 production aircraft. The first of these flew late in 1950 and deliveries to USAF Air Defense Command began soon afterwards, the first Scorpion squadrons being assigned to Arctic defence zones such as Alaska, Iceland and Greenland. The first production model of the Scorpion the F-89A, was powered by two Allison J35-A-21 turbojets with reheat and carried a nose armament of six 20mm cannon. The F-89B and F-89C were progressive developments with uprated Allison engines, while the F-89D had its cannon deleted and carried an armament of 104 folding-fin air-to-air rockets in wingtip pods. Additional fuel tanks under the wings gave an 11% range increase over the F-89C and the aircraft was fitted with an automatic fire control system. The F-89H, which followed the F-89D into production, was armed with six Hughes GAR-1 Falcon missiles and 42 FFARs, and could also carry the MB-1 Genie nuclear AAM. The Falcons were housed in the wingtip pods and were extended prior to firing. The F-89H's armament was fired automatically, a sighting radar and fire control computer forming a fully integrated attack system. Earlier Scorpion variants, brought up to F-89H standard under a USAF modernisation contract that lasted into 1958, were designated F-89J. The F-89F and F-89G were proposed modifications which never left the drawing board, while the XF-89E was an experimental aircraft serving as a test bed for the Allison J71 turbojet.

The Scorpion was retired from first-line service in 1961-2, being replaced by the F-102 and F-106, but it remained in operational service for some years more with the 101st, 115th, 119th, 120th 132nd, 141st, 142nd, 148th and 158th Fighter Groups of the Air National Guard.

Northrop F-5

Role: Tactical Strike/Reconnaissance
Operational: 1964-
Data: F-5A

Engines: Two General Electric J85-GE-13 turbojets rated at 4,080lb thrust with reheat
Span: 25ft 3in
Length: 47ft 2in
Weight: 8,085lb (empty)
20,677lb (max loaded)
Crew: 1
Max speed: 790mph at sea level
Service ceiling: 50,000+feet
Range: 1,387 miles max
Weapons: Two 20mm M-39 cannon and up to 6,000lb of external offensive stores

USA

In 1955 a team of designers and engineers from the Northrop Corporation carried out a fact-finding tour of Europe and Asia, their object being to examine the air defence needs of both NATO and SEATO. As a result, the Northrop N156 was conceived — a relatively simple and cheap combat aircraft capable of undertaking a variety of tasks. At the end of 1958, Northrop received a Department of Defense contract for three prototypes, the first of which flew on 30 July 1959, powered by two General Electric YJ85-GE-1 turbojets, and exceeded Mach 1 on its maiden flight. After nearly three years of intensive testing and evaluation, it was announced on 25 April 1962 that the N156 had been selected as the new all-purpose fighter for supply to friendly nations under the Mutual Aid Pact, and the aircraft entered production as the F-5A, the first example flying in October 1963. The F-5A entered service with USAF Tactical Air Command at Williams AFB, Arizona, in April 1964, and this was used as a base for training the pilots of foreign air forces to which the aircraft was to be supplied.

The first overseas customer was the Imperial Iranian Air Force, which formed the first of seven F-5A squadrons in February 1965. The Royal Hellenic Air Force also equipped two squadrons in 1965, and Norway received 108 aircraft from 1967, these being equipped with arrester hooks and assisted take-off for short field operations. Between 1965 and 1970 Canadair Ltd built 115 aircraft for the Canadian Armed Forces under the designation CF-5A/-5D, these using Orenda-built J85-CAN-15 engines. Other nations using the type were Ethiopia, Morocco, South Korea, the Republic of Vietnam, Nationalist China, the Philippines, Libya, the Netherlands, Spain, Thailand and Turkey. The F-5A was evaluated by the USAF in Vietnam, 12 aircraft of the 10th Fighter Commando Squadron flying up to 33 combat sorties a day during the trial period. These aircraft were later transferred to the 522nd Squadron of the Republic of Vietnam Air Force.

Variants of the basic F-5A were the F-5B dual fighter-trainer, with two seats in tandem, the F-5A-15, powered by higher-rated J85-GE-15 turbojets, and the RF-5A reconnaissance variant. The

105 aircraft for the RNethAF were designated NF-5A/-5B.

The F-5E Tiger II was selected in November 1970 as a successor to the F-5A series, and Northrop had already built and flown an improved version of the basic F-5 in March 1969, the new aircraft powered by two General Electric YJ85-GE-21 engines rated at 5,000lb thrust each. During an intensive flight test programme the aircraft reached a maximum speed of Mach 1.6 and proved highly manoeuvrable, an asset improved on production machines with the aid of manoeuvring flaps — full-span leading edge flaps working in conjunction with trailing edge flaps and operated by a control on the throttle quadrant. The first prolduction F-5E flew on 11 August 1972 and deliveries were made to the USAF's 425th Tactical Fighter Squadron in March 1973. Overseas air forces using the F-5E include Brazil, Chile, Nationalist China, Iran, Jordan, Kenya, South Korea, Malaysia, Saudi Arabia, Singapore, Switzerland and Thailand. The F-5F is a two-seat version, fulfilling a similar role to the F-5B. T-38 Talon trainer derivative is described separately.

Panavia Tornado

Role: Multi-Role Combat
Operational: 1979-

Engines: Two Turbo-Union RB199-34R-2 turbofans rated at 8,500lb thrust (14,500lb with reheat)
Span: 45ft $7\frac{1}{4}$in (fully spread)
28ft $2\frac{1}{2}$in (fully swept)
Length: 54ft $9\frac{1}{2}$in
Weight: 22,000-23,000lb (empty)
38,000-40,000lb (max loaded)
Crew: 2
Max speed: 1,320mph at 36,000ft
Service ceiling: 60,000ft (approx)
Range: Not available
Weapons: Two 27mm IWKA-Mauser cannon in lower fuselage; Sidewinder, Sky Flash, Sparrow and Aspide 1A air-to-air missiles; AS30, Martel, Kormoran and Jumbo air-to-surface missiles; and a variety of conventional or nuclear free-falling bombs

UK/West Germany/Italy

In March 1969, an International European consortium known as Panavia Aircraft GmbH was formed to design and develop a multi-role combat aircraft for eventual service with the air forces of the United Kingdom, West Germany, Italy, and the German Navy, the three aircraft manufacturers involved being the British Aircraft Corporation, Messerschmitt-Bölkow-Blohm and Aeritalia. A supersonic two-seat variable-geometry aircraft, MRCA — subsequently named Tornado — is capable of undertaking six major tasks: close air support, interdiction, air superiority, interception, naval strike and reconnaissance. The first prototype (01), which was assembled by MBB, flew for the first time on 14 August 1974 and was followed by eight more flying prototypes, each being allocated to a different sector of the flight test programme. The 10th aircraft was used for static tests and the next six were pre-production machines, the first flying on 5 February 1977. An initial batch of 40 production

Tornados was ordered, followed by a further 110 in May 1977. Deliveries of the first examples of an initial total of 385 Tornados for the Royal Air Force were scheduled to begin late in 1978, an international operational conversion unit being formed at RAF Cottesmore, and the Tornado GR1 will eventually replace the Vulcans and Buccaneers of Strike Command's Nos 9, 12, 15, 16, 35, 44, 50, 101 and 617 Squadrons, beginning in 1979. An air defence version (ADV) of the Tornado for the RAF, equipped with Sky Flash advanced AAM, will eventually replace the Phantom, and the type will also supplant the Buccaneer in the maritime strike role. First deliveries to the Luftwaffe will also begin in 1979, when the aircraft will start to replace the F-104G Starfighters of Fighter-Bomber Wings 31, 32, 33 and 34. 211 Tornados are envisaged for the Luftwaffe, plus 113 for the German Navy, where the type will equip Marinefliegergruppen (MFG) 1 and 2. The Italian Air Force is to receive 100 Tornados, and these will replace the F-104Gs and Fiat G-91s in service with the 20th, 102nd, 154th and 186th Gruppi in the air superiority, ground-attack and reconnaissance roles.

Republic F-84 Thunderjet

Role: Single-Seat Fighter-Bomber
Operational: 1947-70
Data: F84G

Engines: One 5,600lb thrust J35-A-29 turbojet
Span: 36ft
Length: 38ft
Weight: 11,095lb (empty)
18,645lb (normal loaded)
Crew: 1
Max speed: 622mph at sea level
Service ceiling: 40,500ft
Range: 2,000 miles at 483mph
Weapons: Six 0.5in machine guns, two 11.5in
16 5in or 32 HVAR rockets, two 1,000lb bombs or one 2,000lb free-falling tactical nuclear weapon

USA

The Republic F-84 Thunderjet, which provided many of NATO's air forces with their initial jet experience and which was also the first fighter-bomber capable of carrying a tactical atomic bomb, began life in the summer of 1944, when Republic Aviation's design team investigated the possibility of adapting the airframe of the P-47 Thunderbolt to take an axial-flow turbojet. This proved impractical, and in November 1944 design of an entirely new airframe was begun around the General Electric J35 engine. The first of three XP-84 prototypes (45-59475) was completed in December 1945 and made its first flight on 28 February 1946 from Muroc Air Force Base, powered by a 3,750lb thrust J35-GE-7 turbojet. On 7 September that year, the second prototype (45-59476) established a US speed record of 611mph.

The three prototypes were followed by 15 YP-84As for USAF evaluation. These were powered by an Allison-built J35-A-15 engine and carried an armament of six .5in M2 machine guns. Delivered in the spring of 1947, they were later converted to F-84B standard. The F-84B was the first production model, featuring an ejection seat, M3 machine guns with a higher rate of fire, and underwing points for rocket racks. Deliveries of the F-84B began in the summer of 1947 to the 14th Fighter Group at Dow Field, and 226 were built. The F-84C, of which 191 were built, was externally similar to the F-84B, but incorporated an improved electrical system and an improved bomb-release mechanism. It was powered by a J35-A-13C engine, and production began in April 1948.

The next model to appear, in November 1948, was the F-84D, which had a strengthened wing and a modified fuel system. 151 were built. It was followed, in May 1949, by the F-84E, which in addition to its six 0.5in machine guns could carry two 1,000lb bombs, two 11.75in rockets or 32 5in rockets. The F-84E saw considerable active service in Korea from December 1950, with the 27th Fighter Escort Group and the 48th and 59th Fighter Bomber Wings. Although the F-84 was generally inferior to the MiG-15, it gave a good account of itself on the few occasions when the Russian jets challenged it, and Thunderjet pilots were credited with the destruction of six MiGs over Korea. In the last year of the war, F-84s played a prominent part in interdiction operations against North Korea's communications system, synthetic oil plants and irrigation dams.

A total of 843 F-84Es was built, and it was intended that this variant should be supplanted by the swept-wing F-84F. Teething troubles with the latter, however, led to the development of a further F-84 version, the F-84G. This was manufactured in greater quantity than any other Thunderjet model,

3,025 being built. Most of the F-84Gs went to NATO air forces; Greece received 250, Italy 250, Holland, Norway, Portugal and Denmark received 200 each, while smaller numbers were supplied to France, Turkey, Yugoslavia, Nationalist China and Thailand. The F-84G was fitted with flight refuelling equipment, and during one trial a Thunderjet remained airborne for over 12 hours, being refuelled in flight four times. In 1952, F-84Gs made non-stop flights from California to Hawaii, from Hawaii to Midway, and from Midway to Japan with the aid of flight refuelling.

Long after their retirement from the squadrons of the USAF and the ANG, F-84Gs continued to render sterling service overseas. A few were still serving in Yugoslavia and Thailand in the early 1970s.

Republic F-84F Thunderstreak USA

Role: Single-Seat Fighter-Bomber
Operational: 1954-74
Data: F84F

Engines: One 7,220lb thrust Wright J65-W-3 turbojet
Span: 33ft 7in
Length: 43ft 4in
Weight: 19,340lb (loaded)
28,000lb (max loaded)
Crew: 1
Max speed: 695mph at sea level
Service ceiling: 46,000ft
Range: 2,000 miles with max external fuel
Weapons: Six .5in Colt-Browning machine guns (four in RF-84F) and up to 6,000lb of external stores, including two 1,000lb bombs and eight HVAR rockets

Towards the end of 1949 Republic Aviation launched a proposal for a high-speed, swept-wing derivative of the F-84 Thunderjet. The new design was conceived at a time when US Government expenditure on new combat aircraft was strictly limited, so to cut costs it was decided to utilise 60% of the F-84's components, including the fuselage. By fitting swept flying surfaces and installing an uprated engine, it was believed that overall performance could be substantially improved.

The prototype XF-84F flew for the first time on 3 June 1950, only 167 days after it was ordered. It was powered by a 5,200lb thrust Allison J35-A-25 turbojet, and was originally designated YF-96A. Initial flight tests showed that the aircraft was underpowered, and had it not been for the outbreak of the Korean War, which released emergency funds for combat aircraft development, the F-84F would probably have gone no further. As it was, the design was modified to take the more powerful Wright J65 engine, a licence-built version of the Bristol Siddeley Sapphire, and the XF-84F flew in this configuration on 14 February 1951. The first production F-84F-1-RE flew on 22 November 1952 and the type was officially accepted by the USAF the following month. The first USAF unit to equip with the F-84F, in 1954, was the 407th Strategic Fighter Wing, and despite its high performance, weight and landing speed (155-165mph) American pilots soon got used to it and established a number of noteworthy records. In March 1955, for example, a Tactical Air Command Thunderstreak using flight refuelling set a new US transcontinental record by flying from Los Angeles to New York in 3hr 44min at an average speed of 652mph, and a few months later 12 F-84Fs of the 27th Strategic Fighter Wing flew the 5,118miles from London to Austin, Texas, in 10hr 48min.

The F-84F replaced the earlier Thunderjet with several NATO air forces, giving many European pilots their first experience of modern, swept-wing jet aircraft. The Thunderstreak equipped the 4th and 9th Escadres of the French Air Force, Nos 31, 32, 33, 34 and 35 Wings of the Luftwaffe, Gruppi 20, 21, 22, 101, 102, 154, 155 and 165 of the Italian Air Force, the 1st 2nd, 3rd, 23rd, 27th and 31st squadrons of the Belgian Air Force, as well as four Royal Netherlands AF squadrons, three Greek AF Wings and nine Turkish AF squadrons. F-84Fs served with the Belgian and Turkish Air Forces until well into the 1970s, and with the Air National Guard following retirement from first-line USAF service. Production of the F-84F ended in August 1957, with the completion of the 2,711th aircraft.

In February 1952 a reconnaissance version, designated YRF-84F and named Thunderflash, made its first flight. Of a total of 715 RF-84Fs produced,

286 were supplied to foreign air forces. Apart from USAF service, the Thunderflash was used by the French AF's 33rd Reconnaissance Wing, Aufklärungsgeschwader 51 and 52 of the Luftwaffe, the Belgian AF's 42nd Reconnaissance Squadron, the 3rd Tactical Air Reconnaissance Brigade (Italy),

the 729th Squadron Royal Danish AF, No717 Sqn Royal Norwegian AF, No306 Sqn RNethAF, and by Turkey, Greece and Nationalist China (one squadron each). The RF-84F differed visually from the F-84F in having a 'solid' nose housing cameras and air intakes at the wing roots.

Republic F-105 Thunderchief

USA

Role: Single-Seat Strike Fighter
Operational: 1958-
Data: F-105D

Engines: One Pratt & Whitney J75-P19W turbojet rated at 17,200lb thrust (24,500lb with reheat)
Span: 34ft 11in
Length: 67ft
Weight: 28,000lb (empty)
52,546lb (max loaded)
Crew: 1
Max speed: 1,390mph at 36,000ft
855mph at sea level (without stores)
Service ceiling: 50,000ft
Range: 2,390 miles with max external fuel
Weapons: Up to 16 250lb, 500lb or 750lb bombs, nine 1,000lb bombs or four Bullpup ASMs; nine LAU-18/A rocket batteries; one M-61 Vulcan rotary cannon.

Although beset by continual difficulties and delays during its early development career, the Republic F-105 Thunderchief emerged as the workhorse of the USAF's Tactical Air Command during the 1960s. The F-105 was conceived as a successor to the F-84F Thunderstreak at a time when the US Department of Defense was giving top priority to building up the American nuclear deterrent, and consequently the evolution of a supersonic strike fighter came low down the list of considerations. Nevertheless, in March 1953 the Department of Defense ordered an initial batch of 37 aircraft for evaluation, this being reduced to 15 aircraft in February the following year. To add to Republic's problems, the DoD instructed that four of these aircraft were to be powered by Pratt & Whitney J75 engines instead of the planned J57. In September 1954 the number of aircraft ordered was cut still further to three, and it was not until February 1955

that the order was raised to 15 once more.

The first of two YF-105 prototypes flew on 22 October 1955, powered by a P&W J-57-P-25, and a third aircraft flew on 26 May 1956. Designated YF-105B-1-RE, this employed the Pratt & Whitney J75-P-3 and was the first of a pre-production batch of 12 machines for test purposes. During 1956 the F-105 was evaluated in competition with its main opponent, the North American F-107, and the Republic design proved superior on most counts. As a result, the F-105B was ordered into production in January 1957, deliveries of operational aircraft beginning in May 1958 to the 4th Tactical Fighter Wing. Only 75 F-105Bs were built, this variant being replaced on the production line in 1959 by the all-weather ground-attack F-105D version.

The F-105D, which first flew on 9 June 1959 and entered service with Tactical Air Command the following year, embodied what was at the time the most advanced automatic navigation system in the world, a combination of the Doppler APN-131, the NASARR R-14A all-purpose radar, and the General Electric FC-5 flight control system. Its ASG-19 Thunderstick fire control system permitted either automatic or manual weapons delivery in modes ranging from over-the-shoulder toss to retarded lay-down. 610 F-105Ds were built, and although the aircraft was initially unpopular, mainly because of early snags with its avionics systems, it proved its worth over Vietnam, where it flew more than 75% of USAF strike missions with an abort rate of less than 1%. For the largest and heaviest single-seat fighter-bomber in the world, it also showed an astonishing ability to absorb tremendous battle damage and still get back to base.

Several two-seat versions of the F-105 were proposed, the first of which, the F-105C and F-105E, were both cancelled before completion, the few F-105E examples under construction being finished as

F-105Ds. The only two-seat variant to enter production was the F-105F, which first flew on 11 June 1963. The F-105F, of which 143 were built, had full operational capability and was assigned in small numbers to each F-105D squadron. In Vietnam, F-105Fs frequently led strikes, providing accurate navigation to the target. F-105Fs were among the first Thunderchiefs to be fitted with 'Wild Weasel' ECM equipment, designed to jam North Vietnamese SAM search radar. A total of 21 squadrons used the F-105F, as well as three ANG units.

In its F-105D version, the Thunderchief served with the 4th, 8th, 18th, 23rd, 36th, 49th, 57th, 108th, 140th, 347th, 355th, 388th and 6441st Tactical Fighter Wings, and with the 4520th Combat Crew Training Wing.

Ryan FR-1 Fireball

USA

Role: Naval Fighter
Operational: 1945-47

Engines: One 1,350hp Wright Cyclone R-1820-72W radial engine in the nose. One 1,600hp thrust General Electric J31-GE-3 turbojet in the tail
Span: 40ft
Length: 32ft 4in
Weight: 7,635lb (empty)
9,862lb (normal loaded)
Crew: 1
Max speed: 426mph at 18,100ft (both engines)
Service ceiling: 40,000ft
Range: 1,430 miles max (Cyclone only)
Weapons: Four .5in machine guns in wings; one 1,000lb bomb or eight 60lb RPs

Design work on the Ryan Model 28, or FR-1, was initiated in 1943, and the aircraft was in production before the end of the war in the Pacific. It was the first aircraft to enter service in which a piston engine was combined with a turbojet, using both powerplants for take-off, climb and combat and having the ability to fly and land with either engine shut down. The prototype XFR-1 flew for the first time on 25 June 1944 and the first delivery of an operational FR-1 was made to Navy Fighter Squadron VF-66 in March the following year. Only 69 aircraft were built, including four prototypes, and the Fireball's service career was very short, the last examples being retired from Navy Squadron VF-1E at the end of June 1947. Proposed variants were the XFR-2, XFR-3 and XFR-4, with different engine installations, and a redesigned version, the XF2R-1, flew in November 1946. This had a General Electric XT31-GE-2 turboprop in place of the FR-1's piston engine, resulting in a longer fuselage and larger vertical tail surfaces. The XF2D-1 did not enter production.

SAAB 18

Sweden

Role: Bomber/Reconnaissance
Operational: 1944-59
Photo: B18
Data: B18B

Engines: Two 1,475hp DB605B radials
Span: 55ft 9in
Length: 43ft 5in
Weight: 13,430lb (empty)
19,390lb (loaded)
Crew: 3
Max speed: 355mph
Service ceiling: 32,100ft (B18A: 26,200ft)
Range: 1,620 miles (B18A: 1,370 miles)
Weapons: Two 13.2mm and one 7.9mm machine guns; up to 3,300lb of bombs; 12 10cm, eight 14.5cm or two 18cm rockets

The SAAB 18 originated in a 1939 Swedish Air Force requirement for a reconnaissance aircraft, this being altered later to dive-bomber. Two prototypes were ordered and the first flew on 19 June 1942, powered by two Swedish-built Pratt & Whitney R-1830 radial engines. Because of licence production difficulties, however, it was a copy of the Twin Wasp which was adopted in the first production version, the SAAB 18A, which entered service in 1944. 60 SAAB 18As were built. The aircraft carried a crew of three and, with its twin-engined, twin-finned configuration bore a strong resemblance to the Dornier Do17, its main distinctive feature being the cockpit, which was offset to port to give the pilot a better downward view. A few early SAAB 18s were converted to the reconnaissance role as the S18A; these were equipped with radar and carried either Ska5 or Ska13 cameras.

The next variant, the SAAB 18B, was powered by 1,475hp Daimler-Benz DB605B engines, bringing about a marked improvement in performance. The

B18B entered service with the Flygvapnet in 1946 and 120 were built. In 1949, all B18Bs in service were modified retrospectively to take SAAB-designed ejection seats. The final variant, the T18B, flew in July 1945 and was originally intended as a torpedo bomber, although it actually entered service as an attack aircraft with a 57mm Bofors cannon under the nose in addition to two forward-firing 20mm cannon. 62 aircraft were built before production ended in 1948, and both the B18B and the T18B remained in service until the mid-1950s, when the former was replaced by the Vampire FB50 and the latter by the A32A Lansen. The last S18A reconnaissance aircraft served until May 1959, when their task was taken over by the S32C Lansen.

SAAB J-21A/21R   Sweden

Role: Interceptor/Fighter
Operational: 1945-53 (J-21A)
1950-56 (J-21R)
Data: J-21A

	J-21A	**J-21R**
Engines:	One Daimler-Benz DB605B liquid-cooled developing 1,475hp	One 3,000lb thrust Goblin DGn2 or 3,300lb Goblin 3 turbojet
Span:	38ft 1in	37ft 4in
Length:	34ft 3in	34ft 8in
Weight: (loaded)	9,150lb	9,370lb
Crew:	1	1
Max speed:	398mph at 15,000ft	497mph at 26,250ft
Service ceiling:	32,000ft	39,370ft
Range:	600 miles	447 miles at 26,250ft on internal fuel, 845 miles with external tanks
Weapons:	One 20mm Hispano cannon and four Browning 12.7mm machine guns	One 20mm Bofors cannon and four 13.2mm Bofors machine guns augmented as necessary by a belly pack housing eight machine guns; 10 10cm, five 18cm or 10 8cm rockets in the ground-attack role

Designed in 1941 to meet an urgent need for a modern, home-produced fighter to equip Sweden's Air Force, the SAAB J-21A was unique in many respects. It was the only twin-boom, pusher-engined fighter to be produced in quantity during World War II; it was the second fighter to be fitted with an ejection seat (the first being Germany's Heinkel He219); and it was the last piston-engined combat aircraft to be built in Sweden.

Originally designated L-21, the 'L' denoting SAAB's factory at Linköping, the fighter made its first flight on 13 July 1943, powered by a Daimler-Benz DB605 liquid-cooled engine. This in itself caused problems, because the first batch of DB605 engines imported from Germany proved to be defective, having been sabotaged by forced-labour factory workers who believed them to be destined for the Luftwaffe.

The J-21A was a cantilever low-wing monoplane with an advanced all-metal flush-riveted stressed-skin wing employing a new high speed aerofoil section. The fuselage nacelle was also of all-metal

flush-riveted construction, and the pilot's cockpit, which was placed well forward of the wing leading edge, offered excellent all-round visibility, the canopy sides being bulged to improve downward and rearward vision. The windscreen was of 150mm armoured glass and 20mm armour plate protected the pilot, who was equipped with a SAAB-designed cartridge type ejection seat — the latter having been adopted as the only sure means of clearing the propeller blades. The nose of the fuselage nacelle housed a gun battery of one 20mm Hispano cannon and two 12.7mm Brownings, and a 12.7mm Browning was also installed in each tailboom where it joined the wing leading edge.

Despite a few initial snags, flight testing of the J-21A was generally successful, the aircraft proving easy and pleasant to fly. The prototypes and the initial batch of production aircraft were powered by imported DB605B engines, but subsequent aircraft were fitted with DB605Bs built under licence by the Svenska Flygmotor AB and these machines were designated SAAB-21A-2. The first Swedish Air Force

unit to equip with the new aircraft, late in 1945, was F9 at Gothenburg, and before production of the J-21 ended in 1948 a total of 298 aircraft had been delivered in addition to the three prototypes. Some aircraft were converted to the ground-attack role by the addition of wingtip tanks and underwing weapon racks, and these were designated SAAB-21A-3.

The SAAB-21B was a projected development that envisaged the use of a Rolls-Royce Griffon engine and the installation of a pressurised cockpit with a bubble-type canopy, but this project was overtaken by the jet age. Instead, it was decided to convert four SAAB-21A airframes to take the de Havilland Goblin turbojet, a move that made it necessary to redesign the SAAB-21's rear fuselage, as the Goblin had a greater diameter than the DB605B engine. The tailplane was also raised to give clearance for the jet exhaust. The conversion process, in fact, caused more problems than had been anticipated. It had been hoped that the SAAB-21A's wing and tail structure could be used in the jet-engined version,

but after trials the whole wing had to be restressed and the tail unit stiffened. The undercarriage also had to be modified because of the change in thrust line, and the air intakes, situated above the wing aft of the cockpit, were of low efficiency.

Designated J-21R, the Goblin-engined version flew for the first time on 10 March 1947, but because of the snags encountered the first production deliveries did not take place until 1949, and it was not until the following year that the first Royal Swedish Air Force unit, F10, re-equipped with the type. The initial order called for 120 J-21Rs, but in the event only 60 were produced, the type giving way to the more modern SAAB J-29. The J-21Rs that equipped F10 were converted as ground-attack aircraft and allocated to Squadron F7, where, under the designation A-21R, they provided Swedish pilots with invaluable experience of jet operations and laid the foundation for the entry into service of more advanced types.

SAAB J-29 Sweden

Role: Single-Seat Fighter
Operational: 1951-64
Data: J-29F

Engines: One 5,000lb thrust (6,500lb with reheat) SFA-built DH Ghost 50 turbojet (Swedish designation: RM2)
Span: 36ft 1in
Length: 33ft 2½in
Weight: 9,479lb (empty)
13,360lb (normal loaded)
Crew: 1
Max speed: 658mph at 5,000ft (clean)
Service ceiling: 47,000ft
Range: 1,677 miles max
Weapons: Four 20mm Hispano cannon + AA rockets, eight 150mm rockets in ground-attack role

The SAAB J-29, which began life on the drawing boards of its parent company in October 1945, had the distinction of being the first swept-wing jet fighter of European design to enter service after World War II. The first of three prototypes was test flown on 1 September 1948, powered by a De Havilland Ghost turbojet rated at 4,400lb thrust, and a production prototype made its first flight in July 1950. All production aircraft were equipped with a

5,000lb thrust Ghost 50 engine built under licence in Sweden by Svenska Flygmotor AB (SFA). The first production model, the J-29A, began to enter service with Day Fighter Wing F13 at Norrköping in May 1951, and the aircraft's tubby appearance — the result of the fuselage being tailored to accommodate the larger diameter of the centrifugal-type Ghost engine — soon earned it the affectionate nickname of 'Tunnan' (Barrel).

Other variants of the basic design followed quickly. The second production version was the J-29B, which had increased internal fuel tankage and provision for two drop tanks, increasing the maximum range to 1,677 miles; the A-29 was a ground-attack variant, identical to the J-29B, but fitted with underwing racks for 14 14.5cm Bofors air-to-surface rockets or alternative stores. The S-29C was a specialised photographic reconnaissance version carrying up to six fully automatic cameras and improved avionics; this made its first flight in June 1953, with deliveries starting before the end of that year, and was followed by an experimental version — the J-29D, fitted with an afterburner. Designed by the Royal Swedish Air Board and developed by SFA, the afterburner, increased the thrust of the Ghost turbojet to 6,500lb and boosted the J-29's initial climb rate from 7,500ft/min to

nearly 15,000ft/min. The J-29D first flew in March 1954, and while flight testing was being carried out another intercepter variant made its appearance: the J-29E, fitted with a modified outer wing featuring an extended 'saw tooth' leading edge and giving a higher critical Mach number and improved transonic flight characteristics.

The fifth and last production version, the J-29F, combined the refinements of both the J-29E and J-29D, and began to enter service with Flygvapnet fighter wings late in 1954. Many J-29Bs were subsequently brought up to J-29F standard, long after the production of new aircraft ended in April 1956, and the type — supplemented by four squadrons of Hawker Hunters — remained the

Flygvapnet's main first-line equipment until well into the 1960s, when it was gradually replaced by the J-35 Draken. The J-29 saw a limited amount of active service during the Congo Crisis of 1962-63, when Fighter Squadron F22 was sent to the Congo with nine J-29Bs and two S-29Cs as part of the United Nations peace-keeping force. In a series of effective air strikes on Kolwezi airfield in December 1962/January 1963, these aircraft completely eliminated the air combat strength of the rebel Katangese government.

The SAAB J-29 became the first Swedish combat aircraft to be exported, several being delivered to the small Austrian Air Force.

SAAB 32 Lansen Sweden

Role: Fighter/Ground-Attack
Operational: 1955-
Photo: A32
Data: A32A

Engines: One 8,050lb thrust (9,920lb with reheat) SFA RM5 (licence-built RR Avon 100) turbojet
Span: 42ft 7$\frac{3}{4}$in
Length: 49ft 2$\frac{1}{2}$in
Weight: 15,400lb (empty)
22,000lb (normal loaded)
Crew: 1
Max speed: 700mph at sea level

Service ceiling: 49,210ft
Range: 2,000 miles max
Weapons: Four 20mm cannon and two Type 304 ASMs; four 550lb bombs; two 1,100lb bombs; 12 18cm rockets or 24 13.5/15cm rockets

In the autumn of 1946, the Svenska Aeroplan AB began design studies of a new turbojet-powered attack aircraft for the Swedish Air Force, and two years later the Swedish Air Board authorised the construction of a prototype under the designation P1150. This aircraft, now known as the A32 Lansen (Lance) flew for the first time on 3 November 1952, powered by a 7,500lb thrust Rolls-Royce Avon RA7R

turbojet, three more prototypes were built, and one of these exceeded Mach 1 in a shallow dive during the test programme on 25 October 1953. The Lansen entered quantity production that year and entered Flygvapnet service in 1955, the first unit to receive the type being Attack Wing F17. The Lansen subsequently equipped three more attack wings, F6, F7 and F14, these forming the Royal Swedish Air Force's strike force, Eskader 1.

The A32A attack variant was followed on the production line by the J32B all-weather fighter variant, which flew for the first time on 7 January 1957. A two-seater, the J32B was powered by an 11,250lb thrust RM6 (licence-built Avon RA28) turbojet and carried an improved armament, navigation equipment and fire control system. A third variant, the S32C, was a reconnaissance aircraft and flew for the first time on 26 March 1957. The Lansen began to give way to the A37 Viggen in Sweden's ground-attack units during 1971, but was still an important item on the Swedish Air Force's first-line inventory in 1978.

SAAB 35 Draken
Sweden

Role: Fighter
Operational: 1960-
Photo and Data: J35F

Engines: One Svenska Flygmotor (RR Avon 300-series) RM6C turbojet rated at 12,790lb thrust (17,650lb with reheat)
Span: 30ft 10in
Length: 50ft 4in
Weight: 16,800lb (empty) 22,900lb (normal loaded)
Crew: 1
Max speed: 1,320mph at 36,100ft
Service ceiling: 60,000ft
Range: 1,100 miles with external tanks
Weapons: One 30mm Aden M/55 cannon; two Rb27 and two Rb28 AAMs; two 1,100lb bombs, nine 220lb bombs or 12 13.5cm Bofors rockets (in attack role)

Designed from the outset to intercept transonic bombers at all altitudes and in all weathers, SAAB's versatile J35 Draken was probably, at the time of its service debut, the finest fully integrated air defence system in Western Europe. The first of three prototypes of this unique 'Double-delta' fighter flew for the first time on 25 October 1955, and the initial production version, the J35A, entered service with the Swedish Air Force early in 1960. The J35A was powered by a Svenska Flygmotor RM6B (Rolls-Royce Avon 200) turbojet rated at 15,200lb thrust with reheat, as were the next two production versions, the J35B — basically a J35A with a new fire control system and improved electronics — and the Sk35C, a two-seat trainer which first flew in December 1959. The J35D, which had a more powerful RM6C (Avon 300) engine, flew in December 1960, and most earlier models were modified to J35D standard. The S35E was a reconnaissance version of the J35D, with camera equipment in the nose.

The major production version of the Draken was the J35F, which was virtually designed around the Hughes HM-55 Falcon radar-guided air-to-air missile and was fitted with an improved S7B collision-course fire control system, a high capacity data link system integrating the aircraft with the STRIL 60 air defence environment, an infra-red sensor under the nose and PS-01/A search and ranging radar. The SAAB 35X export version was externally similar to the J35F, but had a greatly increased range and attack capability. Fifty-one were supplied to Denmark under the designations F35XD (fighter-bomber version, TF35XD (two-seat trainer) and RF35XD (reconnaissance version), these equipping Nos 725 and 729 Squadrons. The other export customer for the Draken was the Finnish Air Force, whose No 11 Squadron was operating 27 aircraft of this type in 1978. These were made up of 12 J35Ss, assembled in Finland, six ex-Swedish J35BSs originally supplied to Finland for training and subsequently purchased, three S35Cs and six J35Fs.

In 1978, some 300 Drakens were in front-line service with the Swedish Air Force in the interceptor role, equipping Fighter Wings F1, F4, F10, F12, F13, F16, F17 and F21, a total of 17 squadrons. Total production of the Draken was approximately 600 aircraft.

SAAB 37 Viggen Sweden

Role: Multi-Role Combat
Operational: 1971-

Engines: One Volvo Flygmotor RM8A (Swedish-developed P&W JT8D-22) rated at 14,770lb thrust (26,015lb with reheat) Note: JA37/37X has an uprated RM8B (28,108lb thrust with reheat)
Span 34ft 9¼in
Length: 53ft 5¾in (inc probe)
Weight: 45,195lb (max loaded)
Crew: 1 (Sk37: 2)
Max speed: Mach 2+ at altitude
Service ceiling: 60,000ft
Range: 1,200 miles
Weapons: (Attack mission) Rb04C or Rb05A attack missiles or pods housing six 13.5cm or 19 7.7cm rockets, or 30mm Aden cannon, or 1,000lb bombs on five external stations; (Intercept mission) Rb24 (Sidewinder), Rb27 or Rb28 (Falcon) AAMs

One of the most potent combat aircraft of the 1970s, the SAAB 37 Viggen (Thunderbolt) was designed to carry out the four roles of attack, interception, reconnaissance and training, and — like the earlier J35 Draken — is a fully integrated part of the Swedish STRIL 60 air defence control system. Powered by a Swedish version of the Pratt & Whitney JT8D turbofan engine with a powerful Swedish-developed afterburner, the aircraft has excellent acceleration and climb performance and can operate from runways only 1,640ft in length. Part of its design requirement, in fact, was that it should be capable of operating from sections of Swedish motorways. The first of seven prototypes flew for the first time on 8 February 1967, followed by the first production AJ37 single-seat all-weather attack variant in February 1971. Deliveries of the first AJ37s to the Swedish Air Force began in June that year, the first unit to re-equip being F7 Wing, and by mid-1978 two more wings, F6 and F15, were also operating the type.

The JA 37 single-seat interceptor version, production of which began in 1974, is due to equip eight squadrons from 1978 to 1985, replacing the J35F Draken, and about 180 are expected to be built. The SF37 is a single-seat all-weather armed photo-reconnaissance variant, which began to replace the S35E Drakens of F21 in April 1977 and also equips a squadron of F13, while the SH37 is an all-weather maritime reconnaissance version designed to replace the S32C Lansen, in service with F13 and F17. The Sk37 is a tandem two-seat version, used as a conversion trainer with F7 and F15 in mid-1978; it also retains a secondary attack role. The SAAB 37X is a proposed export version, generally similar to the JA37.

SEPECAT Jaguar
France/UK

Role: Tactical Strike
Operational: 1973-
Photo: S(O)1
Data: GR Mk 1/Jaguar A

Engines: Two Rolls-Royce/Turbomeca Adour
Mk 102 turbofans rated at 5,115lb thrust (7,305lb
with reheat)
Span: 28ft 6in
Length: 50ft 11in
Weight: 15,432lb (empty)
24,000lb (normal loaded)
Crew: 1
Max speed: 840mph at sea level
Service ceiling: 50,000ft
Range: 2,614 miles (ferry, with external fuel)
Weapons: Two 30mm cannon (DEFA or Aden); up
to 10,000lb of bombs, ASMs or rockets

In May 1966 Breguet Aviation and the British
Aircraft Corporation formed a company known as
SEPECAT (Société Européenne de Production de
l'Avion Ecole de Combat et Appui Tactique) for the
design and production of a supersonic strike
fighter/trainer for the French Armed Forces and the
RAF. Known as Jaguar, the new aircraft was
developed from the earlier Breguet Br121 strike
fighter project, and the development schedule called
for the type's entry into service with the Armée de
l' Air in 1972 and the RAF in 1973.

The first Jaguar variant to fly was the French two-
seat advanced trainer, the prototype (E-01) making
its first flight on 8 September 1968. Forty examples
of this version, designated Jaguar E-1, were ordered,
the first production machines entering service with

Escadrille 1/7 in 1972. A second unit, Escadrille
3/11, formed in January 1975. The French single-
seat tactical support version, designated Jaguar A,
flew for the first time on 23 March 1969; 160 were
ordered, the first of which were asssigned to
Escadrille 1/7 'Provence' in June 1973. Other units
equipping with the Jaguar A since then were 2/7
'Argonne', 3/7 'Languedoc', 3/11 'Corse', 1/11
'Roussillon', 2/11 'Vosges' and 3/3 'Ardennes'.

The British tactical support version, designated
Jaguar S — or Jaguar GR Mk 1 in RAF service —
first flew on 12 October 1969. Equipped with a
digital computer controlling an advanced intertial
navigation and weapon-aiming system (NAVWASS),
the GR1 entered service with the Jaguar OCU at
Lossiemouth, Scotland, in October 1973, and the
first operational RAF Jaguar squadron, No 54,
formed there the following March. Other RAF units
subsequently re-equipping with the type were Nos 2,
6, 14, 17, 20, 31 and 41 Squadrons, Nos 2 and 41
operating in the reconnaissance role. The total
number of Jaguar GR1s in RAF service (mid-1978)
was 165. The Jaguar B (Jaguar T Mk 2) is the RAF's
operational trainer version, which first flew on
30 August 1971. 37 had been delivered by the end
of 1976, completing the T Mk 2 order.

The Jaguar International is an export version,
similar to the Jaguar S but with more powerful
Adour engines. In 1977 12 aircraft were supplied to
the Sultan of Oman's Air Force and the Ecuadorean
Air Force. Under the terms of a 1968 agreement
signed by the British and French Defence ministries,
202 Jaguars were built for the RAF and 200 for the
French Air Force. A proposed variant for the French
Navy, designated Jaguar M, was abandoned in
1973.

Shin Meiwa PS-1
Japan

Role: Long-Range Maritime Patrol
Operational: 1973-

Engines: Four 2,850ehp Ishikawajima-built General
Electric T64-IHI-10 turboprops
Span: 108ft 8¾in
Length: 109ft 11in
Weight: 58,000lb (empty)
79,365lb (normal loaded)
Crew: 10
Max speed: 340mph at 5,000ft
Service ceiling: 29,500ft
Range: 1,347 miles (normal)
Weapons: Various ASW stores in upper deck
weapons bay aft of tactical compartment

In 1966, the Shin Meiwa Industry Co Ltd was awarded a contract to develop a STOL long-range anti-submarine flying boat for the Japan Maritime Self-Defence Force under the designation PX-S. Shin Meiwa had already carried out research into such a project for seven years beforehand, and during this period the company rebuilt a Grumman Albatross as a flying scale model of the new design, with the designation UF-XS. The first full-scale PX-S prototype flew for the first time on 5 October 1957, followed by a second aircraft on 14 June 1968. Both aircraft were handed over to the 415th Flight Test Squadron of the JMSDF at Iwakuni for service trials, and two pre-series machines were built, these being

designated SS-2 by Shin Meiwa and PS-1 by the JMSDF. Ten production aircraft were built, and the 31st Maritime Air Group became operational with the type on 1 March 1973 at Iwakuni. The PS-1 has a very low landing and take-off speed, and is designed to dip its sonar equipment into the sea during repeated landings and take-offs, even in rough wave conditions. In July 1972, Shin Meiwa began design work on a further variant, the PS-1S (SS-2A), an amphibian intended primarily for the air-sea rescue role. Powered by four T64/P4C turboprops developing 3,400hp, the prototype flew for the first time on 16 October 1964. Its designation was later changed to RS-1 and, finally, US-1.

SNACAC NC900

Role: Single-Seat Fighter
Operational: 1945-46

Engines: One 2,100hp BMW 801D-2 radial
Span: 34ft 5½in
Length: 29ft
Weight: 7,000lb (empty)
9,750lb (loaded)
Crew: 1
Max speed: 408mph at 20,600ft
Service ceiling: 37,400ft
Range: 500 miles
Weapons: Four 20mm MG 151 cannon and two 13mm MG 131 machine guns

Following the withdrawal of German forces from French territory late in 1944, the aircraft factory of

Germany (French-built)

the SNCA du Centre at Cravant, near Auxerre, which had retained a clandestine production facility during the occupation, began manufacture of the Focke-Wulf Fw190A-5 fighter under the designation NC900. The first French-built machine flew for the first time on 16 March 1945 and a total of 64 were produced, these being both the Fw190A-5 and A-8 variants. The type was generally unsuccessful, mainly because the BMW 801D-2 radial engines used by SNAC had been assembled from components manufactured in France during the occupation and had been tampered with by French workers. No funds were available to manufacture new components and the majority of NC900s soon became unserviceable through engine seizure. A few, however, served operationally for a brief period with GCIII/5 'Normandie-Niemen', somewhat strange bedfellows for that unit's Yak-3s.

Sud-Aviation S04050 Vautour

Role: Interceptor/Close Support
Operational: 1956-
Data: IIN

Engines: Two 7,720lb thrust SNECMA Atar 101E3 turbojets
Span: 49ft 6½in
Length: 51ft 1in
Weight: 23,150lb (empty)
33,069lb (normal loaded)
Crew: 2
Max speed: 686mph at sea level
Service ceiling: 50,000ft
Range: 3,700 miles (max ferry)
Weapons: Four 30mm DEFA 552 cannon in nose; two MATRA 104A rocket packs with 232 68mm

France

SNEB rockets; four MATRA 116E underwing pods with 19 rockets, for four MATRA 510, 511 or 530 AAMs

Designed from the outset to carry out three tasks — all weather interception, close support and high altitude bombing — the S04050 Vautour was the product of a French Air Force specification issued in 1951. The prototype flew on 16 October 1952, powered by two 5,280lb thrust SNECMA Atar 101B turbojets, followed by a second and third prototype with Atar 101Cs and Armstrong Siddeley Sapphire ASSa6s. Six pre-production aircraft were ordered for service evaluation, the first flying in March 1955. All but one were powered by 6,615lb thrust Atar 101Ds, the sole exception using 9,260lb thrust Rolls-Royce Avons.

Two production versions were ordered, the Vautour IIB (light bomber) and the IIN (all-weather interceptor). 40 IIBs were ordered in 1955, the first series production aircraft flying on 3 July 1957, and the type entered service in December that year with the 92e Escadre de Bombardement (1/92 'Bourgogne' and 2/92 'Aquitaine') at Bordeaux. All Vautours in French service were powered by the SNECMA Atar 101E3.

Seventy examples of the Vautour IIN were ordered, the first entering service with the 6e Escadre de Chasse in 1956. The next Vautour IIN unit was the 30e Escadre de Chasse, 3/30 'Lorraine' receiving the type at Tours in 1957, 1/30 'Loire' at Creil in February 1961, and 2/30 at Reims in 1962. GC 2/30 inherited the traditions of the famous 'Normandie-Niemen' Regiment of World War II and

retained its Vautours until 1974, when they were replaced by Mirage F-1Cs. Some of the surplus IINs were allocated to GB 2/92 at Bordeaux, this being the last French Air Force unit to use the type. In 1958 Sud-Aviation developed the final version of the Vautour, the IIBR. This was a bomber-reconnaissance variant with CSF radar, flight refuelling equipment and a fuselage camera pack. A few were converted to the flying tanker role in support of the Mirage IV nuclear strike force.

The close support version of the Vautour, the IIA, did not enter service with the French Air Force, but 20 were supplied to the Israeli Air Force, together with four IINs. The IAF's Vautours saw combat during the Six-Day War of June 1967, and some were later converted to the ECM role. Both the IIA and IIB versions were single-seaters.

Sukhoi Su-7B/Su-17   USSR

Role: Tactical Fighter-Bomber
Operational: 1960-
NATO Code-Name: Fitter
Data: Su-17

Engines: One 17,200lb thrust Lyulka AL-21F-3 turbojet (25,000lb with reheat)
Span: 45ft 11¼in
Length: 50ft 6¼in
Weight: 22,046lb (empty)
41,887lb (max loaded)
Crew: 1
Max speed: Mach 2.17 at height
Service ceiling: 59,050ft
Range: 1,300 miles with max external fuel
Weapons: One 30mm NR-30 cannon in each wing root; up to 11,023lb of underwing stores, including bombs, rockets and ASMs

First seen in prototype form at the 1956 Tushino Air Display, the Sukhoi Su-7 was subsequently built in large numbers and was the standard tactical fighter-bomber with Russia's Frontovaia Aviatsiya throughout the 1960s. Designated Fitter-A under the NATO reporting system, the aircraft features sharply-

swept (60-degree) wings and carries a considerable range of underwing stores, including rocket packs and bombs, as well as two external fuel tanks under the fuselage. For short-field take-off, there is provision for two solid-fuel rockets under the rear fuselage. The basic Su-7 has undergone a number of modifications during its service career and later production aircraft are fitted with two large brake parachutes and a revised cannon installation, possibly housing twin-barrel 23mm weapons in place of the more usual 30mm. Late production aircraft are designated Su-7BM, the M standing for Modifikatsirovanny. About 400 Su-7s were still in service with the Soviet Air Force in 1977 and the type has been exported to Cuba, Czechoslovakia, Egypt, East Germany, Hungary, India, Iraq, Poland, Syria and North Vietnam. Egyptian Air Force Su-7s saw combat during the Six-Day War of 1967 and the Yom Kippur War of 1973, while Indian Air Force machines attacked Pakistani ground targets in the 1971 conflict.The Su-7U, code-named Moujik, is a tandem two-seat trainer version which made its first public appearance in 1967.

Another Su-7 variant which appeared in 1967 was the Su-17 'Fitter-B', which was identical with the Su-7 except for the wing panels, which were

moveable outboard of the main undercarriage. This variable-geometry version entered service with the Soviet AF in the early 1970s, the VG configuration offering a considerable improvement in take-off and landing performance. Operational Su-17s incorporate a number of refinements and are known by the NATO code-name of Fitter-C and -D, the latter variant having a small radome under the nose and laser rangefinding equipment. Su-17 attack units were widely deployed in eastern Europe in 1977-78. A slightly modified export version, with some equipment deleted, is designated Su-20/22.

Sukhoi Su-9/Su-11 — USSR

Role: All-Weather Fighter
Operational: 1959-
NATO Code-Name: Fishpot
Photo: Su-11
Data: Su-9 (estimated)

Engines: One 19,840lb thrust Lyulka AL-7F turbojet
Span: 27ft 8in
Length: 55ft
Weight: 20,000lb (empty)
30,000lb (loaded)
Crew: 1
Max speed: 1,190mph at 40,000ft
Service ceiling: 55,000ft
Range: 900 miles with external fuel
Weapons: Four 'Alkali' radar-homing AAMs, or two 'Anab' infra-red homing AAMs

One of the new generation of Soviet combat aircraft which came as a considerable shock to western observers at the Tushino Air Display in May 1956, the Sukhoi Su-9 single-seat all-weather interceptor used basically the same fuselage and tail unit as the Su-7B ground-attack aircraft, but featured a delta wing similar to that of the MiG-21. The type entered service with the Societ Air Force in 1959, production aircraft differing somewhat from the prototypes in that they were fitted with a conical radome in the centre of a small-diameter air intake (the early examples, dubbed Fishpot-A, having a very small radome mounted above the intake). The first production variant, code-named Fishpot-B, carried four 'Alkali' radar-homing AAMs on underwing pylons and, like the Su-7, two fuel tanks were mounted side-by-side under the fuselage.

The Su-11, first seen publicly in 1967, is an improved version with an uprated Lyulka AL-7F-1 turbojet and a lengthened fuselage, the nose cone being enlarged to accommodate more advanced AI radar. This variant is code-named Fishpot-C and carries an armament of two 'Anab' missiles. In 1977, about one-quarter of the IA-PVO's interceptor squadrons were still equipped with either the Su-9 or Su-11. A tandem two-seat trainer version of the Su-9 is code-named 'Maiden'.

Sukhoi Su-15

Role: All-Weather Interceptor
Operational: 1968-
NATO Code-Name: Flagon

Engines: Two unidentified turbojets, possibly of Lyulka design
Span: 30ft (Flagon-D, -E and -F: 34ft 6in)
Length: 68ft
Weight: 35,275lb (max loaded)
Crew: 1
Max speed: Mach 2.3 at 36,000ft
Service ceiling: 65,000ft
Range: 1,100 miles
Weapons: One AAM under each wing; side-by-side pylons under centre fuselage for additional weapons or fuel tanks

First identified in 1967 when 10 examples appeared at the Domodedovo Air Display, the Sukhoi Su-15

USSR

was developed in response to a Soviet Air Force requirement for a large, long-range single-seat all-weather fighter to succeed the Su-11. The initial production version, Flagon-A, is thought to have been built in small numbers only and to have entered service with the IA-PVO sometime in 1968. The Flagon-B, which was also displayed at Domodedovo in July 1967, was an experimental STOL version with three vertically-mounted jet lift engines in the centre fuselage, while the Flagon-C was a two-seat trainer version. The Flagon-D was similar to the early production model but featured a compound sweep wing in place of the Flagon-A's 'straight' delta configuration, and the new planform was retained on the Flagon-E, which was the major production version and entered service with the IA-PVO in 1973. The latest operational version, Flagon-F, has a new radome and uprated engines. Between 700 and 800 Su-15s were thought to be serving with the Soviet Air Force in 1978.

Sukhoi Su-19

Role: Tactical Strike
Operational: 1975-
NATO Code-Name: Fencer

Engines: Two 17,200lb thrust (25,000lb with reheat) Lyulka AL-21F turbojets
Span: 56ft 3in (spread)
31ft 3in (swept)
Length: 69ft 10in
Weight: 68,000lb (loaded)
Crew: 2
Max speed: Mach 1.2 at sea level
Service ceiling: 60,000ft +
Range: 500 miles, low-level with full weapons load
Weapons: One GSh-23 twin-barrel 23mm cannon; up to 10,000lb of offensive stores under wings and fuselage

USSR

In the same category as the General Dynamics F-111, the Sukhoi Su-19 is a variable-geometry tactical strike aircraft which was first identified in 1974. The type entered operational service with the Soviet Air Force a year later and about 300 were in use by the end of 1977, equipping first-line tactical squadrons in European Russia. Some units are also reportedly deployed in East Germany. Very little information had been released about the Su-19 up to the middle of 1978, but its engine layout is similar to that of the Su-15 Flagon and the two-man crew is seated side-by-side in an apparently roomy cockpit. Wing leading-edge sweep appears to be about 70 degrees in the fully-swept position, and 23 degrees in the fully spread position.

Supermarine Attacker

Role: Carrier-Borne Strike Fighter
Operational: 1951-58
Specification: E1/45

Engines: One 5,000lb thrust RR Nene 3 (F1 and FB1); one 5,100lb thrust RR Nene 102 (FB2)
Span: 36ft 11in
Length: 37ft 6in
Weight: 8,434lb (F1), 9,910lb (FB2)
Weight loaded: 11,500lb (F1), 12,300lb (FB2)
Crew: 1
Max speed: 590mph at sea level
Service ceiling: 45,000ft
Range: 590 miles normal, 1,190 miles with belly tank
Weapons: Four 20mm cannon, eight 60lb rockets or two 1,000lb bombs

At the end of World War II, the Royal Navy carried out deck-landing trials with both Meteor and Vampire jet fighters, specially modified for carrier

UK

operation. Neither type proved suitable, however, and the Navy was forced to look elsewhere to meet its needs. Accordingly, an order was placed for two prototypes of a navalised version of the Supermarine Attacker, the prototype of which — designed to specification E10/44 — flew on 27 July 1946. The first prototype of the naval variant, to specification E1/45, made its first flight on 17 June 1947, and in November 1949 it was decided to order sufficient Attackers to equip three first-line Fleet Air Arm squadrons, the RAF having in the meantime decided to abandon the landplane version in favour of the Vampire and Meteor, over which it had no performance advantage.

The initial order called for 60 Attacker F1s, the first production machine flying in April 1950. Because the aircraft was required to act in the strike role as well as in that of interceptor, its wing — the design of which was based on the piston-engined Supermarine Spiteful — had to be strengthened to accommodate underwing rocket rails and bomb racks, and because of these modifications it was not

until August 1951 that the first Attackers entered service with No 800 Squadron at Ford, in Sussex, making that unit the Fleet Air Arm's first operational jet squadron. A second squadron, No 803, was formed in November 1951, the two units having eight Attackers each. Both squadrons — No 800 with Attacker FB1s and No 803 with F1s — went aboard HMS *Eagle* in September 1952 and spent a month working into the routine of carrier life. During this time a third Attacker squadron, No 890, was formed at Ford, but it was disbanded again only weeks later and its aircraft allocated to Nos 800 and 803.

Meanwhile Supermarine's had produced a new version of the Attacker, the FB2, powered by a Rolls-Royce Nene 102 in place of the earlier Nene 3 and

featuring modified ailerons and cockpit hood; 85 were ordered, and these began to re-equip the Attacker squadrons in May 1953. Both units spent a good deal of time afloat in HMS *Eagle*, No 803 having a four-month spell ashore at Hal Far, Malta, in the summer of 1954, but by the autumn of that year they had exchanged their Attackers for Sea Hawks. The Attacker continued to serve as an operational trainer with No 736 Squadron and with fighter squadrons of the RNVR until the latter were disbanded in 1957.

Thirty-six Attackers were also delivered to the Pakistan Air Force in 1952-53 and continued in service until the late 1950s, when they were replaced by F-86F Sabres.

Supermarine Scimitar UK

Role: Carrier-Borne Strike Fighter
Operational: 1958-66
Specification:

Engines: Two 11,250lb thrust Rolls-Royce Avon 202 turbojets
Span: 37ft 2in
Length: 55ft 4in
Weight: 33,000lb (normal loaded)
Crew: 1
Max speed: 710mph at 10,000ft
Service ceiling: 50,000ft
Range: 1,500 miles (max)
Weapons: Four 30mm Aden cannon and 48 2in FFARs in underwing pods, or four Sidewinder AAMs; four 1,000lb bombs or four Bullpup ASMs

The Supermarine Scimitar was the end product of a lengthy evolutionary process dating back to 1945 and the Supermarine 505, a carrier-based fighter project which was revised several times, its design becoming successively the Types 508, 525 and 529.

The design finally crystallised in the Type 544, the first of three prototypes flying on 20 January 1956. The type was ordered into production for the Fleet Air Arm as the Scimitar F1 and the first production aircraft flew on 11 January 1957, powered by two Rolls-Royce Avon 202 turbojets rated at 11,250lb thrust each. The first Scimitars were delivered to No 700X Trials Flight in August 1957 and No 803 Squadron formed with the type in June 1958, followed by Nos 807, 800 and 804 Squadrons. 100 Scimitars were originally ordered but this was later reduced to 76, the last aircraft being delivered in September 1960. In 1962 the Scimitar was modified to carry the Bullpup ASM, and its striking power was further extended by provision for four Sidewinder AAMs in addition to its four 30mm cannon. The type was progressively phased out of service with the introduction of the Buccaner S1 and by 1966 it had been withdrawn from first-line service as a strike aircraft, although some Scimitars were converted to the tanker role and others were allocated to Nos 736 and 764 Squadrons for use as operational trainers.

Supermarine Spitfire/Seafire (postwar) UK

Role: Fighter
Operational: 1938-55 (Spitfire)
1942-54 (Seafire)
Photo: PR19
Data: Spitfire Mks 21-24

Engines: One Rolls-Royce Griffon 61 or 85 engine developing 2,050hp
Span: 36ft 11in
Length: 32ft 8in
Weight: 7,160lb (empty)
9,900lb (normal loaded)
Crew: 1
Max speed: 450mph at 19,000ft
Service ceiling: 43,000ft
Range: 965 miles with auxiliary tank
Weapons: Four 20mm Hispano Mk II cannon

Although Supermarine's excellent Spitfire and its naval counterpart, the Seafire, will always be remembered for the sterling service they rendered in all theatres during World War II, both types continued in production for some time after the conflict and remained important combat aircraft on the inventories of several air forces during the postwar years. In Britain, Spitfire F21s and 22s equipped 13 squadrons of the Royal Auxiliary Air Force between 1946 and 1950, while in the Far East the Spitfires of No 155 Squadron flew several strikes against Indonesian extremists in November 1945. In 1948 the Spitfires of Nos 28 and 60 Squadrons struck at terrorist hideouts in Malaya, the last Spitfire mission in this trouble spot being flown by a 60 Squadron aircraft on 1 January 1951. Several Spitfire PR19s operated in the photo-reconnaissance role with No 81 Squadron in Singapore until April 1954, while in Hong Kong Spitfire 24s served with No 80 Squadron and the Hong Kong Auxiliary Air Force until 1955. In Burma, ex-RAF Spitfire F18s and LF9s, together with 20 ex-FAA Seafire IIIs, entered service with the air force of a newly-independent Burma between 1948 and 1954 and were used in counter-terrorist operations for some years. It was in Israel, however, that the Spitfire saw most postwar combat, with Egyptians

and Israeli Spitfire LF9s battling for air supremacy from the moment Israel became independent in May 1948. Several RAF Spitfires were also lost during the conflict, some when Egyptian aircraft strafed Tel Aviv (the home of Nos 32 and 208 Squadrons) and four FR18s of 208 Squadron when they were attacked by Israeli Spitfires over the Sinai. Apart from the Commonwealth Air Forces, all of which used Spitfires in considerable numbers, Spitfires were also supplied to Czechoslovakia, which received some LF9s in 1945; France, which received 172 LF9s in 1945-46, some of these being used operationally in Indo-China with GC 1/7 and II/7; Italy (110 LF/HF9s, some of which were supplied to Israel); Greece (77 LF9s in 1946-49); Belgium (Mks 14 and 16 in 1948-51); Turkey (198 LF9s in 1947-48); Argentina (one HF9); Denmark (36 HF9s); Thailand (30 Mk 14s); and Syria, which was the last Middle East air force to use the type.

In 1949, the Seafire 47s of the Fleet Air Arm's No 800 Squadron took part in anti-communist attacks in Malaya, and the following year they were the first British aircraft to see action in Korea. In the UK Seafires formed the equipment of three RNVR squadrons until 1951, when they were replaced by Sea Furies. 12 de-navalised Mk III Seafires were supplied to the Irish Air Corps in 1947.

Supermarine Swift

Role: Fighter/Reconnaissance
Operational: 1954-61
Specification: E41/46
Photo: F Mk 3
Data: FR Mk 5

Engines: One 9,450lb thrust Rolls-Royce Avon 114 turbojet
Span: 32ft 4in
Length: 42ft 3in
Weight: 13,000lb (empty)
21,400lb (loaded)
Crew: 1
Max speed: 685mph at sea level
Service ceiling: 55,000ft
Range: 950 miles
Weapons: Four 30mm Aden cannon

Although held by many to be a failure, the Supermarine Swift — which traced its lineage through a number of experimental jet aircraft to the

UK

famous Spitfire — can lay claim to fame on several counts. Not only was it at one time the World Air Speed Record holder, but it was also the first British fighter capable of supersonic performance and the first swept-wing type to enter service with the RAF. Its direct line of descent went back to 1946 and the Supermarine 510, an experimental version of the Attacker with swept wings which made its first flight on 29 December 1948, powered by a Rolls-Royce Nene II turbojet. The 510 was followed by the Type 535, which was identical except for a longer nose and tricycle undercarriage. This flew for the first time on 23 August 1950 and was in turn developed into the Type 541, which became the Swift prototype. Two Type 541 prototypes were in fact ordered, the first (WJ960) flying on 1 August 1951 and the second (WJ965) on 18 July 1952. The aircraft was ordered into priority production for the RAF as a high-altitude interceptor even before the first prototype had flown, the first order for 100 machines being placed in November 1950 at the height of the Korean crisis. This was followed by a further order for

50 aircraft in January 1951, and between that date and August 1953 production orders were increased to a total of 492, including 17 for the Ministry of Supply.

An initial series of 20 Swift F Mk 1s was built, the first flying on 25 August 1952 powered by a Rolls-Royce Avon RA7 developing 7,200lb thrust. Several of these were subsequently modified: WK195 became the Swift F Mk 3 prototype, WK197 was fitted with a ventral fuel tank, WK198 became the Swift F Mk 4 prototype, WK199 was fitted with four 30mm cannon instead of the usual two, WK200 became the Swift FR Mk 5 fighter-reconnaissance prototype, and WK201 was equipped with four machine guns and a ventral tank. The Swift F Mk 1 entered service with No 56 Squadron RAF in February 1954 and was followed by the Swift F Mk 2, with an armament of four 30mm cannon. Both these variants, however, were found to be unsuitable for their primary role of high-level interception, being prone to tightening in turns and suffering frequent high-altitude flameouts as a result of shock waves entering the air intakes when the

cannon were fired. Thirty-nine F1s and F2s were delivered to the RAF, being supplanted on the production line by the F3 (25 built) and the F4 (44 built), the latter being fitted with a moveable tailplane.

In February 1955 the Air Ministry concluded that the Swift could not be relied upon to carry out its primary role, and its day as a fighter was at an end, the type being replaced by the Hawker Hunter in RAF Fighter Command. Nevertheless, it was recognised that the Swift had a future as a low-level tactical reconnaissance aircraft, and 70 FR Mk 5s were built, the first entering service with No 2 Squadron in Germany in April 1956, followed by No 79 later that year. The FR5 remained in first-line service until 1961, when it was replaced by the Hunter FR10.

Other Swift variants were the PR Mk 6, a high-altitude strategic reconnaissance version whcih was abandoned, and the F7, 12 of which were built. These were used to test air-to-air missiles by the Guided Weapons Development Squadron at RAF Valley.

Tupolev Tu-2
USSR

Role: Attack Bomber
Operational: 1943-60
NATO Code-Name: Bat

Engines: Two 1,850hp ASh-82FN radials
Span: 61ft 10½in
Length: 45ft 3in
Weight: 18,200lb (empty)
22,884lb (normal loaded)
Crew: 4
Max speed: 340mph at 17,715ft
Service ceiling: 31,170ft
Range: 1,243 miles with a 3,000lb bomb load
Weapons: Two 20mm ShVAK cannon in wing roots; single 12.7mm machine guns in dorsal and ventral positions; normal bomb load of 2,205lb, maximum 6,614lb

First entering service in quantity with units of the Soviet Air Force's Frontovaia Aviatsiya in 1943, the twin-engined Tupolev Tu-2 attack bomber was one of the types which finally enabled the Russians to gain air superiority during the savage battles of 1944. By the end of hostilities over 1,100 had been delivered and development still continued, several

derivatives of the basic design having already been tested. These included the Tu-2D, a long range version with a greater span and additional fuel tanks, the Tu-2T torpedo-bomber for the Soviet Navy, and the Tu-2Sh, a ground attack variant with a solid nose housing two 37mm or 45mm cannon. By the time production ended in 1947 some 3,000 Tu-2s had been built and the type equipped the majority of Soviet Bloc attack squadrons well into the 1950s. Chinese Communist Tu-2s were encountered frequently during the Korean War and considerable numbers were destroyed by UN pilots. On one occasion (30 November 1951) F-86 Sabre pilots of the 4th Fighter Interceptor Group shot down eight out of a formation of 12 Tu-2s south of the Yalu, together with three escorting La-9 fighters.

During the postwar years Tu-2s were flown with several experimental engine installations. One variant, designated UTB, was converted by Sukhoi as an instructional training bomber and fitted with 700hp ASh-21 engines instead of the usual 1,850hp ASh-82FNs, some examples being supplied to the Polish Air Force. The Tu-2's robust airframe made it an ideal test-bed, and it was used in this capacity for some time after its retirement from operational service.

Tupolev Tu-4   USSR

Role: Strategic Heavy Bomber
Operational: 1948-68
NATO Code-Name: Bull

Engines: Four 2,200hp 18-cylinder radials (copies of Wright Cyclone R-3350)
Span: 141ft 3in
Length: 99ft
Weight: 74,500lb (empty)
120,000lb (loaded)
Crew: 10-14
Max speed: 357mph at 30,000ft
Service ceiling: 33,600ft
Range: 3,250 miles (normal)
Weapons: 12 .5in machine guns and one 20mm cannon; up to 12,000lb of bombs or maritime stores

In the summer and autumn of 1944, three Boeing B-29 Superfortresses, operating out of advanced bases in China, made emergency landings on Soviet territory following attacks on Japanese targets. For the Russians, the arrival of the B-29s was providential, for the Soviet Union had no truly long-range strategic bomber and it was estimated that it would be at least 1950 before an indigenous design could be brought into service. It was therefore decided to copy the B-29 down to the minutest detail, thus enabling the Soviet aviation industry to avoid most of the technical problems inherent in designing a modern, complex bomber from scratch. The programme was given the highest priority by Stalin himself. The task of copying the B-29's airframe was assigned to Andrei N. Tupolev's design bureau, while the job of reproducing the aircraft's Wright Cyclone R-3350 motors fell to Arkadii M. Shvetsov's engine design bureau. A major portion of the aviation industry was involved in the programme, as well as numerous research institutes whose task it was to develop new production techniques, materials, electronics and so on. Two of the impounded B-29s were stripped down to the last rivet, while the third was retained for flight testing. The prototype Tu-4, as the B-29 copy was designated, was allocated to the NII V-VS (the Soviet Air Force Test Centre) in the summer of 1946, followed by a second aircraft some weeks later. An initial batch of 20 pre-series aircraft was built, and the first series production aircraft were issued to the squadrons of the Dalnaya Aviatsiya (Long-Range

Aviation) at the beginning of 1948. By this time the Tu-4's existence had already been revealed publicly, three pre-series aircraft having carried out a flypast at the Tushino air display in August 1947.

The service introduction of the Tu-4 was not without its problems, early series aircraft suffering from continual troubles with the Ash-73TK engines, the remote-controlled defensive armament and the pressurisation system. Most of these troubles resulted from the crash development programme, during which some snags inevitably went unnoticed, but the more serious among them were ironed out when quality production control was tightened up. Nevertheless, it was the middle of 1949 before the first DA Air Division was declared fully operational with 90 Tu-4s. By the end of the year 300 aircraft were in service, together with a small number assigned to the AV-MF, the Soviet Naval Air Arm, for long-range maritime patrol.

Several advanced Tu-4 derivatives were proposed by Tupolev in the early 1950s (see Prototypes Section) but these were shelved when it was decided to concentrate on the development of long-range jet and turboprop-powered bombers. This decision, however, meant that the Tu-4 remained first-line equipment in the DA up to 1960, and in fact the much-publicised U-2 reconnaissance photographs shown to the world by the Russians in May of that year revealed a line-up of Tu-4s on a Soviet airfield.

Some Tu-4s were used as test-beds for equipment destined for new types such as the Tu-20 and Mya-4. One Tu-4, for example, was fitted with a bogie-type undercarriage and wingtip outriggers, similar to that employed by the Mya-4, and was also equipped with RATOG developing a thrust of 20,000lb. Other Tu-4s were used for flight refuelling experiments, and many were taken on to the inventory of the Soviet Air Force Transport Command when they were retired from the DA. Transport Tu-4s were modified by the addition of underwing containers, with a consequent adverse effect on performance, and they were retired from service with the advent of the Antonov An-12. Maritime Tu-4s were also retired in the early 1960s.

A number of Tu-4s were supplied to Red China, and these formed the nucleus of a small strategic bombing force. A handful of Tu-4s were still known to be serving with the Chinese People's Air Force in 1968.

Tupolev Tu-14   USSR

Role: Naval Attack Bomber
Operational: 1950-64
NATO Code-Name: Bosun

Engines: Two 5,950lb thrust Klimov VK-1 turbojets
Span: 70ft
Length: 68ft
Weight: 33,500lb (empty)
57,000lb (max loaded)
Crew: 4
Max speed: 528mph
Service ceiling: 36,900ft
Range: 1,750miles

Weapons: Four forward-firing 12.7mm machine guns; two 23mm cannon in tail position; up to 6,700lb of bombs, torpedoes or mines

Like Ilyushin's Il-28, the Tupolev Tu-14 was designed to meet a Soviet Air Force requirement for a light jet attack bomber to replace the ageing Tu-2 with the Frontovaia Aviatsiya. Bearing the manufacturer's designation Tu-81, the prototype flew for the first time in 1949, some months later than the Il-28, and was powered by two Klimov VK-1 (Rolls-Royce Nene) turbojets, plans to use the RR Derwent as an alternative powerplant having been abandoned. In the event, the Il-28 was selected as the principal Soviet Air Force tactical jet bomber, but the Tu-14's greater endurance, together with a long weapons bay capable of accommodating torpedoes and a variety of other maritime stores, made it suitable for the naval attack role and it was chosen to equip the light bomber squadrons of the A-VMF, the Soviet Naval Air Arm. Of conventional design, with underslung engines, a straight wing and swept tailplane, the Tu-14 was built in considerable numbers and also served in the photo-reconnaissance and electronic intelligence roles, being eventually phased out of service in the mid-1960s.

Tupolev Tu-16 USSR

Role: Bomber/Reconnaissance
Operational: 1955-
NATO Code-Name: Badger

Engines: Two Mikulin AM-3M turbojets, each rated at 20,950lb thrust
Span: 110ft
Length: 120ft
Weight: Empty not known
150,000 (normal loaded)
Crew: 7-10, depending on mission
Max speed: 587mph at 35,000ft
Service ceiling: 42,650ft
Range: 3,000 miles with max bomb load
Weapons: Two 23mm Nudelman-Rikhter cannon in dorsal and ventral barbettes; two 23mm in tail position; one fixed 23mm on starboard side of nose (early versions only; up to 19,800lb of conventional or nuclear weapons in internal bomb bay; subsonic ASMs or trans-sonic rocket missiles under wings)

First seen publicly at the Tushino Air Display in May 1954, the Tupolev Tu-16 flew for the first time in 1952 under the manufacturer's designation Tu-88, and was destined to become the most important bomber type on the inventories of the Soviet Air Force and Naval Air Arm for well over a decade. Some 2,000 were built, and half of these were still believed to be serving in one role or another in 1977-78. The first strategic bomber version was the Badger-A (to use the NATO reporting system), and in addition to serving in large numbers with the Soviet Air Forces this type was also supplied to Iraq (nine) and Egypt (30). All 30 of the Egyptian aircraft and one of the Iraqi machines were destroyed during the Arab-Israeli Six Day War. The Badger-B was similar, but was equipped to carry two swept-wing anti-shipping missiles (code-name: Kennel) on underwing pylons. Twenty-five Badger-Bs were supplied to Indonesia in 1961, equipping two squadrons.

The Badger-C, first identified in 1961, was equipped with a large stand-off bomb similar in configuration to the American 'Hound Dog'. This weapon, code-named Kipper, was stated to be primarily for anti-shipping use. The Badger-C had a large nose radome, and the nose armament of one fixed 23mm cannon, a feature of earlier variants, was deleted. The Badger-D was a maritime reconnaissance version with an enlarged radome under the nose and electronic surveillance equipment in blisters under the fuselage. The Badger-E was basically a Badger-A with a battery of cameras in the bomb bay for high-altitude maritime photo-reconnaissance, while the Badger-F was fitted with an electronic reconnaissance pod under each wing. About 150 Badger-Cs, Ds, Es and Fs were operational with the Soviet Naval Air Arm in 1977, and five hundred Badger-As were still believed to be in service with the Soviet Air Force in a wide variety of roles, ranging from flight refuelling tankers (with wingtip-to-wingtip refuelling equipment) to crew trainers.

The latest variant, the Badger-G, carries two rocket-powered 'Kelt' anti-shipping missiles on underwing pylons, and about 250 are thought to be in service with the Soviet Naval Air Arm. 25 were also supplied to Egypt, and some of these saw action during the Yom Kippur War of October 1973, launching a number of 'Kelts' against targets in Sinai. Tu-16s make regular maritime surveillance and electronic intelligence flights over the North Atlantic and Mediterranean areas, the type used mainly for these missions being the Badger-F. About 60 Tu-16s were built in Communist China from 1968, and equip that country's small strategic bomber force.

Tupolev Tu-22

USSR

Role: Bomber/Reconnaissance
Operational: 1962-
NATO Code-Name: Blinder
Data: Estimated

Engines: Two unidentified turbojet engines rated at approx 27,000lb thrust with reheat
Span: 90ft 10½in
Length: 132ft 11½in
Weight: not known empty
185,000lb (loaded)
Crew: 3
Max speed: 990mph at 40,000ft
Service ceiling: 60,000ft
Range: 4,000 miles with one in-flight refuelling
Weapons: One 23mm cannon in remotely-controlled tail barbette; free-falling nuclear or conventional weapons, or one recessed 'Kitchen' stand-off missile with a range of approx 460 miles

First shown publicly in pre-series form at the 1961 Tushino Air Display, the Tu-22 was the first supersonic bomber to enter service with the Soviet Air Forces. The first operational version, code-named Blinder-A, was produced in limited numbers only, its range of about 1,400 miles falling short of planned strategic requirements. The second variant, Blinder-B, was fitted with a flight refuelling probe and was equipped to carry an air-to-surface stand-off missile (NATO code-name: Kitchen) recessed in the weapons bay. This version, some 200 of which are believed to have been built, was intended primarily for the Soviet Naval Air Arm in the anti-shipping role, and carried a nose-mounted search radar. Twelve examples were supplied to the Libyan Air Force. The Blinder-C is a maritime reconnaissance version carrying a battery of six cameras in the weapons bay and is equipped for the electronic surveillance and ECM role. Between 60 and 70 were in service with the Soviet Naval Air Arm in 1978, operating mainly over the Baltic and Black Sea areas. The Blinder-D is a two-seat operational trainer version, and a further variant has been identified with air-to-air missiles. The latter's operational status is uncertain, but small numbers are believed to be serving in the long-range air defence role.

Tupolev Tu-26

Role: Variable-Geometry Strategic Bomber
Operational: 1975-
NATO Code-Name: Backfire
Data: Estimated

Engines: Unidentified, but probably two Kuznetsov turbofans developing 44,090lb thrust with reheat
Span: 113ft (fully spread)
86ft (fully swept)
Length: 132ft
Weight: 270,000lb (max loaded)
Crew: 4
Max speed: Mach 2.5 at altitude
Service ceiling: 65,000ft
Range: 6,000 miles
Weapons: Variety of free-falling or stand-off air-to-surface missiles, including the AS-6 (NATO Code-name: Kingfish) liquid-fuel rocket weapon with mid-course guidance and active radar homing, designed for low-level nuclear or conventional strike at a range of up to 155 miles from the parent aircraft

In the autumn of 1969, official US sources stated that the Soviet Union was developing a new supersonic variable-geometry medium bomber, presumably to supplant or complement the Tu-22 Blinder in service with the Soviet Air Forces. In July 1970, intelligence satellite data confirmed that the aircraft existed in prototype form, and it was later identified as a twin-engined Tupolev design. About a

USSR

dozen machines were flying by the end of 1973, and the type's designation was reported to be Tu-26.

The Tu-26's design bears some resemblance to that of a Tupolev supersonic bomber prototype built and flown in the late 1950s under the manufacturer's designation Tu-98 (NATO code-name: Backfin). Tu-26 design requirements called for a maximum over-the-target speed in the order of Mach 2.5, a maximum unrefuelled range of up to 6,000 miles at high altitude and low-level penetration capability. Again according to US sources, early production Tu-26s (Backfire-As) fell short of the range requirement, but the subsequent model, the Backfire-B, is believed to meet all operational demands. The Backfire-A had large undercarriage fairings on the wing trailing edges, but these are eliminated in the Backfire-B and the latter version also has an increased wingspan.

Both versions of the Backfire entered service with the Soviet Air Force in 1975, and towards the end of that year some maritime reconnaissance/strike units of the Soviet Naval Air Arm also re-equipped with the type. About 120 Backfire-As and -Bs were believed to be in service in 1978, and eventual total production is estimated at 400 aircraft. The Backfire is likely to remain one of the most important items on the Soviet inventory throughout the 1980s, being the only modern Soviet bomber capable of attacking targets on the North American continent without refuelling. In the low-level naval strike role, it also poses a considerable threat to NATO maritime power.

Tupolev Tu-28

Role: Long-Range Interceptor
Operational: 1962-
NATO Code-Name: Fiddler
Data: Estimated

Engines: Two unidentified afterburning turbojets with a maximum rating of approx 27,000lb thrust
Span: 65ft
Length: 85ft
Weight: 78,000lb (normal loaded)
Crew: 2
Max speed: 1,150mph at 36,000ft
Service ceiling: 65,620ft
Range: 3,100 miles with max fuel
Weapons: Four 'Ash' air-to-air missiles on underwing pylons

USSR

Originally thought to be a Yakovlev design when it first appeared publicly at Tushino in 1961, the Tupolev Tu-28P is the largest fighter to enter operational service anywhere in the world. The suffix 'P' (Perekhvatchik= Interceptor) is interesting, because when this is applied to Soviet aircraft designations it indicates that a type has been *adapted* as a fighter. It is possible, therefore, that the Tu-28 was originally designed as a low-level strike aircraft, possibly in the anti-shipping role, and that its adaptation as a fighter came as a result of a pressing Soviet Air Force requirement for an aircraft capable of intercepting Strategic Air Command's B-52s while the latter were still outside stand-off missile launch range.

Since its entry into full operational service in 1962, the Tu-28P has been given a progressively

heavier armament, the latest version carrying four air-to-air missiles. The aircraft has full all-weather capability and advanced AI radar housed in a large ogival nose radome. Some have been converted to the electronic countermeasures role, with ECM equipment in a ventral pack. It is possible that the Tu-28P is gradually being replaced as a long-range interceptor by a version of the Tu-22 'Blinder', as the latter is replaced in turn by the Tu-26 Backfire VG bomber.

Tupolev Tu-95   USSR

Role: Long-Range Strategic
Attack/Maritime Reconnaissance
Operational: 1956-
NATO Code-Name: Bear
Data: Bear-D

Engines: Four Kuznetsov NK-12 turboprops uprated to 14,795eshp
Span: 180ft
Length: 150ft
Weight: 340,000lb (loaded)
Crew: 10-13
Max speed: 620mph
Service ceiling: 40,000ft
Range: 7,800 miles max
Weapons: Twin 23mm cannon in dorsal, ventral and tail positions. Internal provision for variety of maritime stores, including nuclear and conventional free-falling weapons

In 1952 the lessons of the Korean War were already bringing about profound changes in combat aircraft design policy in both East and West. One of the principal conclusions was that piston-engined bombers such as the B-29 and its Soviet copy, the Tu-4, could no longer survive in an environment dominated by jet fighters. Accordingly, the Soviet design bureaux of Tupolev and Myasishchev were each selected to develop a new and fast strategic heavy bomber, potentially capable of attacking North America across the Pole. Originally, the emphasis was placed on the four-jet, swept-wing design proposed by Myasishchev, which was to emerge as the Mya-4 'Molot' (NATO code-name: Bison). The main reason for this was the belief that Tupolev's turboprop-powered design would be limited to Mach 0.76.

The Tupolev aircraft, designated Tu-95, was certainly radical, with four turboprops mounted on a swept wing. The Kuznetsov-designed engines were developed to a specification that called for 12,000shp at sea level and 8,000shp at Mach 0.85 and 36,000ft, the weight (minus propeller) being limited to 5,130lb. The aircraft specification envisaged a maximum speed of Mach 0.85, a radius of action of 4,000 miles and an economical cruising speed of Mach 0.7 at 36,000ft with a payload of 11,000lb.

To bring the project to fruition as quickly as possible, Tupolev's team retained the structural techniques evolved in producing the Tu-4 and its derivatives. The fuselage was basically that of the Tu-85 (see Prototypes Section), married to swept flying surfaces. It was of semi-monocoque construction with three pressurised compartments; those situated immediately fore and aft of the bomb-bay were linked by a tunnel, while the third, in the extreme tail, was isolated. Defensive armament comprised a remote-controlled rear dorsal turret with two 23mm cannon, a rear ventral turret and a tail turret with two 23mm guns each. All these weapons were controlled from a single post with two observation blisters situated on either side of the fuselage under the tailplane.

Development of the Mya-4 and the Tu-95 proceeded in parallel, several prototypes of each being built for evaluation, and it was intended that both types should take part in the Tushino flypast in May 1954. Some delay was experienced with the Tu-95's engines, however, and in the event only the Myasishchev design was test flown in time. Flight tests of the Tu-95 began in the summer of 1954, and seven pre-series aircraft made an appearance at Tushino on 3 July 1955. By this time the importance of the turboprop-powered bomber was growing, for the performance of the four-jet Mya-4 had fallen considerably short of expectations and as a result production orders were cut back drastically. Even though the Tu-95's Kuznetsov NK-12 engines were

still causing problems, developing only 8,000-9,000shp in practice instead of the expected 12,000, it was realised that the Tupolev design would form the mainstay of the Dalnaya Aviatsiya's strategic air divisions for at least the next decade.

The Tu-95 entered service with the DA in the second half of 1956. Two years later, reconnaissance flights by U-2 aircraft revealed that the number of Tu-95s deployed on Soviet airfields far exceeded that of the Mya-4, and that consequently it was the Tupolev aircraft which presented the greatest long-range threat to North America. Several different versions of the Tu-95 were identified during the years that followed, some of them serving with the Soviet Fleet in the maritime reconnaissance role. The original Bear-A version was followed by the Bear-B, which was first seen in 1961; this was fitted with a flight refuelling probe and a large under-the-nose radome, and carried an air-to-surface missile ('Kangaroo'). The Bear-C was generally similar except for streamlined blisters on both sides of the rear fuselage.

The Bear-D, which was first photographed by US icebreakers off Severnya Zemlya in August 1967, had a number of important modifications, including a large ventral radome for X-band radar and several new electronics blisters. This variant operates in conjunction with Soviet submarines and surface vessels, gather visual and electronic intelligence and providing data on potential targets for missile crews at long ranges. The Bear-F, first seen in 1967, was a refined maritime version of the Bear-D, with lengthened fairings aft of the inboard engine nacelles, modified radar installations and stores bays in the rear fuselage in place of the ventral gun turret.

The sixth version, the Bear-E, appears to be a reconnaissance version of the Bear-A, with between six and seven camera ports in the bomb bay.

In 1977 about 100 Tu-95s were still serving with the Soviet Air Force, and a further 60 with the Soviet Naval Air Arm. The latter are frequently employed on electronic reconnaissance missions over all areas where Soviet maritime influence exists.

Tupolev Tu-126   USSR

Role: Airborne Early Warning
Operational: 1967-
NATO Code-Name: Moss

Engines: Four 14,795ehp Kuznetsov NK-12VM turboprops
Span: 167ft 8in
Length: 188ft
Weight: 195,000lb (approx empty)
380,000lb (approx loaded)
Crew: 21-30
Max speed: 550mph
Service ceiling: 30,000ft
Range: 6,000 miles
Weapons: None

First identified in 1968, the Tupolev Tu-126 is a military development of the Tu-114 civil airliner, fitted with a 36-foot lenticular early warning radar scanner above the fuselage. The aircraft is equipped with a flight refuelling probe, and modifications include a ventral tail fin and numerous 'blisters' housing electronic equipment. The Tu-126 is designed to work in conjunction with advanced interceptors such as the MiG-25 Foxbat, and can also operate as an airborne command post in directing strike aircraft. Fewer than 20 Tu-126s were believed to be operational in 1978, most of them in the AWACS role off the coastline of the USSR.

Vickers Valiant   UK

Role: Strategic Medium Bomber
Operational: 1955-1964
Specification: B9/48
Data: Bk 1

Engines: Four Rolls-Royce Avon 204/205 (RA14s/28s)
Span: 114ft 4in
Length: 108ft 3in
Weight: 75,880lb (empty)
138,000lb (loaded)
Crew: Five
Max speed: 554mph at 36,000ft
Service ceiling: 54,000ft
Range: (10,000lb bomb load halfway) 3,450 miles without reserves, 4,500 miles with underwing tanks
Weapons: Conventional, nuclear or thermonuclear free-falling bombs

The Vickers Valiant, the first of the trio of 'V-Bombers' to enter service with the Royal Air Force, was designed to meet the requirements of specification B9/48, and Vickers received an order for two prototypes in April 1948. The first of these, WB210, flew under the designation Type 660 on 18 May 1951, powered by four 6,500lb thrust Rolls-Royce Avon RA3 turbojets, and the name Valiant was officially adopted the following month. In 1952 WB210 was fitted with 7,500lb thrust Avon RA7s, but in January that year the aircraft was destroyed following an engine bay fire. Avon RA7s also powered the second prototype, WB215, which flew for the first time on 11 April 1952, but this was later equipped with 9,500lb thrust Avon RA14s.

The next Valiant to fly was the Type 673 Valiant B2 (WJ954) which made its first flight on 4 September 1953. It differed extensively from earlier prototypes and later production models in that the fuselage ahead of the wing was lengthened by the insertion of a 4ft 6in bay. The airframe was strengthened, extra fuel tankage was installed and the whole aircraft was stressed for high speed operation at low level. The undercarriage configuration was also changed, the main bogie-type assembly retracting rearwards into pods on the wing trailing edges outboard of the engine nacelles.

Maximum design speed of the Valiant B2 was 665mph (Mach .806) at sea level, but during trials the aircraft only attained 552mph at sea level and no further B2s were built.

The first production Type 674 Valiant B1 (WP199) flew on 21 December 1953. This and the next four production machines were powered by Avon RA7s, but subsequent Valiant B1s were equipped with more powerful Avon RA14s and, later, RA28s. A dual-role variant, the Valiant B(PR)1, flew for the first time on 8 October 1954, and 11 of these bomber reconnaissance versions were built at intervals during the production sequence. Two further variants were the B(PR)K1 and BK1, with flight refuelling equipment. The final production Valiant, a BK1 (XD875) flew on 27 August 1957, bringing total production to 107 machines, including three prototypes.

The Valiant entered service with No 138 Squadron at Gaydon in January 1955, and subsequently equipped Nos 7, 18, 49, 90, 148, 199, 207, 214 and 543 squadrons, performing the strategic reconnaissance role with the latter unit. In October 1956 Valiants of Nos 148, 207 and 214

Squadrons saw action during the Anglo-French Suez operation, attacking Egyptian airfields from high altitude. In May 1957 a Valiant of No 49 Squadron dropped the first British H-Bomb over the Christmas Island test range.

During their career, Valiants made several notable long-distance flights. In October 1953 the second prototype aircraft, WB215, took part in the London-New Zealand air race, being specially fitted with underwing fuel tanks; on 9 July 1959 a Valiant of No 214 Squadron made the first non-stop flight from the United Kingdom to Cape Town, being refuelled in the air twice; on 2-3 March 1960 a Valiant of the same unit made the longest non-stop flight by a RAF aircraft, 8,500 miles round the United Kingdom; and in May that year another No 214 Squadron aircraft flew non-stop from the United Kingdom to Singapore.

In 1963 Valiants of RAF Bomber Command were assigned to NATO in the tactical role, but in December 1964 all aircraft of this type were taken out of service some years ahead of schedule as a result of fatigue cracks.

Westland Wyvern UK

Role: Naval Strike Fighter
Specifications: N11/44, F13/44, N12/45, T12/48
Operational: 1953-58
Data: S4

Engines: One 4,110ehp Armstrong-Siddeley Python ASP3 turboprop
Span: 44ft
Length: 42ft 0¼in
Weight: 15,608lb (empty)
24,500lb (max loaded)
Crew: 1

Max speed: 383mph at sea level
Service ceiling: 28,000ft
Range: 904 miles with auxiliary tanks
Weapons: Four 20mm Hispano Mk5 cannon in wings; one torpedo, three 1,000lb bombs, or 16 60lb rocket projectiles

Designed to Specification N11/44, which called for a naval strike fighter capable of operating from both carriers and shore bases, the Westland Wyvern was the world's first operational turboprop-powered combat aircraft. It was also the only turboprop-powered naval strike fighter ever to reach squadron service. The first six prototypes and 10 pre-

production aircraft were fitted with Rolls-Royce Eagle piston engines, but when the RAF — which had shown an interest in the type under specification F13/44 — decided to abandon the Wyvern at the end of 1945, the Naval Staff decided to concentrate further development around the Armstrong-Siddeley Python turboprop.

The first prototype (Eagle-engined) Wyvern TF1 flew on 12 December 1946 and the first Python-engined aircraft on 22 March 1949, one other Wyvern prototype having also flown with a Rolls-Royce Clyde engine. Problems with the power plant caused lengthy delays, and it was not until 1952 that the first Wyverns entered service with Royal Navy trials units. Early Python-engined aircraft were designated TF2 and later redesignated TF4 after some modifications; this designation was changed yet again to S4 in 1953.

The first Fleet Air Arm squadron to equip with the Wyvern S4 was No 813, which was fully operational by September 1953. The unit subsequently embarked in HMS *Albion* and, later, HMS *Eagle*, spending considerable periods ashore while various technical problems were ironed out. A second Wyvern squadron, No 827, formed in November 1954, and this joined No 813 aboard *Eagle*. Both squadrons disbanded in November 1955 and their aircraft were used to form two new squadrons, Nos 830 and 831. During their work-up period both squadrons emphasised close support, including low-level photo reconnaissance.

As part of HMS *Eagle's* carrier air group, No 830 Squadron took part in many strikes on Egyptian targets during the Suez crisis of October 1956, losing two aircraft to flak. Although the Wyverns had performed well in their ground-attack role they had, however, proved extremely vulnerable to ground fire because of their size, and after Suez No 830 Squadron was disbanded, leaving No 831 — aboard HMS *Ark Royal* — as the only operational Wyvern unit afloat. No 813, however, had reformed in November 1956, and embarked in *Eagle* the following summer. No 831 disbanded in December 1957, followed by No 813 in March 1958.

Several second-line units also used the Wyvern. The most important of these were No 703 Squadron, the Service Trials Unit, and No 787 Squadron, the Naval Air Fighting Development Unit. Both squadrons merged during 1955 to form No 700 Squadron, based at Ford, which continued to use Wyverns until 1956. No 764 Squadron, a Fighter Pilot Pool, also had Wyverns on its inventory until it re-equipped with Sea Hawks in 1957. Total Wyvern production was 127 aircraft.

Yakolev Yak-15/Yak-17

Role: Single-Seat Fighter
Operational: 1947-54
Data: Yak-15

Engines: One RD-10 (Junkers Jump 004B) turbojet rated at 1,980lb thrust
Span: 31ft 6in
Length: 28ft
Weight: 5,170lb (empty)
5,800lb (loaded)
Crew: 1
Max speed: 495mph at 10,000ft
Service ceiling: 38,000ft
Range: 460 miles
Weapons: Two 23mm Nudelman-Suranov cannon

Although the Russians tested their first jet engine (the VRD-1, designed by A. M. Lyulka) in 1941, they lagged far behind Britain, Germany and the USA in the field, and when the first German BMW 003A and Junkers Jumo 004A jet engines fell into their hands early in 1945 priority was given to the mass production of copies in the Soviet Union. The programme received a boost with the capture of German aero-engine technicians, who were rushed to the Soviet factories where production of the turbojets had already begun — the BMW 003 under the designation RD-20 and the Jumo 004 under the designation RD-10.

Because of the urgency surrounding the programme — the Soviet Government being desperately anxious to rush a jet fighter into service in an attempt to keep pace with the West — it was decided to adapt an existing fighter airframe to take one of the German turbojets. The type chosen was the Yak-3, the best wartime fighter to emerge from

USSR

Alexander S. Yakovlev's design bureau. Of extremely robust construction, the Yak-3 was nevertheless small and light, factors that compensated for the relatively low power of the Jumo turbojet selected to power the new variant.

Yakovlev took the wings, undercarriage and tail unit of the Yak-3 and married them with a new all-metal fuselage, the 1,980lb thrust Jumo 004B turbojet being mounted below the wing main spar, fed by a small, circular nose intake and exhausting under the rear fuselage. Designated Yak-15, the prototype of the new jet fighter flew for the first time on 24 April 1946. Deliveries to the IA-PVO began early in 1947, production aircraft being powered by the Russian-built RD-10 engine, and the Yak-15 was revealed to the public in August that year at the Tushino air display.

Although the Yak-15 was an interim design, bridging the gap until the advent of more modern jet fighters, it was important in that it provided the Soviet Air Force with the jet experience it so badly needed. Although lacking the sophistication of contemporary western types, it was more manoeuvrable than either the Vampire or the F-80 Shooting Star. Yak-15s served with Russia's satellite air forces, too, and were occasionally encountered over North Korea in the early part of 1953.

In 1948 the Yak-15 was replaced on the production line by the Yak-17, a more modern variant with a 2,200lb thrust RD-10A turbojet, a tricycle undercarriage and redesigned vertical tail surfaces. A two-seat version, the Yak-17UTI, became the Soviet Union's first two-seat jet conversion trainer, and remained in service until replaced by the MiG-15UTI.

Yakolev Yak-23　　　　　　　USSR

Role: Fighter
Operational: 1949-59
NATO Code-Name: Flora

Engines: One 3,500lb thrust RD-500 turbojet
Span: 28ft 6½in
Length: 26ft 7in
Weight: 4,410lb (empty)
7,365lb (normal loaded)
Crew: 1
Max speed: 568mph
Service ceiling: 48,550ft
Range: 750 miles
Weapons: Two 23mm NS-23 cannon mounted in fuselage nose

Developed from the Yak-15/17 series of fighters, the Yak-23 was produced as an insurance against the failure of the more advanced MiG-15 and flew for the first time in 1947, powered by an imported Rolls-Royce Derwent turbojet. When the MiG-15 proved successful, it was decided to produce the Yak-23 in limited quantities for delivery to Russia's satellite air forces. Production Yak-23s were powered by the Soviet copy of the Derwent, designated RD-500, and were fitted with an ejection seat. The type was a mid-wing monoplane of all-metal construction and was used by the air forces of Bulgaria, Poland and Czechoslovakia in the 1950s, many of the examples delivered being produced in Czechoslovakia under the designation S101. Although built in far smaller numbers than the Republic F-84 Thunderjet, the Yak-23 was to the Warsaw Pact what the American aircraft was to NATO, introducing many first-line pilots to jet fighter operation.

Yakolev Yak-25/26/27　　　USSR

Role: Interceptor/Tactical
Reconnaissance
Operational: 1956-74
NATO Code-Name: Flashlight
(Yak 25/27)
Mangrove (Yak-26)
Data: Yak-26

Engines: Two VK-9 (RD-9) turbojets rated at 8,820lb thrust each with reheat
Span: 38ft 6in
Length: 62ft
Weight: 25,000lb (normal loaded)
Crew: 2
Max speed: 720mph at sea level
Service ceiling: 52,000ft
Range: 2,000 miles max
Weapons: One 30mm cannon in fairing on starboard side of fuselage nose

First seen publicly at the Tushino Air Display in 1955, the Yak-25 twin-jet all-weather interceptor was designed to the same specification as the Lavochkin La-200B (see prototypes section) and flew for the first time in 1952, powered by two Milulin AM-5 turbojets. Carrying a crew of two in tandem and featuring a large, rounded nose radome, the Yakovlev aircraft was ordered into full production for the Soviet Air Force, entering service with a development unit in 1955 and becoming fully operational the following year. In 1957, the type was re-engined with Klimov VK-9 turbojets, rated at 6,175lb thrust each, and redesignated Yak-25F. Both versions were known as Flashlight-A under the NATO reporting system. The Yak-25R (Flashlight-B) was a reconnaissance variant, with longer engine nacelles, a radome under the nose and extended chord at the wing root leading edge. The cockpit was redesigned, the second seat being deleted, and the navigator/bomb aimer was housed in a pointed, glazed nose. Like the Flashlight-A, the Flashlight-B was powered by AM-5 and VK-9 engines in turn. The Yak-27 (Flashlight-C) was a development of the basic Yak-25 design, first seen in prototype form in 1956. This modified all-weather interceptor variant featured longer engine nacelles, housing VK-9 turbojets with afterburners, a pointed nose radome and extended wing-root chord. The Yak-26 (NATO Code-name: Mangrove) reconnaissance version was basically a Yak-27 with a glazed nose, similar to that of the Yak-25R, and was built in quantity for the Soviet Tactical Air Force.

One interesting development of the basic Yak-25 was a high-altitude reconnaissance aircraft (NATO Code-name: Mandrake), consisting of a 'Flashlight-A' fuselage married to a new, straight wing spanning approximately 70ft 6in. The Soviet counterpart of the USAF's RB-57F, Mandrake is believed to have become operational in 1963, and to have remained on the Soviet Air Force's first-line inventory for about 10 years.

Yakolev Yak-28　　　　　　USSR

Role: Tactical Strike/Interceptor
Operational: 1961-
NATO Code-Names: Brewer (Yak-28)
Firebar (Yak-28P)
Data: Yak-28P

Engines: Two Tumansky R-37F turbojets rated at 13,200lb thrust with reheat
Span: 42ft 6in
Length: 71ft
Weight: 35,000lb (max loaded)
Crew: 2
Max speed: 730mph at 35,000ft
Service ceiling: 55,000ft
Range: 1,500 miles max
Weapons: Two 'Anab' infra-red AAMs

Although bearing a strong family resemblance to the Yak-25/26/27 series, the Yak-28, which was first revealed at Tushino in 1961, was in fact a

completely new design. The two-seat tactical strike version, code-named Brewer-A, entered service with units of the Soviet Frontal Aviation in 1961, replacing the ageing Il-28. The Brewer-B and -C displayed minor changes from the early production version, while the Brewer-D (Yak-28R) was a reconnaissance version with a battery of cameras in the bomb bay. The Brewer-E, which entered service in 1970, is an electronic countermeasures aircraft,

with the under-fuselage radome deleted and an active ECM pack partly recessed in the bomb bay. The Yak-28P (NATO Code-name: Firebar) is a two-seat all-weather fighter variant, carrying an armament of two 'Anab' AAMs. Late production Yak-28Ps are fitted with a long needle-type nosecone. Both the Brewer-E and the Yak-28P are thought to be conversions of early production Yak-28 airframes, rather than new-build aircraft.

Yakolev Yak-36

Role: VTOL Strike Fighter
Operational: 1976-
NATO Code-Name: Forger

Engines: One primary turbojet developing approx 17,000lb thrust, and two lift-jets rated at approx 5,600lb each
Span: 23ft
Length: 49ft 3in (Forger-B: 58ft)
Weight: 22,050lb (max loaded)
Crew: 1
Max speed: Mach 1.3 at height
Service ceiling: Not known
Range: Not known
Weapons: Variety of gun pods and rocket packs carried under wings

The Soviet union's first operational VTOL aircraft, the Yak-36 was developed from the Yakovlev 'Freehand' experimental VTOL type, two examples of which were displayed at Domodedovo in July 1967. The much redesigned and refined Yak-36 was first

USSR

encountered in operational form in July 1976, when the 40,000ton carrier/cruiser *Kiev* passed through the Mediterranean en route to join the Soviet Northern Fleet at Murmansk. Designed primarily for naval use, the aircraft is of conventional design, with small mid-set delta wings. Main power is supplied by a single large turbojet, without afterburner, and two jetlift engines are fitted in tandem aft of the cockpit. Close observation of the Kiev's complement of Yak-36s (which, according to some sources, possibly belonged to a development squadron) revealed gun pods and rocket packs on four underwing pylons. All observed take-offs were made vertically, and there is no evidence that short take-offs, designed to increase the aircraft's useful load, are standard procedure with the Yak-36. In addition to the basic single-seat strike/reconnaissance version (Forger-A), a two-seat trainer variant (Forger-B) was also seen aboard the *Kiev*. Service status of the Yak-36 in 1978 was uncertain, but the type appears to have plenty of development potential and more advanced versions will doubtless make their appearance on future carrier/cruisers of the 'Kiev' class.

Part Two

Antonov An-2 (NATO Code-Name: Colt)   USSR

Engines: One 1,000hp Shvetsov ASh-62IR radial
Span: 59ft 7$\frac{1}{2}$in
Max Speed: 160mph at sea level

First flown in 1947, the An-2 biplane is a robust utility transport widely used among the Soviet Bloc air forces, mainly for paratroop training.

Antonov An-8 (NATO Code-Name: Camp)   USSR

Engines: Two 5,100eshp Kuznetsov NK-2M turboprops
Span: 98ft
Max Speed: 350mph at sea level

Antonov's first turboprop-powered aircraft, the twin-engined An-8 transport began to enter service with the Soviet Air Force in 1958. The first of five prototypes flew in 1955, and the aircraft was intended primarily as an Li-2 (Soviet-built DC-3) replacement. The AN-8 could carry 75 passengers in the trooping role and was armed with a single 23mm cannon in the tail position. The type failed to meet Soviet AF requirements and was used mainly as a paratroop trainer, although some aircraft were employed on miscellaneous tasks such as monitoring radioactive fallout.

Antonov An-12 (NATO Code-Name: Cub)   USSR

Engines: Four 4,000eshp Ivchenko AI-20K turboprops
Span: 124ft 8in
Max Speed: 373mph at sea level

In 1957 Antonov produced a four-engined derivative of the An-8, designated An-10. Intended as a freighter for Aeroflot, the An-10 was subsequently fitted with an An-8 type rear fuselage to meet military loading requirements, and the new aircraft became the An-12. In addition to fulfilling the role of standard paratroop and freight transport in the Soviet Air Force, the An-12 was supplied to several foreign air forces, including those of India, Algeria, Egypt, Indonesia, Iraq and Poland.

Antonov An-14 (NATO Code-Name: Clod)   USSR

Engines: Two 300hp Ivchenko AI-14RF radials
Span: 72ft 2in
Max speed: 150mph at sea level

A twin-engined light general purpose aircraft, the An-14 Pchelka (Little Bee) flew for the first time on 15 March 1958. It was subsequently used widely as a light transport and communications aircraft by the Soviet and East German armed forces, although it was intended primarily as a commercial machine.

Antonov An-22 (NATO Code-Name: Cock)   USSR

Engines: Four 15,000shp Kuznetsov NK-12MA turboprops
Span: 211ft 4in
Max speed: 460mph at sea level

First revealed at the Paris Air Show in June 1965, the huge An-22 heavy transport serves with both Aeroflot and the Soviet Air Force, where it is used to transport large loads such as missiles on tracked launchers. It can also carry dismantled aircraft, and was used to ferry MiG-25 'Foxbat' aircraft to Egypt in 1971. The An-22 set up several payload-to-height records in October 1967.

Antonov An-24 (NATO Code-Name: Coke)   USSR

Photo: AN-24B
Engines: Two 2,550ehp Ivchenko AI-24A turboprops
Span: 95ft 9½in
Max speed: 335mph at 19,685ft

Designed as a civil feeder-liner, the An-24 is used in some numbers in the military transport role by the air forces of the USSR, Czechoslovakia, Egypt, East Germany, Hungary, North Korea, Poland, Somalia, and North Vietnam. The prototype first flew in April 1960. A few Soviet AF An-24s are equipped as airborne command posts, and at least one was used in this role during the invasion of Czechoslovakia in August 1968.

Beech C-45   USA

Photo: TC-45H
Engines: Two 450hp Pratt & Whitney R-985-B5 Wasp Junior radials
Span: 47ft 7in
Max speed: 230mph at sea level
A military version of the famous Beech Model 18, the Beech C-45G was used extensively by the USAF and many other air forces. Deliveries of the C-45G to the USAF totalled 468, followed by 432 examples of an improved model, the C-45H.

Boeing C-97   USA

Photo: KC-97
Engines: Four 3,800hp Pratt & Whitney R-4360-59B radials
Span: 141ft 3in
Max speed: 375mph

The Mainstay of the USAF's military transport squadrons during the 1950s, the C-97 Stratofreighter was developed from the Model 337 Stratocruiser civil airliner. The 888th and last Stratofreighter was delivered to the USAF in mid-1956. Many were converted to the flying tanker role under the designation KC-97.

Boeing C-135/KC-135

USA

Photo: KC-135A
Engines: Four 13,750lb thrust Pratt & Whitney
J57-P-59W turbojets
Span: 130ft 10in
Max speed: 624mph at 10,000ft

In 1954, the USAF announced its intention to purchase a development of the Boeing 367-80 (prototype 707) jet airliner for use as a tanker-transport. The military version flew for the first time on 31 August 1956 under the designation KC-135A and 820 aircraft were subsequently produced in several variants, including the EC-135 airborne command post and the RC-135 for electronic reconnaissance. 12 examples of a dual tanker-transport version were supplied to France under the designation C-135F. The C-137 Stratolifter long-range transport was developed from the KC-135 and had the flight refuelling equipment removed. Variants included the RC-135 photo-mapping aircraft and the WC-135 for weather reconnaissance.

Boeing VC-137

USA

Engines: Four Pratt & Whitney JT3D turbofans rated at 17,000lb thrust
Span: 145ft 8½in
Max speed: 615mph at 23,000ft

Boeing 707, used mainly for the carriage of VIPs — including the President of the United States — and special freight. The first VC-137A flew on 7 April 1959.

The VC-137, a small number of which were delivered to the USAF, is a military conversion of the

Blackburn Beverley

UK

Engines: Four 2,850hp Bristol Centaurus 173 radials
Span: 162ft
Max speed: 238mph at 5,700ft

Developed from the Blackburn and General Aircraft Universal Freighter, the Beverley C1 military transport entered service with RAF Transport Command in April 1956 and equipped three squadrons until replaced by the Lockheed Hercules a decade later. The Beverley could carry 94 fully-equipped troops or a 29,000lb payload.

Breguet Br941

France

Engines: Four 1,500shp Turbomeca Turmo IIID3 shaft turbines
Span: 76ft 8½in
Max speed: 285mph

The Breguet 941 was a STOL transport project, first flown on 1 June 1961. Four pre-series aircraft were evaluated by the Armeé de l'Air's 62e Escadre de Transport, but the type did not enter production.

Bristol 170 Mk 31 Freighter

UK

Engines: Two 2,000hp Bristol Hercules 734 radials
Span: 108ft
Max speed: 225mph

Although the Bristol 170 was designed originally as a military transport, it was not adopted by the RAF. Nevertheless, the type was supplied to a number of overseas air forces, including Pakistan and New Zealand.

Bristol Britannia C1/C2

UK

Photo: Britannia 307F
Engines: Four 4,445ehp Bristol Siddeley Proteus 225 turboprops
Span: 142ft 3½in
Max speed: 404mph

The Britannia C1, which flew for the first time on 29 December 1958, was developed from the Britannia 310 civil airliner and entered service with No 99 Squadron, RAF Transport Command, in 1959, followed by No 511 Squadron. 23 Britannias were delivered, including three C2s, the latter differing from the C1 in having only the forward section of its fuselage floor strengthened for heavy loads, being intended mainly for trooping.

Canadair CC-106 Yukon

Canada

Engines: Four 5,730ehp Rolls-Royce Tyne 515/10 turboprops
Span: 142ft 3⅔in
Max speed: 352mph at 25,000ft

Royce Tynes. 12 Yukons were delivered to the RCAF, equipping No 426 Squadron.

Derived from the Bristol Britannia, the CC-106 Yukon (CL-44-6) flew for the first time in November 1959. Apart from the fuselage, which was appreciably longer than the Britannia's, the Yukon differed from its parent aircraft in its engines, which were Rolls-

CASA 207 Azor

Spain

Engines: Two 2,040hp Bristol Hercules 730 radials
Span: 91ft 2in
Max speed: 285mph at 6,100ft

First flown on 28 September 1955, the C207 Azor equipped Nos 351 and 911 Squadrons of the Spanish Air Force, 20 aircraft being delivered. The Azor could carry out a variety of tasks, ranging from VIP transport to paratrooping.

141

Convair R4Y-1/C-131A

USA

Photo: C-131A
Engines: Two 2,500hp Pratt & Whitney R2800 radials
Span: 105ft 4in
Max speed: 313mph

Developed from the Model 340 Convair-Liner, the R4Y-1 was a cargo, personnel and air ambulance transport for the US Navy. The USAF's version, the C-131A Samaritan, was similar. Other variants were the R4Y-1Z executive transport and the R4Y-2, which was developed from the Model 440.

Dassault MD315 Flamant

France

Engines: Two SNECMA 12S engines rated at 580hp
Span: 67ft 10in
Max speed: 236mph

First flown in November 1948, the Dassault Flamant was in widespread use with the French armed forces for many years, some 300 being built. The type was employed in a variety of roles, ranging from navigation/bombing trainer to 10-seat transport.

Dassault Mystere 20 (Falcon 20)

France

Engines: Two General Electric CF700-2D-2 turbofans
Span: 53ft 6in
Max speed: 404mph at sea level

Designed as a light twin-jet executive transport, the Mystere 20 flew for the first time on 4 May 1963. Examples are in service with the Armée de l'Air and several foreign air forces, both as VIP transports and navigational trainers. Aircraft marketed in the USA are known as Fan Jet Falcons.

De Havilland Comet Mks 2/4

UK

Photo: Comet 4B
Data: C2
Engines: Four 7,300lb thrust Rolls-Royce Avon 117/8 turbojets
Span: 115ft
Max speed: 508mph

In June 1956 No 216 Squadron, RAF Transport Command, became the world's first jet transport squadron, equipping with eight Comet C2s at RAF Lyneham. Later, the RAF also acquired five Comet 4Cs, designating these C4s. The RAF Comets were used on high-speed, long range mixed passenger and freight services. Other Comets used by the RAF were the T2 trainer and the 2R electronic reconnaissance variants.

De Havilland Devon

UK

Engines: Two 340hp DH Gipsy Queen 70s
Span: 57ft
Max speed: 210mph

A military version of the DH104 Dove Series 4, the eight-passenger Devon C1 was used for communications duties with the RAF and many overseas air forces. The Sea Devon was a variant for the Fleet Air Arm

De Havilland Heron

UK

Photo: C4
Engines: Four 250hp DH Gipsy Queen 30s
Span: 71ft 6in
Max speed: 220mph

First flown on 10 May 1950, the 14/17-seat DH114 Heron appeared in two versions, the Series 1 with a fixed undercarriage and the Series 2 with retractable gear. The latter was adopted as a light four-engined transport by several overseas air forces in small numbers, among them Federal Germany, Ceylon, Iraq, Jordan and South Africa, and three examples served with the RAF Queen's Flight.

De Havilland Canada DHC-2 Beaver

Canada

Engines: One Pratt & Whitney R-985 Wasp Junior developing 450hp
Span: 48ft
Max speed: 179mph

The seven-seat DHC-2 Beaver flew for the first time on 16 August 1947 and more than 1,500 were subsequently produced, serving on liaison and army co-operation.duties in many parts of the world. The aircraft was designated L-20 in USAF service. Fourteeen were still serving with Britain's Army Air Corps in mid-1978, these aircraft having Alvis Leonides engines in place of the original P&W Wasp Junior.

De Havilland Canada DHC-3 Otter

Canada

Engines: One 600hp Pratt & Whitney R-1340 radial
Span: 58ft
Max speed: 153mph

First flown in December 1951, the DHC-3 Otter utility transport is designated U-1A in US Army service and, apart from the Canadian Armed Forces, serves with the air forces of Australia, Burma, Chile, Colombia, Ghana, Indonesia, India and Norway. Tasks range from transport to search and rescue and paratroop dropping.

De Havilland Canada DHC-4 Caribou

Canada

Engines: Two 1,450hp Pratt & Whitney R-2000-7M2 radials
Span: 95ft 7½in
Max speed: 216mph at 6,500ft

Designated CC-108 in the Canadian Armed Forces and CV-2 or C-7 in US Army service, the DHC-4 Caribou was first flown in July 1958. The US Army obtained 159, most of which were later transferred to the USAF. Other nations using the Caribou in a military role include Ghana, Kuwait, Zambia, India, Australia, Kenya, Malaysia, Tanzania, Spain, Muscat and Oman, Uganda, Abu Dhabi and Thailand.

De Havilland Canada DHC-5 Buffalo

Canada

Engines: Two General Electric T64 turboprops
Span: 96ft
Max speed: 271mph at 10,000ft

Developed in response to a US Army requirement for a STOL tactical transport, the DHC-5 Buffalo was an enlarged version of the Caribou, the prototype flying in April 1964. Designated CC-115 in the Canadian Armed Forces and C-8A in US Army service, the aircraft was used extensively in Vietnam. Examples were also supplied to Brazil and Peru.

De Havilland Canada DHC-6 Twin Otter

Canada

Engines: Two 652eshp Pratt & Whitney PT6A-27 turboprops
Span: 65ft
Max speed: 220mph at 10,000ft

A twin engined STOL transport, first flown in May 1965, the DHC Twin Otter was supplied to the Canadian Armed Forces (CC-138), the US Army (UV-18A) and to the air arms of Argentina, Chile, Ecuador, Jamaica, Panama, Paraguay, Peru, and Norway. 600 examples had been built by the beginning of 1978.

Dornier Do27

West Germany

Engines: One 340hp Lycoming GSO-480-B
Span: 29ft 4½in
Max speed: 141mph at 3,280ft

First flown in June 1955, the Do27 — Dornier's first postwar design to enter quantity production — saw widespread service with several air arms, 428 being delivered to the Federal German Luftwaffe. Military versions of the Do27 may be used for the passenger/freight transport, liaison, observation, ambulance and rescue roles. The type was built under licence in Spain as the CASA C127.

Dornier Do28 Skyservant

Engines: Two 290hp Lycoming IO-540As
Span: 45ft 3½in
Max speed: 174mph at sea level

Developed from the Do27, the twin-engined Do28, which first flew in April 1959, was supplied to the Luftwaffe for liaison and light transport duties, some being internally converted as VIP transports. The type was exported to several foreign air forces, including that of Israel.

Douglas C-118

USA

Photo: C-118B
Engines: Four 2,500hp Pratt & Whitney R-2800-52W radials
Span: 117ft 6in
Max speed: 360mph

The C-118 was the military transport version of the DC-6, which in turn was developed from the DC-4 (C-54) Skymaster. The C-118 was intended mainly as a freighter, but could be quickly converted to the troop transport role. The US Navy version was designated R6D-1, and the VC-118 was a VIP transport. 166 were built.

Douglas R4D-8

USA

Engines: Two 1,535hp Wright R-1820-80 radials
Span: 90ft
Max speed: 270mph

Known as the Super DC-3, the R-4D-8 was so extensively modifed that it was practically a new design, its wing and tail surfaces differing considerably from those of the earlier DC-3/C-47 series. About 100 were delivered to the US Navy.

Douglas C-124 Globemaster

USA

Engines: Four 3,800hp Pratt & Whitney R-4360-63A radials
Span: 174ft 1½in
Max speed: 304mph

The C-124 was an extensively modified version of the C-74 Globemaster I, 14 of which were delivered to the USAF. The C-124 was the largest heavy cargo and troop transport in production in the early 1950s, being able to carry 200 fully-equipped troops, and was widely used on airlift operations during the Korean War. The two production versions were the C-124A and C-124C, the latter having more powerful engines. 445 were built.

Douglas C-133 Cargomaster

USA

Engines: Four Pratt & Whitney T34-P-7W/9W turboprops
Span: 179ft 8in
Max speed: 355mph

First flown on 23 April 1956, the giant C-133 entered service with the USAF Military Air Transport Service in 1957 and subsequently equipped the 1st and 84th Air Transport Squadrons. The type was produced in two variants, the C-133A and -B. Most C-133s were equipped to transport Atlas and Minuteman ICBMs.

Fairchild C-82/C-119

USA

Engines: Usually Pratt & Whitney R-4460s or R-3350s
Span: 109ft 3in
Max speed: 281mph at 18,000ft

The Fairchild Corporation's first operational postwar transport design, the C-82 soon gave way to a modified version known as the C-119. Over 1,300 were subsequently built, and the C-119 saw widespread service with the USAF, the US Navy (as the R4Q), and the air forces of Belgium, Brazil, Canada, Nationalist China, India, Italy, Morocco and Norway. Some USAF C-119s were specially modified for reconnaissance satellite recovery.

Fairchild C-123 Provider

USA

Span: 110ft
Max speed: 253mph

The C-123 was developed from the experimental Chase XG-20 transport glider, two examples of which were built in 1948. One was fitted with P&W R-2800 engines and became the XC-123 Avitruc; the other was tested with four J47 turbojets and became the sole C-123A. The aircraft entered production as the C-123B and 302 were built between 1954 and 1958, the great majority by the Fairchild Corporation. Of these, six went to Saudi Arabia, 18 to Venezuela, and others to Thailand and South Vietnam. Fifty or so C-123Bs were used by the USAF in Vietnam (315th Air Command Group). In 1978 the type was still being used by the 315th and 439th Tactical Airlift Wings of the USAF Reserve, the 144th Tactical Airlift Squadron of the ANG, and the US Coast Guard.

Fiat (Aeritalia) G222

Italy

Engines: Two Fiat-built General Electric T64 turboprops
Span: 94ft 2in
Max speed: 336mph

Flown for the first time on 18 July 1970, the Aeritalia G222 general purpose transport has replaced the Fairchild C-119s with the Italian Air Force's No 2 Squadron and also serves with No 98 Squadron, both units belonging to the 46th Brigade. 61 aircraft have been delivered, including three for ECM and radio calibration duties. The type also serves with the Argentine Army and the United Arab Emirates Air Force (1978).

Fokker F27M Troopship

Span: 95ft 2in
Max speed: 340mph

The Fokker Troopship is the military version of the F27 Friendship, with accommodation for 45 airborne troops, 13,800lb of freight or 24 stretchers. The type is in service with the RNethAF, Argentina, Indonesia and the Sudan.

Grumman Albatross

USA

Engines: Two Wright R1820 radials
Span: 96ft 8in
Max speed: 236mph

First flown in October 1947, the Grumman Albatross, an amphibian, entered US military service in July 1949. Over 500 were built, including the HU-16A/B version for USAF air-sea rescue duties, the HU-16C for the US Navy and Coast Guard, and the HU-16D for the utility transport role with the USN.

Grumman TF-1 Trader

USA

Engines: Two Wright R-1820 radials
Span: 69ft 8in
Max speed: 280mph at sea level

Developed from the S2F Tracker, the TF-1 (C-1A) entered service with the US Navy in 1956 as a carrier on-board delivery (COD) aircraft. On 26 June 1958 a TF-1 of VR-21 delivered a J34 engine to the USS *Yorktown*, 300 miles at sea, in the first delivery of an aircraft engine by air to a carrier. A further variant was the TF-1Q electronic countermeasures aircraft, which entered service with All-Weather Attack Squadron 35 in January 1957.

Grumman C-2A Greyhound

USA

Engines: Two Allison T56 turboprops
Span: 80ft 7in
Max speed: 352mph

The C-2A was evolved from the E-2A Hawkeye to supplement the TF-1s of the US Navy's Carrier On-Board Delivery Force. The type flew for the first time in November 1964 and deliveries to the fleet began in 1966. Twelve C-2As were in service in 1978.

Handley Page Hastings

UK

Span: 113ft
Max speed: 348mph

First flown on 7 May 1946, the Handley Page Hastings was the mainstay of RAF Transport Command for 10 years. The first squadron to receive it, in October 1948, was No 47, and this unit took part in the Berlin Airlift. One hundred Hastings C1s and 42 C2s were built, the latter powered by four Bristol Hercules 106 engines in place of the C1's Hercules 101s. After their retirement from transport duties, some Hastings were used for bombing training, radio/radar trials and weather reconnaissance.

Hawker Siddeley Andover/HS 748

UK

Span: 98ft 3in
Max speed: 302mph at 15,000ft

A rear-loading military transport, the Andover C Mk 1 was developed from the commercial Hawker Siddeley 748, the prototype flying in December 1963. The first of 31 production Andover C Mk 1s was delivered to No 46 Squadron RAF in 1966, followed by No 52 Squadron. The Andover CC Mk 2 was a VIP version of the basic HS748, two being delivered for service with the Queen's Flight. Twelve Andovers were still in RAF service in mid-1978. A military transport version of the basic HS748, the 748M, is built under licence by HAL in India.

Hawker Siddeley Argosy

UK

Engines: Four Rolls-Royce Dart Mk 101 turboprops
Span: 115ft
Max speed: 290mph

Developed from the Armstrong Whitworth 650 Argosy passenger-freight transport, the HS660 Argosy C Mk 1 flew on 4 March 1961, the first of 56 aircraft entering service with No 114 Squadron in March 1962; the type also equipped No 267 Squadron. The Argosy was prematurely retired in the early 1970s because of the decline in RAF transport movements.

Hunting Percival Pembroke/Sea Prince

UK

Engines: Two 540hp Alvis Leonides
Span: 64ft 6in
Max speed: 224mph

Developed from the Prince Series III light passenger transport, the Pembroke C Mk 1 has served as a light transport and communications aircraft with the RAF for nearly three decades, all machines having had their main spars renewed. In mid-1978, the type was in use with Nos 32 and 207 Squadrons, and with No 60 Squadron in RAF Germany. The Pembroke's naval counterpart is the Sea Prince C1/C2, which has a lower all-up weight.

1A35 Huanquero

Argentina

Engines: Two IAR-19A radials
Span: 64ft 3½in
Max speed: 225mph

A light military transport for the Argentine Air Force, the IA35 first flew in Septembeer 1953. Several variants were produced, including the IA35-III ambulance and the IA-35-IV photographic aircraft.

IA50 GII

Argentina

Engines: Two Turbomeca Bastan VI-A turboprops
Span: 64ft 3¼in
Max speed: 310mph

First flown in April 1963, the IA50 GII is a twin-engined light transport. In mid-1978, IA50 GIIs (14 transports, two survey and one VIP aircraft) were serving with the Argentine Air Force's 1 Brigade Aerea.

Ilyushin Il-12/Il-14 (NATO Code-Names: Coach Il-12 , Crate Il-14)

USSR

Photo: Il-14P
Span: 69ft 11in
Max speed: 254mph (Il-12), 268mph (Il-14)

The Il-12, which flew for the first time in 1946, was the standard Soviet twin-engined military and civil transport aircraft of the postwar years. It carried five crew and up to 32 passengers, and was used by most Soviet Bloc countries. It was gradually replaced in service by the Il-14 which flew in 1950 with up-rated Ash-82T radial engines and which was widely exported. Apart from the Soviet Union, countries using the Il-14 in the military transport role in 1978 included Afghanistan, Albania, Algeria, Bulgaria,

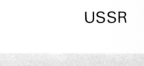

China, Congo Republic, Cuba, Egypt, Ethiopia, East Germany, Iraq, North Korea, Mongolia, Romania, South Yemen and Yugoslavia.

Ilyushin Il-18 (NATO Code-Name: Coot)

USSR

Photo: Il-18D
Engines: Four Ivchenko AI-20 turboprops
Span: 122ft 8½in
Max speed: 466mph

Although primarily a commercial transport, the Il-18 Moskva is used by the Soviet Air Force as a personnel transport and freighter.

Ilyushin Il-76 (NATO Code-Name: Candid)

USSR

Engines: Four Soloviev D-30KP turbofans
Span: 165ft 8in
Max speed: 500mph

First flown on 25 March 1971, the Il-76 has gradually superseded the Antonov An-12 in the Soviet Air Force's transport units, the military version being fitted with a tail gun position. The type has also been evaluated as an M-4 'Bison' replacement in the flight refuelling role.

Kawasaki C-1

Japan

Engines: Two Mitsubishi (Pratt & Whitney) JT8D-M-9 turbofans
Span: 100ft 4¾in
Max speed: 501mph at 25,000ft

Designed to replace the elderly Curtiss C-46Ds in service with the Japanese Air Self-Defence Force, the C-1 first flew on 12 November 1970. 26 were ordered, and these equip Nos 1, 2 and 3 Squadrons of the JSDF's Transport Wing.

Lockheed C-121

USA

Photo: C-121C
Engines: Four Wright R-3350 radials
Span: 123ft 5in
Max speed: 376mph

The Lockheed C-121 was a military transport version of the famous Model 1049F Super Constellation. Variants included the C-121C, the PC-121A and -B long-range personnel and cargo models, and the R7V-1 for the US Navy. By the mid-1960s, most C-121s in USAF service had been relegated to the Air Force Reserve and the Air National Guard.

Lockheed C-130 Hercules

USA

Span: 132ft 7in
Max Speed: 384mph (C130E/H)

One of the most versatile tactical transport aircraft ever built, the Lockheed C-130 Hercules flew for the first time on 23 August 1954, and many different variants have been produced in the quarter-century since then. The initial production versions were the C-130A and B, of which 461 were built, and these were followed by the major production variant, the C-130E, 510 of which were produced. Other versions include the AC-130E close support 'gunship', the WC-130E weather reconnaissance aircraft, the KC-130F assault transport for the USMC, the HC-130H for aerospace rescue and recovery, the C-130K for the Royal Air Force, and the LC-130R, which has wheel/ski landing gear. Apart from the USA and Great Britain, nations using the Allison T56-powered Hercules in 1978 included Argentina, Australia, Belgium, Bolivia, Brazil, Canada, Chile, Denmark, Gabon, Greece, Indonesia, Israel, Italy, Jordan, South Korea, Libya, Morocco, New Zealand, Nigeria, Norway, Pakistan, the Philippines, Portugal, Saudi Arabia, South Africa, Spain, the Sudan, Sweden, Turkey, the United Arab Emirates, Venezuela and Zaire.

Lockheed C-140 Jetstar

USA

Engines: Four Pratt & Whitney JT12A turbojets
Span: 54ft 5in
Max speed: 403mph

The C-140 is the military version of the Lockheed Model 1329 jet utility transport. Five C-140As are used by the USAF Communications Service, and eleven VC-140Bs are in service with the Special Air Missions Wing of MATS as VIP transports.

Lockheed C-141 Starlifter

USA

Engines: Four Pratt & Whitney TF33 turbofans
Span: 160ft 1in
Max speed: 570mph

First flown on 17 December 1963, the C-141A Starlifter was designed to provide the USAF Military Air Transport Service a high-speed global airlift and strategic deployment capability. Deliveries of the C-141A began in April 1965 to the 44th Air Transport Squadron, and in 1978 271 were in service with 13 squadrons of Military Airlift Command. The C-141's main cabin can accommodate 154 troops or 123 fully-equipped paratroops.

Lockheed C-5A Galaxy

USA

Engines: Four General Electric TF39 turbofans
Span: 222ft 8½in
Max speed: 571mph

The largest transport aircraft in service anywhere in the world, the C-5A Galaxy was first flown on 30 June 1968 and the first aircraft was delivered to Military Airlift Command in December 1969. The Galaxy carries a crew of five, with provision for 270 troops on the lower deck and 75 on the upper. The lower deck, however, is intended for freight, and could, for example, accommodate 10 Pershing missiles with their launch vehicles, or two Iroquois helicopters and an M-60 tank. Four squadrons of Military Airlift command were equipped with 76 C-5As in 1978.

Max Holste 1521 Broussard

France

Engines: One 450hp Pratt & Whitney
R-985 Wasp radials
Span: 45ft 1in
Max speed: 161mph

The Broussard was the French Armed Forces' standard light utility transport for many years, until its role was gradually taken over by helicopters. In the army co-operation role, the type saw widespread service in Algeria. More than 400 were built, of which 335 were delivered to the French forces. Examples were supplied to several countries within the French sphere of influence.

Nord 2501 Noratlas

France

Engines: Two SNECMA-produced Hercules radials
Span: 106ft 7½in
Max speed: 273mph

First flown on 10 September 1949, the Nord Noratlas was still the mainstay of France's Military Air Transport Command (CoTAM) in 1978, with 120 aircraft equipping four squadrons. The type was also used by the Federal German Luftwaffe and the Israeli Air Force.

Northrop C-125 Raider

USA

Engines: Three Wright R-1820 radials
Span: 86ft 6in
Max speed: 201mph

Developed from the Northrop N-23 Pioneer of 1946, the C-125 Raider was ordered into production for the USAF as a short-field light cargo transport in 1948.

The first YC-125 flew in August 1949, but the USAF requirement was filled by transport helicopters and the 23 aircraft delivered were used as engine ground trainers after only a short spell in the transport role. The aircraft were later declared surplus and sold privately.

Scottish Aviation Pioneer

UK

Engines: One 520hp Alvis Leonides 502/7 radial
Span: 49ft 9in
Max speed: 145mph

The standard RAF light utility transport during the 1950s, 44 Scottish Aviation (Prestwick) Pioneer CC1s were built. The aircraft could carry four troops or two stretcher cases.

Scottish Aviation Twin Pioneer

UK

Engines: Two Alvis Leonides 514/8As
Span: 76ft 6in
Max speed: 165mph

The triple-finned Twin Pioneer STOL light transport could carry 12 troops, 12 stretchers, 10 paratroops or 3,400lb of freight. 31 were delivered to the RAF and served into the 1970s, mainly in the Middle East.

Short Belfast

UK

Engines: Four Rolls-Royce Tyne turboprops
Span: 158ft 9½in
Max speed: 360mph

Designed to carry heavy loads such as missiles, guns and fighting vehicles, the Short Belfast flew for the first time on 1 May 1964 and 10 aircraft were subsequently delivered to No 53 Squadron, RAF Air Support Command. The type was retired in 1976.

Transall C-160

France/West Germany

Engines: Two Rolls-Royce Tyne turboprops
Span: 131ft 3in
Max speed: 333mph

Developed to meet the joint transport requirements of the French and West German Air Forces, the C-160 Transall first flew in February 1963. In 1978, 46 Transalls equipped three squadrons of the French Air Transport Command, two Tactical Transport Wings of the Luftwaffe (76 aircraft) and one squadron of the South African Air Force's Air Transport Command (9 aircraft). The aircraft can carry 93 troops or up to 81 fully equipped paratroops, or a cargo load of up to 35,270lb.

Vickers Valetta

UK

Engines: Two Bristol Hercules radials
Span: 89ft 3in
Max speed: 294mph

Developed from the Vickers Viking civil airliner, the Valetta C1 medium-range transport was widely used by RAF Transport Command in the 1950s. The type could carry 34 passengers. The Valetta T3 was a conversion used to train navigators.

Vickers VC-10

UK

Engines: Four Rolls-Royce Conway turbojets
Span: 146ft 2in
Max speed: 620mph

Designated VC-10 C Mk 1, 14 examples of this four-jet airliner were delivered to No 10 Squadron, RAF Air Support Command, between 1966 and 1968. The aircraft have a nose probe for flight refuelling. In 1978 it was announced that some of the RAF's VC-10s were to be converted as flight refuelling tankers to supplement the existing fleet of Victor K2s.

Part Three

Aero 3 / Yugoslavia

A low-wing monoplane basic trainer, the Aero 3 succeeded the earlier Aero 2 in service with the Yugoslav Air Force from 1957.

Aero L-29 Delfin
/ Czechoslovakia

A two-seat basic and advanced jet trainer, the L-29 first flew in April 1959 and subsequently served in large numbers with all Warsaw Pact air forces and some overseas air forces, including Syria, Uganda and Indonesia.

Aero L-39 / Czechoslovakia

Designed to succeed the L-29, the L-39 flew in November 1968. Re-equipment of Warsaw Pact training squadrons with the type was proceeding in 1978.

AISA I-115 / Spain

Designated E6 in Spanish Air Force service, the I-115 replaced the Bücker Jungmann biplane as Spain's standard primary trainer in the 1950s. The type was a tandem two-seat long-wing monoplane.

Auster Mks 6-9 / UK

The Auster AOP Mks 6 and 9 were both Army Co-Operation versions of the famous high-wing light aircraft, the Mk 9 featuring considerable redesign. The T7 was a training variant, used by the Army Air Corps and the air arms of Iraq, Jordan and Rhodesia.

Avro Anson T20-22 / UK

The Anson T20, T21 and T22 were navigational and radio training versions of the celebrated 'Faithful Annie'. Over 11,000 Ansons were built in Britain and Canada, production ending in 1952.

Avro Athena / UK

Designed as an advanced trainer, the Athena was not a success and only a small number saw service with the RAF, these being used as gunnery trainers.

Beech T-34 Mentor / USA

First flown in December 1948, the T-34 was developed from the civilian Beechcraft Bonanza and was built in large numbers, serving with the US services and with many countries in the American sphere of influence.

Boulton Paul Balliol / UK

Originally designed to be powered by a turboprop engine, the Balliol in fact entered RAF service powered by a Rolls-Royce Merlin. An advanced trainer, the RAF variant was designated T2 and served during the 1950s. The Fleet Air Arm version was designated T21. The Balliol also served with the Royal Ceylon Air Force.

Canadair CL-41 / Canada

First flown in January 1960, the CL-41 was produced both as a basic jet trainer and a counter-insurgency trainer, the latter being designated CL-41G. These are used in the ground-attack role by the Royal Malaysian Air Force. In 1978, about 85 CL-41s (CT-114s) were serving with the Canadian Armed Forces.

Cessna T-37 / USA

The first purpose-built jet trainer to be used by the USAF, the T-37 flew on 12 October 1954. The type has also been supplied to many foreign air forces. The A-37 is a counter-insurgency version, which was used extensively in Vietnam.

Cessna 337 Super Skymaster / USA

Used for training and communications with a number of air forces, the military version of the 4-6 seat executive aircraft is also produced as the 0-2, carrying out forward air control duties.

Commonwealth CA-25 Winjeel / Australia

The standard primary trainer with the Royal Australian Air Force for many years, the CA-25 was eventually replaced in the mid-1970s. Sixty-two aircraft were built.

De Havilland Chipmunk / Canada/UK

Originally developed by de Havilland (Canada), the Chipmunk T10 was developed by the parent company to meet RAF basic training requirements, which it carried out until replaced by the Scottish Aviation Bulldog in the 1970s. The type was also supplied to many overseas air forces. Canadian-built Chipmunks carried the designation T30.

De Havilland Vampire T11 / UK

First flown on 15 November 1950, the T11 advanced jet trainer saw widespread service throughout the world. It was used by most Commonwealth air forces, and other users included Austria, Burma, Chile, Finland, Indonesia, Iraq, the Lebanon, Rhodesia, Sweden, Switzerland, Eire, South Africa, Venezuela, Jordan and India. The export version was designated T55.

Fanaero-Chile Chincol / Chile

Produced as a basic trainer for the Chilean Air Force, the Chincol flew for the first time in 1955 and 50 were subsequently built.

Fiat G46 / Italy

Used in some numbers as a basic trainer by the Italian Air Force during the postwar years, the G46 was also exported to Egypt, Argentina and Austria.

Fiat G59 / Italy

Derived from the wartime G55 Centauro fighter, the G59 was used as an advanced trainer with the Italian Air Force until the early 1960s, in both single- and double-seat versions.

Fiat G80/82 / Italy

First flown in December 1951, the Fiat G80 fighter trainer was powered by a DH Goblin turbojet. The G82 was a development powered by a Rolls-Royce Nene. Both variants served with the Italian Air Force until replaced by the Fiat G91T.

Fokker S11 Instructor / Holland

Holland's first indigenous postwar primary trainer, the S11 served with the air forces of the Netherlands, Brazil, Israel and Italy, where it was produced under licence as the Macchi M416.

Fokker S14 / Holland

The first jet aircraft designed and built in Holland, the S14 flew on 20 May 1951, powered by a Rolls-Royce Derwent turbojet. It was also the first jet aircraft anywhere in the world to be designed specifically for the training role. The S14 served in small numbers with the RNethAF into the 1960s as a conversion trainer.

Fouga Magister / France

Famous as the equipment of the French 'Patrouille de France' and the Belgian 'Diables Rouges' aerobatic teams, the Fouga Magister was one of the most successful jet trainers ever developed, seeing widespread service with the French and several other air forces. In the light ground-attack role, the Magister distinguished itself in the Arab-Israeli war of 1967, carrying out devastating rocket attacks against Egyptian armour in Sinai.

Fuji T1F / Japan

Designed to replace the T-6G basic trainer, the prototype T1F jet trainer flew for the first time on 8 January 1958. Designated T1A/T1B, the type was in service with the JASDF in 1978. The aircraft has provision for underwing stores, including Sidewinder AAMs, gun pods and rockets.

Handley Page (Reading) Marathon / UK

First flown in May 1946, the Marathon served briefly with the RAF in the early 1950s as a navigational trainer, until replaced by the Vickers Varsity. The aircraft's service designation was T11.

Handley Page Jetstream / UK

After a protracted development career, beset by difficulties and disappointments — such as the cancellation of a USAF order — the Handley Page Jetstream was selected by the RAF as a Varsity replacement in the multi-engine training role. Deliveries began in 1973, and totalled eight aircraft.

Hawker Siddeley (DH) 125 Dominie / UK

Developed from the HS125 twin-jet executive aircraft, the Dominie T Mk 1 replaced the Vickers Varsity in RAF service as an advanced navigational trainer. Nineteen aircraft were on the RAF inventory in 1978. Military versions of the HS125 have been supplied to several countries, including Brazil, Ghana, Argentina, Malaysia and South Africa.

Hawker Siddeley Gnat T Mk 1 / UK

Developed from the Folland Gnat lightweight fighter, the two-seat Gnat T Mk 1 replaced the Vampire T11 as the RAF's standard advanced jet trainer from 1962, the prototype having flown in August 1959. The type is familiar world-wide through its use by the RAF aerobatic team, the Red Arrows.

Hawker Siddeley Hawk / UK

Designed as a Gnat and Hunter replacement, the HS Hawk trainer and strike aircraft began to enter RAF service in October 1976, and 175 will eventually be delivered. Export versions of the Hawk carry up to 5,600lb of external stores. 50 Hawks have been ordered by Finland, deliveries beginning in 1980, and the Finns plan to acquire an eventual total of 100 aircraft, most assembled under licence. The type has also been ordered by Indonesia.

Hindustan HT-2 / India

The all-metal HT-2 basic trainer entered production for the Indian Air Force in 1953, and about 160 were built. 12 were supplied to Ghana. In 1980-81, the type is due to be replaced in IAF service by a new trainer, the HPT-32.

Hindustan HJT-16 Kiran Mk II / India

Flown for the first time in September 1964, the Kiran Mk II is a basic jet trainer for the Indian Air Force. About 130 were ordered, half of which had been delivered by mid-1978.

Hispano HA-100 Triana / Spain

A radial-engined advanced trainer, the HA-100 was designed to supplement the Spanish Air Force's fleet of T-6 Texans, but served only in small numbers in the early 1960s.

Hispano HA-200 / Spain

The HA-200 advanced jet trainer, 62 of which were in Spanish Air Force service in 1978, was also built under licence in Egypt under the name 'Al Kahira' (Cairo). The HA-220 is a close support version, equipping the Spanish AF Tactical Air Command's No 214 Squadron.

Hunting Percival Prentice / UK

Designed to specification T23/43, the Percival Prentice flew on 31 March 1946 and the type entered RAF service as the Prentice T1. It was also used widely by the air forces of Argentina, India and the Lebanon.

Hunting Percival Provost / UK

The Percival Provost, designed to specification T16/48, flew for the first time on 23 February 1950 and replaced the Prentice with the RAF's basic training schools. As the T53, the type was also supplied to Burma, Iraq and the Sudan, while the T51 and T52 were used by Eire and Rhodesia.

Hunting Percival (BAC) Jet Provost / UK

The Jet Provost was designed as an ab initio jet trainer, replacing the piston-engined Provost, and served with the RAF in three versions, the Mks 3, 4 and 5. The latter has a redesigned nose and pressurised cockpit. The BAC Strikemaster is a ground attack version of the T5, with provision for various underwing offensive loads, and is used by several foreign air forces, including those of Saudi Arabia, South Yemen, Oman, Kuwait, Singapore, Kenya and New Zealand.

Ikarus Trainers / Yugoslavia

The Yugoslav aircraft industry produced several indigenous training aircraft during the postwar years, the first of which was the Type 213 Vihor basic trainer. A development of this basic design was the radial-engined Type 522 advanced trainer, which entered service with the Yugoslav Air Force in 1957. The Type 214 was a twin-engined bombing/-navigational trainer.

Lockheed T-33/T1A / USA

The most widely used advanced trainer in the world, the Lockheed T-33 flew in 1948 and was developed from the F-80 Shooting Star. The type was designated T-33A in USAF service and T-33B (T2-V) with the US Navy and Marine Corps. It is estimated that some 90% of the free world's military jet pilots trained on the T-33 during the 1950s and 1960s. About 5,700 T-33s were built in the USA alone, and other under licence in Canada and Japan. The US Navy's version of the T-33A, the TV-1, entered service in 1957 and featured extensive cockpit redesign. It was used as a deck landing and navigational trainer.

Maachi MB326 / Italy

First flown on 10 December 1957, the MB326 strike/trainer is the Italian Air Force's basic training type and has been widely exported. Countries using the aircraft, several versions of which have been produced, in the dual ground-attack/training role include Tunisia, Ghana, Argentina, Brazil, Zaire, Zambia, Australia and South Africa, where the aircraft is built under licence as the Impala. The MB326K is a single-seat variant of the basic two-seat design.

Morane-Saulnier MS472 Vanneau / France

Derived from the prewar Morane 406 fighter, the MS472 served as an advanced trainer with the French Air Force until the early 1960s, when the last examples were phased out of service in North Africa.

Morane-Saulnier MS733 Alcyon / France

The MS733 served as a basic trainer with the French Air Force during the 1950s, and was finally declared obsolete in 1962. Some examples were also supplied to Cambodia.

Morane-Saulnier MS760 Paris / France

Suitable for both the basic training and liaison roles, the MS760 could also be used as an armament trainer. Employed in small numbers by the Armée de l'Air and the Aeronavale, this twin-jet type has been produced in two, four- and six-seat versions. It was built under licence in Brazil, and was also supplied to the Argentine Air Force.

Nord 3202 / France

A two-seat primary trainer, the Nord 3202 served with the training establishments of the Aviation Legere de l'Armée de Terre (ALAT) from the late 1950s, and a few were still used in 1978 to give pilots fixed-wing experience before converting to helicopters.

North American T-28 / USA

Designed to replace the T-6 Texan, the NAA Model 159 (XT-28) flew for the first time in September 1949. The T-28 was adopted by several air forces, including Argentina, South Korea, Cambodia, Ethiopia, Ecuador, Laos, the Philippines and Mexico. A single-seat COIN version, the T-28D, was produced in 1962, and this variant was exported to Bolivia, Thailand, Zaire and South Vietnam.

North American T-39 / USA

The NA T-39 Sabreliner entered service with the USAF Air Training Command in 1961. Several variants were produced, some serving as crew trainers for the F-105. The T-39D was a variant for the US Navy. 191 examples were built for the US armed forces.

North American T-2A Buckeye / USA

Designed to meet a requirement for a jet trainer for the US Navy, the T-2 (formerly T2J-1) Buckeye entered US Navy service in 1958. 217 T-2As were built, followed by 100 T-2Bs and 144 T-2Cs. The type was powered by two Pratt & Whitney J60 turbojets.

Northrop T-38 Talon / USA

First flown in April 1959, the T-38 became operational with the USAF in March 1961 and 1,138 were subsequently delivered. Some of these were used by NASA as astronaut checkout aircraft; others served with USAF air combat schools to simulate Soviet MiG-21s.

Piaggio P148 / Italy

Designed as a primary trainer, the P148 entered service with the Italian Air Force in 1952, and 100 aircraft were subsequently delivered.

Piaggio P149 / Italy

Developed from the fixed-undercarriage P148 of 1951, the P149 basic trainer was used by both the Italian Air Force and the Federal German Luftwaffe, 262 aircraft having been acquired by the latter for training and liaison. In 1978 the type was still flying with the Luftwaffe's Air Cadets Regiment on air experience flights.

Pilatus P-3 / Switzerland

Entering service with the Swiss Air Force in 1956, the P-3 is used to train pilots from the primary to the jet conversion stage. About 120 aircraft were in service in 1978, including some earlier P-2s.

PZL M-4 Tarpan / Poland

Intended for both civil and military use, the Tarpan primary trainer was produced in 1963. A further version was the M-4P all-weather navigational trainer.

PZL TS-8 Bies / Poland

Built in substantial numbers during 1957-62, the Bies (Daredevil) was the Polish Air Force's standard basic trainer until supplanted by the turbojet-powered Iskra. The type was still serving in some numbers in 1978.

PZL TS-11 Iskra / Poland

First flown in 1961, the Iskra (Spark) was Poland's first indigenous jet aircraft and entered service with the Polish Air Force in 1963. Several hundred examples were built.

SAAB Safir / Sweden

Adopted by the Swedish Air Force as its standard primary trainer in the early 1950s, the SAAB-91 Safir also served with a number of foreign air forces, including Ethiopia. Replaced by the Bulldog in the basic training role, the surviving Swedish Air Force Safirs were turned over to liaison duties.

SAAB MFI-15 / Sweden

Designed for pre-selection training and army co-operation duties, the MFI-15 flew for the first time in July 1969. The type did not enter quantity production.

SAAB 105 / Sweden

First flown in 1963, the SAAB 105 twin-jet advanced trainer is known as the Sk60 in Swedish Air Force service, 150 having been delivered. The type, several versions of which were built, also equips two light ground attack wings of the Austrian Air Force (1978).

Scottish Aviation Bulldog / UK

A military version of the Beagle Pup, the Bulldog prototype flew on 19 May 1969. The type serves as a standard piston-engined primary trainer with the Royal Air Force and the air arms of Sweden, Kenya and Malaysia. The Bulldog is designated Sk61 in Swedish service.

Short Sturgeon / UK

Originally designed as a naval attack aircraft, the twin-engined Short Sturgeon entered service with the Royal Navy as a fast multi-purpose gunnery training and target aircraft. Designated Sturgeon TT2, the type was issued to both carrier-borne units and shore establishments, serving during the 1950s.

SIPA S12 / France

Derived from the wartime Arado Ar396, the S12 served in substantial numbers with the Armée de l'Air during the 1950s as a basic trainer. A further variant, the SIPA 121, was used in the light attack role in Algeria.

Soko Galeb / Yugoslavia

First flown in May 1961, the Soko Galeb (Seagull) jet basic trainer equips the training squadrons of the Yugoslav Air Force, some 60 examples having been delivered. The J-1 Jastreb (Hawk) is a single-seat light attack variant.

Vickers Varsity / UK

Based on the design of the Vickers Valetta, but with a tricycle undercarriage, the twin-engined Varsity remained the RAF's standard multi-purpose crew trainer for twenty years, until it was eventually replaced by more modern types such as the HS125 Dominie and HP Jetstream. 163 were built.

Yakovlev Yak-11 (NATO Code-Name: Moose) / USSR

Developed from the wartime Yak-9 fighter series, the Yak-11 basic trainer was supplied in large numbers to Soviet Bloc air forces during the late 1940s. It was built under licence in Czechoslovakia as the C11.

Yakovlev Yak-12 / USSR

First flown in 1946, the Yak-12 high-wing monoplane was widely used as a trainer and four-seat liaison aircraft by the Soviet and satellite air forces.

Yakovlev Yak-18 (NATO Code-Name: Max) / USSR

The Yak-18 primary trainer first entered service with the Soviet Air Force in 1946, and was subsequently used in large numbers throughout the Communist-aligned world. The Yak-18U was a much redesigned version, featuring a nosewheel undercarriage.

158

Index

Combat Aircraft